MUSIC AND MORE

MUSIC AND MORE

ESSAYS, 1975 - 1991

Samuel Lipman

NORTHWESTERN UNIVERSITY PRESS

Evanston, Illinois

Northwestern University Press
Evanston, Illinois 60201

The essays collected in this volume were first published in *Commentary*, The *New Criterion*,
and The *New York Times*. "Say No to Trash" copyright © 1989 by
The New York Times Company; reprinted by permission.

Printed in the United States of America

Library of Congress Cataloging-in-Publication Data

Lipman, Samuel.
    Music and more : essays, 1975-1991 / Samuel Lipman.
      p. cm.
    Includes bibliographical references.
    ISBN 0-8101-1051-2 (alk. paper). — ISBN 0-8101-1076-8 (pbk. :
alk. paper)
      1. Music—History and criticism. 2. Art and society. I. Title.
ML60.L468 1992   92-15703
780—dc20   CIP
                           MN

The paper used in this publication meets the minimum requirements of American Standard
for Information Sciences—Permanence of Paper for Printed Library Materials, ANSI Z39.48-1984.

To Frederick F. Greenman, Jr.

Contents

Contents

Acknowledgments

So many people have meant so much to me over the years in which these essays were written that I scarcely know where to begin, or where to end.

Michael Joyce, James Piereson, and Richard Larry have been constant friends and counselors and, through their continuing interest in *The New Criterion*, have made possible the majority of the essays that make up this book. At *The New Criterion* I am also indebted to the valiant help and high kindness of Roger Kimball, Christopher Carduff, Robert Richman, Marge Danser, Erich Eichman, and Donna Rifkind; several of these essays were edited with stringency and exactitude by our much mourned assistant managing editor, Eva Szent-Miklosy. At *Commentary*, my thanks, as always, go to Neal Kozodoy and Brenda Brown for their editorial care and wisdom. To Howard Shanet, the redoubtable historian of the New York Philharmonic, I am indebted for the title of this book and much encouragement besides. Here, perhaps, is the best place to state that I have not made any attempt to rewrite these essays; save for minor changes in style, corrections of misprints, and several corrections of fact, they are presented here as originally printed.

To my dear friends Hilton Kramer, the editor of *The New Criterion*, and Norman Podhoretz, editor-in-chief of *Commentary*, I freely acknowledge a personal debt that goes far beyond their massive contributions to my literary and intellectual development. Over the years—and it is now a decade since I began my work for *The New Criterion* and almost two decades since I first appeared in *Commentary*—they have been not just close associates but comrades-in-arms. We have not yet won the greatest of our battles but, oh my, what a wonderful noise we've made!

At Northwestern University Press, I want to thank its former director, Jonathan Brent, with whom I first discussed this book; in the course of its preparation for the press, I have enjoyed the solicitude and close attention of Susan Harris and Lee Yost, and the careful copyediting of Barbara Folsom. I also want to mention the extraordinary interest that Joseph Epstein, the editor of *The American Scholar*, has taken in my work and in helping to get it published.

I have dedicated this book to Frederick F. Greenman, Jr. He has been more than a friend to me; in a way that does not need to be spelled out here, he has been a lifesaver. To my old friend Omus Hirshbein, who has spent his life fighting for the music he and I believe in, I give thanks, both in my name and (or so I think) in music's, too.

To my wife, Jeaneane, and to my son, Edward, I give my love, as they have so bounteously given me theirs.

INTRODUCTION

The Culture of
Classical Music Today

Let me begin with the good news. Over the past decade, classical music—Western, dead-white-European-male music, if you will—has become more popular in America than ever. The evidence of this popularity is to be found everywhere. There are more composers, more performers, more new works being written, more new and old works being played, and more students studying to be performers. There are more symphony orchestras, more opera companies, more professional choruses, and more large music schools. Audiences for live concerts and operas have been steadily increasing for many years; it is also demonstrably true that the so-called CD revolution has resulted in the sale of extra millions of classical-music recordings to millions of music listeners both young and old. Along with all the purchases of CDs (and video cassettes and laser discs), of course, go sales of billions of dollars' worth of new and newer hi-fi hardware, some of which at least is used to play classical music. Nor can the extraordinary reach of opera broadcasts on public television, and on various cable channels too, be ignored; PBS broadcasts from the Metropolitan Opera are seen by millions of viewers in the United States, and now by millions abroad on their own government-run TV channels. Furthermore, the Met now has ambitious plans for gala pay-per-view television broadcasts, from which it is hoped that the company will draw large revenues. Even in the trend-conscious academy, the study of great music, not just as notes and sounds but as ideas and influences, has become the rage in all the most prestigious schools.

And then there is the pervasion of classical music as an integral part of the ambiance of our daily—and nightly—lives. What used to be derogated as elevator music has become *classical* elevator music; no visit to a pricey restaurant is complete without a sonic background of the *Four Seasons* of Vivaldi or any of several particularly familiar piano concertos of Mozart. Bach turns up frequently in television commercials, and has even been known to provide an accompaniment to scoreboard displays on televised baseball games. What is true in restaurants, TV commercials, and baseball games is equally true in department and specialty stores, and in all manner of business offices.

Then, too, there are the commercial indicia of popularity. It may all be put crassly, but not inaccurately: never has more money been made from classical music by its practitioners, and from music by those who arrange for its commercial exposure. Performers' fees, like ticket prices, are very high. The most famous conductors earn in excess of $1,000,000 each year; it is not uncommon for guest conductors to earn well in excess of $20,000 for each week they conduct. The tenor Luciano Pavarotti, it is said, can command a fee of more than $100,000 for a single concert appearance, and a favorite instrumentalist like Itzhak Perlman can receive $35,000 or more for each of his concerts. Columbia Artists Management, Inc., the largest arranger of classical concerts and media events in the world, seems a veritable paragon of year-to-year growth. Administrative salaries in the nonprofit organizations that solicit contributions from the public (as well as sell tickets) are high too: salaries of top orchestra managers (now called "Managing Directors") often reach, with benefits, perquisites, and expense accounts, levels well above $200,000 annually.

In recounting all the good news, it would hardly be fair to omit the fact that over the past two decades even large American corporations have flocked to support orchestras and opera companies, and have in many cases taken great pride in associating their good corporate names with musical culture. In an even larger way, senior business executives have been, and are today, willing to sit on musical boards and contribute their economic expertise to the running of these cultural enterprises. In general, contributions to music, not just from business but from foundations and private sources, have been going up, and even the present recession has not noticeably reduced these gifts.

I have just defined popularity in market terms. Large scale of activity, wide availability of product, increasing level of expenditures, existence of powerful institutions, stable base of support: all these testify to the kind of success that comes only from providing a lot of people with what a lot of people want. From this point of view, I can do no better than return to the statement with which I began—undoubtedly, classical music is more popular today than ever before.

Should we then not rejoice? After all, something that is beautiful—by the most elevated criteria one of the enduring monuments of Western civilization—has become a part of the lives of countless people, filling their hours by beguiling their ears. Great music—and we can be in no doubt that, for example, Vivaldi, Bach, and Mozart created great music—has become diffused throughout much of American society and life. What more could music, and therefore those who love music, ask?

But if we go beyond this notion of popularity as an end in itself and ask just *what* is now so popular about classical music, we begin to find bad news rather than good. What if we ask, not about the popularity of the constituent elements of music, but about the quality of their achievement and the health of their condition? What, in other words, if we attempt an artistic evaluation of the state of classical music today?

Perhaps the best place to start this evaluation is with new music. Here the situation is now, and has been for many years, in the highest degree hypertrophic: untold numbers of new works are indeed being written, and have been written, by untold numbers of composers. A remarkable percentage of these new works receive performances, and a remarkable percentage of the composers who write them manage to make a living out of pursuits—usually teaching—associated with composition. Alas, the result of all this activity, all the grants for new music, all the publicity surrounding its public performance, all the passionate encomia new music receives not just as sound but even more as ideology, is—nothing. Absolutely nothing.

Merely a description of the musical repertory—the pieces the best musicians want to play and the most musically committed audiences want to hear—says it all. The slightly less than two hundred and fifty years from the rise of Bach to the end of World War II contains, with remarkably few exceptions, our entire musical repertory of choice. Even the exceptions—chiefly late Prokofiev and Shostakovich—now seem more than ever to have been fully rooted in the musical life of the earlier years of our century. Of the myriad of composers who have grown up since World War II, nothing remains but entries in our ever-larger musical encyclopedias, along with listings of compositions played once and, very likely, nevermore.

During this period of almost a half-century since 1945, there have been numerous highly touted developments in musical composition. In these years, we have seen and heard total serialism—the extension of Arnold Schoenberg's twelve-tone method to all the parameters of music, including duration, dynamics, and timbre; compositions full of screeches, whistles, and roars, produced and reproduced on magnetic tape; chance music, in which the performer was called upon to be the composer as well; conceptual music (a close relative of chance music), in which written instructions of performance replaced any notes at all; the use of oriental chanting and instruments; minimalism, in which the ceaseless repetition of simple chords and rhythms served to produce works of extreme length and utter boredom; and most recently, I suppose, neoromanticism, the notion that anytime a composer said, "Let there be melody and harmony," lo, there was melody and harmony. The most famous names among the protagonists of these compositional schools have been such stars as Karlheinz Stockhausen, Pierre Boulez, John Cage, Philip Glass, and now John Adams; so far as their compositions are concerned, all their reputations, and all their long-lived careers, have not sufficed to put a single one of their works into the repertory of mainstream classical music.

Sadly, so complete has been the failure of all these new compositions that they have dragged down with them one of the true bright spots of twentieth-century music—American compositions of the 1930s, 1940s, and early 1950s. The objections of both musicians and audiences to the prevailingly amelodic and perversely dissonantal characteristics of the

European music of the post–World War II period—and of the American music from the mid-1950s on written under this European influence—have placed even the great achievements of (to name only a few) the Americans Roy Harris, Samuel Barber, Howard Hanson, Walter Piston, William Schuman, and David Diamond under the cloud of what is derisorily called "modern music." The only exception to this summary rejection of American music has been Aaron Copland, and even his position in the repertory now seems ever more exclusively based on his easy-to-take ballet scores rather than on his concert music. And what is true of these well-known American composers whose work is now in a condition of desuetude is vastly more true of such immensely gifted later composers as (again to name only two) Andrew Imbrie and William Bergsma.

A special word is in order for the condition of new opera. Here, in this most problematic and expensive of musical forms, there have been two "stars" since World War II: the English Benjamin Britten and the American Philip Glass. Yet Britten's two most successful works, *Peter Grimes* (1945) and *Billy Budd* (1951), go back at least forty years; none of his later works, very much including *Death in Venice* (1973), has been anything more than a succès d'estime. In the case of Glass's several works, only *Einstein on the Beach* (1976), his collaboration with the director/designer Robert Wilson, has managed to stick in the memory, vastly more for Wilson's staging than for Glass's music. Elsewhere with Glass, the Gandhi pageant *Satyagraha* (1980) and the incredibly static *Akhnaten* (1984) seemed more like *tableaux morts* than flesh-and-blood operas. The current hotshot, of course, is John Adams, whose *Nixon in China* (1987), a collaboration with the avant-garde director Peter Sellars, appealed to an audience of "cutting-edge" dance and theater types; as always with trendy new music, the missing element in the audience was music lovers.

Although new operas are commissioned and usually performed by the company doing the commissioning, by far the largest number of opera companies in this country—including the giant of them all, the Metropolitan Opera—concentrate their efforts on the standard works by the same few composers that have always made up their repertories. The winners, now as before, are the most-celebrated operas of Mozart,

Verdi, and Puccini, and, of course, "*Cav* and *Pag*"—*Cavalleria rusticana* and *Pagliacci*. The way these winners are sold, by small opera company after small opera company, is vulgar in the extreme: every opera, whatever its particular plot and mood, is described as an exciting story of love and intrigue, guaranteed to keep the audience on the edge of their seats.

From composers and their compositions, it is but a short jump to performers. Here a sharp distinction must be drawn between Americans and Europeans. Early in his career, it seemed that the meteoric rise of Leonard Bernstein would pave the way for a new generation of American masters of the baton. But despite the existence of Bernstein as a role model, the number of American conductors leading major American orchestras remains vanishingly small: David Zinman in Baltimore, Leonard Slatkin in Saint Louis, Gerard Schwarz in Seattle, and, in opera, James Levine at the Metropolitan. Elsewhere, the list of conductors, in place or appointed, is totally European (or, in one case, Asian): New York (Kurt Masur), Boston (Seiji Ozawa), Philadelphia (Wolfgang Sawallisch), Cleveland (Christoph von Dohnányi), Chicago (Daniel Barenboim), Los Angeles (Esa-Pekka Salonen), and Washington (Mstislav Rostropovich). In San Francisco, the American-born Herbert Blomstedt is entirely a product of European musical life, and in Pittsburgh Lorin Maazel, though trained in this country, made his initial conducting reputation entirely abroad.

At least in our best orchestras, symphony musicians are now remarkably well paid; in these major ensembles, annual incomes of more than $50,000 (with benefits extra), and with substantially more for solo players, are the rule rather than the exception. And yet there is everywhere a feeling of discontent with the orchestral player's lot. Conductors are in general not highly respected; management is often seen as the enemy, plotting to get more work out of the musicians, with diminished job security and worsened working conditions. Though orchestra players now live well, their job satisfactions seem low. They resent the routinized nature of their tasks, and they have little feeling that they are making great music. One telling sign of their discontent is the small amount of time the finest orchestral players now give to the study and playing of great chamber music—not for money, but for their own pleasure. All in all, membership in an orchestra is now seen as a dead-end street—a well-paying job, to be sure, but nevertheless a dead-end.

Among singers, the story is rather more encouraging. Since the nineteenth century, American vocal artists have found it possible to make national and even international careers; one thinks of such past greats as Rosa Ponselle, Lawrence Tibbett, Richard Crooks, Richard Tucker, and Leonard Warren. In recent years, one thinks immediately of Leontyne Price, Sherrill Milnes, Samuel Ramey, and now Thomas Hampson. Less famous American singers are busy, and actually much in demand. But despite their justified successes, it cannot be said that any American singer since World War II has placed a personal stamp on any single role in a standard European opera, let alone on any great opera composer's oeuvre. Whether one thinks of Verdi or Puccini or Wagner, the commanding interpretations—the interpretations in which the singers place their mark on our perception of the characters they portray—remain those accomplished by such European singers of the fairly recent past as (again to name only a few) Maria Callas, Tito Gobbi, Hans Hotter, and Elisabeth Schwarzkopf.

Our instrumentalists have hardly fared so well as our singers. Our only analogue to Leonard Bernstein in his role as a conductor has been the pianist Van Cliburn. This once-young Texan, trained entirely in this country, rocketed to stardom with his unexpected victory in the 1958 Tchaikovsky Competition in Moscow; by this triumph he inherited the mantle of the leader of the American school of piano playing from the tragically short-lived William Kapell, who had perished in an airplane crash in 1953. But it was already unsettling that the chief critical praise lavished on Cliburn emphasized not how he sounded like an American pianist—steely fingered, sharp-rhythmed, and clangorous in tone—but how his playing was a throwback to an older European style, riper, richer, and more romantic—that is, less materialistic. But Cliburn's great start quickly took him in the direction of becoming a popular entertainer, of no influence over his fellow pianists and other musicians. And since Cliburn, only Murray Perahia among American pianists has made a truly important international career—and Perahia's career is almost entirely the result of his long residence in London.

Among string players in America, the great names that came forward in the 1960s and 1970s were those of Israeli violinists Itzhak Perlman and Pinchas Zukerman; though both are American residents and trained here, they seem additions to American musical life rather than constituents of it. Much the same can be said of the Japanese violinist Midori, a successful concert artist before her teens and now, about twenty years old, seemingly at the top of her career. Of the most successful string players now in this country, only the American cellist of Chinese parentage Yo-Yo Ma seems a truly functioning part of our musical life.

For many years, American music lovers were justly proud of their great orchestras. In the 1920s and 1930s, Leopold Stokowski's Philadelphia Orchestra and Serge Koussevitzky's Boston Symphony Orchestra were of world-class stature; in the first half of the 1930s, the same could be said of Arturo Toscanini's New York Philharmonic and then, a bit later, of his NBC Symphony. Though the Philadelphia retained its beautiful sound under Stokowski's successor, Eugene Ormandy, much of the musical excitement engendered by Stokowski was soon dissipated; the Boston Symphony's unique combination of brilliance and depth of sonority did not survive Koussevitzky's supersession by Charles Munch in the 1940s. Only George Szell's Cleveland Orchestra of the 1950s and 1960s joined the class of immortals, and indeed to date it has been the last American orchestra to do so.

As a whole, American orchestral life over the past two or three decades, and very much continuing into the present, has been a sad story of a rough-hewn efficiency in performance, achieved at the cost of tonal refinement, ensemble precision, individual character, and musical vitality. Zubin Mehta's long tenure at the Philharmonic, now fortunately concluded, seemed disastrous in its coarseness and vulgarity, both for the orchestra itself and for the Philharmonic's core audience. The Philadelphia, under Riccardo Muti during the 1980s, almost completely lost its hitherto jealously guarded tonal profile. The Boston Symphony, giving one routine performance after another, has ceased to be a factor on the international scene, despite its supposedly charismatic leader, Seiji Ozawa. Of the greatest American orchestras of the past, only the Cleveland under Christoph von Dohnányi manages to sustain a deserved reputation for interesting programs played in an interesting manner.

In the world of opera, I can only speak of the Metropolitan and the New York City Opera. In this age of the cheap American dollar, the Metropolitan is now a prime tourist attraction. Many, if not most, performances are sold out, and good seats for any performance, at whatever price, are hard to come by. Its shop and mail-order sales are booming, and the Met's house magazine, *Opera News*, now under the strong editorship of Patrick Smith, has no less than 120,000 subscribers. Furthermore, with the excellent players Levine has brought in, the Met orchestra has become under his training a force to be reckoned with not only in the opera house but as a distinctive ensemble ranking with the best orchestras in the world today. The result of this newfound power of the Met has been a spate of artificial-sounding Met opera recordings, conducted by Levine, appearing on the German Deutsche Grammophon and the Japanese Sony Classical labels. Because of its ability to record, the Met is able to engage on a long-term basis the most successful singers in the world, including Luciano Pavarotti and Plácido Domingo. But all this activity and prosperity cannot hide the fact that the Met's performances are in large measure undistinguished vocally, without any permanently redeeming value provided by the Met's growing indulgence in gargantuan and costly new productions. Although Levine insists on conducting the most important works and new productions himself, the level of conducting on most non-Levine nights at the Met—despite an occasional visit from someone like Carlos Kleiber—is remarkably uninteresting. When Levine is on the podium, his conducting often seems narrowly self-indulgent: for example, his infatuation with slow tempos went far to destroy the Met's *Ring* cycle of the past several years. Though it will indeed be doing a very few new works in the coming seasons, the rules of safety and sameness in repertory, direction, and performance all combine to make the Met a dull, albeit deluxe, company. And as serious listening to the weekly Met radio broadcasts proves, even safety and sameness cannot guarantee minimally acceptable performances in terms of security of intonation and solidity of vocal production.

By contrast, the New York City Opera now gives the impression of fighting for its life. Left in uncertain artistic condition by Beverly Sills when she turned over the company's general directorship to conductor Christopher Keene, the City Opera is saddled with the New York State

Theater, an inconvenient and acoustically unattractive place in which to perform opera. Its long-term financial problems, which had some years ago forced a serious rearrangement in the dates of its seasons, have hardly been eased by Beverly Sills's triumphant entry onto the Metropolitan Opera board; here, her main task will likely be fund-raising for the Met, but not for the New York City Opera, the company which so many years ago gave her operatic birth and for so many years sustained her career. City Opera performances, despite the best efforts of Christopher Keene and a host of other dedicated people, remain very much in the shadow of the Met's vaunted opulence. The City Opera's recent ventures into new opera—one thinks immediately of Anthony Davis's *X*, Dominick Argento's *Casanova*, and Jay Reise's *Rasputin*—have hardly borne fruit. Of all the City Opera initiatives in the past few years, only one—but a big one it was—seemed to make its proper mark: the strikingly well-received production in the fall of 1990 of Schoenberg's *Moses und Aron*, a central work of pre–World War II modernism that the Met should have performed long ago but has sedulously avoided these many years.

For some years now, all these signs of decline in American musical (and operatic) life have been quite clear to all but those optimistic souls who make their meager livings by praise. The answer to this negative perception has been—in addition to various attempts by powerful arts advocates and *apparatchiki* to kill the messengers—to concentrate attention on supposedly authentic modes of performance. Through this device, it was hoped that two inconvenient and highly disturbing facets of contemporary musical life might be elided and thus obscured: the lack of new music and the lack of interesting new performers.

This new way of performing old music has drawn sustenance—inspiration seems too honorific a term—from the rediscovery of seventeenth- and eighteenth-century composition so characteristic of our own century. This unearthing of past musical treasures was important, under the name of neoclassicism, for the creative efforts of such estimable composers as Igor Stravinsky and Richard Strauss. At the hands of such distinctive personalities as the English old-instrument-builder and theorist Arnold Dolmetsch and the magnificent harpsichordist Wanda Landowska, this reclamation unearthed a forgotten genre of masterpieces, and thus enriched our musical vocabulary and sensibility; even the poet Ezra Pound and his friend the violinist Olga Rudge, through their work on behalf of the music of Vivaldi, deserve credit for some of this achievement.

But what started as an artistic crusade by immensely gifted individuals had become, by the 1950s, what might be called the "Business of Baroque"; what increasingly seemed to count was not the quality of the music being rediscovered and performed, or the distinction of the way it was being performed, but rather the worship of musical quaintness and the cultivation of stylistic difference for its own sake. By the 1960s, it had become unfashionable in intellectual circles to play Bach on the piano; even Glenn Gould's marvelous recorded performances of Bach were chiefly admired for how little the instrument he played sounded, at his hands, like a flesh-and-blood piano.

The 1970s and 1980s saw the growth in England of orchestra-sized ensembles dedicated to playing not just Bach on period instruments and in period style but Haydn, Mozart, and Beethoven. At first the leader in this pursuit was the very drab and unexciting Christopher Hogwood, leading a pick-up group appropriately called the Academy of Ancient Music. Soon Hogwood was succeeded by the rather more sparky Roger Norrington, leading yet another pick-up group labeled the London Classical Players and making a great impression, at least on the critics, with fast, light, and inflexible performances of all the Beethoven symphonies. Everywhere there were cries that this was Beethoven as Beethoven had heard his own music: so applauded was Norrington's approach that he even applied his talents to the *Symphonie fantastique* of Berlioz. But as the *réclame* settled, as by now it most certainly has, Norrington's performances stood revealed as made up of equal parts of scrawny and out-of-tune strings and pinched and aggressive winds and brass. In New York, an important sign of the times was the abysmal failure with both public and press in its initial season of the Classical Band, our own version of the authentic-performance phenomenon led by the English baroque specialist Trevor Pinnock.

The ups, and perhaps now downs, of the movement to play old music in such a way as to make it sound new-old, have not been without their influence on the academic study of musicology. On the one hand, the professoriate has leapt into the study of (to use Hogwood's appellation) "ancient music." Theses, dissertations, and published articles and treatises on the proper performance style of music written before 1775 or thereabouts have been pouring out of the educational mill. Furthermore, this concern with how the music written around and before the time of Bach and his sons should be performed has moved forward into the nineteenth century. Not just Mozart but Beethoven, too, has become fair game for musicology. In particular, a thriving scholarly industry has been established in the study of Beethoven's sketchbooks; in this study, particular attention is given to the use of watermark analysis to date the paper on which these sketches were written, and thus to establish the chronological order of the sketches in order to reveal the process of composition. Now all the analytic techniques of musicology are being applied to later music, in particular to Chopin, who has gone in intellectual estimation in only a few decades from rejection as a vapid salon composer to acceptance as the worthy subject of rigorous scholarly-musical analysis. Similarly, a new Verdi edition, closely associated with the musicologist Philip Gossett of the University of Chicago, is laying claim to the establishment of a truly scholarly text, and a proper style of performance, for these core operas of the Italian romantic tradition.

But there is much more going on now in academic musicology than the mere study of how notes should be played and sung. Musicology has become very much a part of semiotics, with such words as "signifier" and "signified" liberally strewn over the newest studies of famous composers. Furthermore, the new rage in musicology is called cultural studies—the placing of music squarely in the politics and sociology of its creation and the conditions under which it became available to the public. Taking over from what used to be called the sociology of knowledge, these new musicologists are not content with discussing the origins of great works of music in their own terms, but go beyond what composers thought they were writing, musicians thought they were performing, and audiences thought they were hearing—and, especially, what patrons thought they were supporting—to see the past of this art in the light of radical contemporary notions of economics and gender.

Thus, in *Music and Society: The Politics of Composition, Performance, and Reception*, published in 1987 by the august Cambridge University Press and edited by Richard Leppert and Susan McClary, one finds such articles as "The Ideology of Autonomous Art," "Towards an Aesthetic of Popular Music," "Music, Domestic Life and Cultural Chauvinism: Images of British Subjects at Home in India," and "Music and Male Hegemony." In "The Blasphemy of Talking Politics during Bach Year," Susan McClary, described as "Associate Professor of Musicology and a member of two research centers (Center for Advanced Feminist Studies and Center for Humanistic Studies, for which she was Acting Director, 1985–86) at the University of Minnesota," explains (or rather explains away) the achievement of Bach in the following manner:

[A]t the same time that this music shapes itself in terms of bourgeois ideology (its goal orientation, obsessive control of greater and greater spans of time, its willful striving, delayed gratification and defiance of norms), it often cloaks that ideology by putting it at the service of an explicit theology. The tonal procedures developed by the emerging bourgeoisie to articulate their sense of the world here become presented as what we, in fact, want to believe they are: eternal, universal truths. It is no accident that the dynasty of Great (bourgeois) Composers begins with Bach, for he gives the impression that *our* [emphasis in the original] way of representing the world musically is God-given. Thereafter, tonality can retain its aura of absolute perfection ("the way music goes") in its native secular habitat. This sleight of hand earned Bach the name "the fifth evangelist" . . .

McClary concludes her long article by putting all her cards on the table:

I would propose the age-old strategy of rewriting the tradition in such a way as to appropriate Bach to our own political ends. Just as Renaissance mannerists justified their subjective excesses by appealing to principles of ancient Greek theory, so each group since the early nineteenth century has found it necessary to kidnap Bach from the immediately preceding generation and to demonstrate his affinity with the emerging sensibility. My portrait of Bach presented earlier clearly exhibits characteristics of the post-modern eclectic, of the ideologically marginalized artist empowering himself to appropriate, reinterpret, and manipulate to his own ends the signs and forms of dominant culture. His ultimate success in this enterprise can be a model of sorts to us all. In actively reclaiming Bach and the canon in order to put them to our own uses, we can also reclaim ourselves.

One of the most interesting aspects of the current trends in musicology is the extent to which it has invaded music criticism. In this century and in our country, music criticism has been the essentially journalistic coverage in venues large or small, popular or elite, of developments in music composition and performance. As the specific gravity, not to mention the attractiveness, of new works dwindled and then vanished, music criticism found itself increasingly focused on performance. And as by the end of the 1960s, traditional performances, along with traditional performers, more and more resembled each other, music criticism began to appear as either an exercise in making pointless distinctions between identical products or an exercise in nostalgia, in which current performances were held up against past recordings and invariably found wanting.

To some extent, the authentic-performance movement, by bringing a new (though really old) musical product into view, did provide critics with something new to write about. But because the authentic-performance movement was so much a creation of academic and quasi-academic thought rather than of autochthonous musical impulses, writing about it, even in the daily press, increasingly required musico-logical training and a musicological bent: of the two, the bent was by far the more important. And so music critics found themselves writing Sunday think-pieces on ornamentation in baroque music, as advocated in the latest academic treatise, or perhaps a music-magazine article discussing Brahms's style of piano playing, as demonstrated on an almost inaudible Edison cylinder recording made by the composer before his death in the 1890s.

Perhaps more significantly, a trend has emerged of late in the bringing into musical journalism of the concerns of the cultural studies now so beloved of the new wave of academic musicologists. An outstanding example of this new attempt to write about music by writing about something else very much not music is the spate of articles in the *New York Times* by University of California music professor Richard Taruskin. This past April, Taruskin questioned the place in the repertory of such beautiful Prokofiev works as *Alexander Nevsky* (1939), the Cello Sonata (1949), and the Seventh Symphony (1951–52) because they were composed, and officially supported, during the Stalin terror. Then, in June, Taruskin claimed that Tchaikovsky's music, seemingly so admired and beloved, was actually under a critical cloud in that "[a]ll of the prejudices commonly directed against woman composers have been directed at him." Taruskin's article then asks, without adducing any evidence to the contrary, "is there any other explanation save latent homophobia for the amazing progress of that notorious tissue of hearsay concerning Tchaikovsky's death (pederastic affairs, threatened exposure, suicide at the behest of some old school chums) in the musical press and even in the scholarly community . . . ?" Here is the bringing up to date of great music with a vengeance, as if all music were present politics.

Underlying this turning to the musicological discussion of performance practice and the bringing into music of the new cultural studies is an appalling constriction of the market for music criticism and, not surprisingly, a loss of any conviction on the part of the critics themselves that there is anyone out there actually reading them. The death of major American music magazines, those dealing both with live performances and with recordings, is now complete; the last to go was the once-distinguished monthly *Musical America*, which has now become what is delicately described as a consumer-oriented trade publication. The space given to daily music-reviewing has in many places become exiguous; even the *New York Times*, long the last courageous holdout against the pressures to limit the coverage of classical music, has drastically reduced its coverage in recent years of debut recitals and concerts given in smaller halls, while at the same time devoting more space to preconcert booster pieces.[1] The once-proud *Washington Post*, for many years the home of the redoubtable critic Paul Hume, has now come very close to being a newspaper without influence in the musical world. *Time* and *Newsweek* now rarely cover classical music, and then only when something of presumably piquant interest occurs.

And then, despite all the glorious numbers, there is the continuing and worsening problem of the musical audience. Perhaps more people indeed are going to classical-music concerts and operas, but even this brute assertion seems hard to take at face value, given the total unreliability of attendance figures so characteristic of arts institutions, arts advocates, and arts poll-takers. However many people there actually are in the seats, and however many people *say* they want to, and do, attend concerts and operas, the fact remains that audiences everywhere are increasingly unsophisticated and uncommitted. Subscription series offered to the public have fewer events on them each year; miniseries are popular, and with their popularity goes the fractionating of musical experience, as fewer people hear an extensive representation either of the work of the musicians they are hearing or of the works that constitute the repertory of great music. Then, too, the young seem curiously absent from musical events, and the audience that does come is ever grayer and will, if not renewed, inevitably disappear.

It is precisely this absence of the young from live classical events that seems most ominous for the future. The music of choice for the upwardly mobile Yuppie young is "easy-listening" music: the stupefying docilities of New Age sounds, the less distinctive forms of minimalism, the more emotionally flattened forms of jazz, and especially the sewing-machine inanities of the lesser baroque composers. Indeed, it is hard to avoid the impression that what appeals to the young about the classical music that does in fact interest them is not this music's contrast and variety, not its attempts to storm the heavens, but rather its sameness. It seems clear that what is precisely so attractive about the baroque music now so much in fashion is its unending surface patterns and repeated, and only slightly altered, harmonic and rhythmic sequences.

Performers everywhere are aware that in order to gain the attention of the audience, it is necessary for them to do ever more, not just *with* the music, but *to* the music. Subtle musical gestures, whether made by instrumentalists, singers, or conductors and orchestras, now have little effect; the music can no longer be allowed to speak for itself and to make its points by clarity, refinement, and structural rigor. Instead, each note must be emotionally milked, each tempo made either much too slow or much too fast, each dynamic made either much too loud or much too soft, each contrast of mood made sharper, and the climax of each phrase exaggerated. Sadly, all these attempts at exaggeration have merely served further to deaden audience reaction, producing, as in the case of Zubin Mehta at the New York Philharmonic, a sense of tiredness and ennui. In a more fundamental sense, the very harmonic code of Western music—the tonal system—now seems to have lost both its power, with unsophisticated audiences, to shock and its former ability, with audiences both knowing and unknowing, to compel attention. Faced with this aural vacuum in their listeners, performers now find the key to success in fancy garb, clothing men in ruffled shirts and women in *louche* pantsuits; among young performers, moussed hair is rapidly becoming the coiffure of public notice for both sexes.

It is difficult to know exactly what has caused the current weakened condition of the audience. Doubtless there are several factors at work: the destruction of classical-music education in elementary and secondary schools; the shift in colleges and universities away from the old, unjustly maligned music-appreciation courses to supposedly rigorous, scholarly courses in music history, theory, and analysis; the calamitously large availability of meretricious pop music, enforced in its circulation by engulfing peer pressure and the unresolved psychosexual yearnings of parents come to maturity in the 1960s; the immense competition for what is now so crassly called the "entertainment dollar" among music, opera, ballet, theater, film, and television.

There is also the current vogue for multiculturalism, the artificial, wholly ideological, and ultimately patronizing urge to advance the cultural products of others at the expense of one's own. In music, this trend has very much weakened the position of the classic masterpieces, in effect forcing a wholesale redefinition of just what one is allowed to call by this term. Doubtless much of the liking for what is now called "world musics" comes from the disaffected young, anxious to break what they see as the shackles of home and nation. In my own experience, the most avid proponents of multiculturalism are those who are paid to promote this cause by public and private funding bodies eager to win publicity and a high reputation for being "politically correct" and on the "cutting edge" of art. A recent example of this organized attempt to reconstitute the body of culture—in this case, great music—is to be found in *Public Money and the Muse*, a book published this past spring by the American Assembly, a public-policy group headquartered at Columbia University.[2] In this book, funded by the Rockefeller and AT&T foundations, Gerald D. Yoshitomi, executive director of the Japanese American Culture and Community Center in Los Angeles, writes (in a chapter on "Cultural Equity"): "All of our children must hear the music of the world's great composers played by outstanding symphony orchestras;

yet we must also broaden our standard definitions of who is to be included in that great composers list." In one sense, though hardly a helpful one, Yoshitomi is right: it is much easier to expand the definition of the word *great* than to produce great art.

It is difficult not to feel that the real life of classical-music lovers now takes place in the privacy of their homes as they listen to the enormous variety of great music available on recordings. Compared to live concerts, recordings are inexpensive; listening to recordings in one's living room is correctly perceived as both a safer and a more comfortable activity than venturing out at night into the center cities where the great concert halls are still located. On new recordings, through splicing and other kinds of doctoring, performances can easily be made to give the impression—though only the impression—of perfection; by comparison, live concerts, by their very nature, are often technically messy affairs. And then, for more knowledgeable listeners, there is the enormous overhang of recordings from the past, made newly available on CDs in quite extraordinary-sounding transfers. These new-old recordings do indeed provide music lovers with some of the greatest—that is, most moving—vocal and instrumental performances of which we can have any knowledge. With the scales thus loaded against new performances and performers, it is no wonder that true music lovers are now so rarely to be found at live concerts.

Given the present importance of recordings in our musical life, a sad word must be said here for the present condition of classical recording in the United States. RCA, responsible through Victor, its predecessor company, for the recordings of Enrico Caruso made in the first two decades of this century, and then, under its present name, for making Arturo Toscanini and Vladimir Horowitz—among many others—available to millions of music lovers, is now owned by Bertelsmann, a German conglomerate; CBS Records, responsible for the wonderful recordings of—again among many others—the Budapest Quartet and Bruno Walter, is owned by Sony, the Japanese electronics and media giant. All the other major record labels available in this country, including Deutsche Grammophon, Philips, Angel, and London, are owned in Europe. The result of this foreign ownership is, quite simply, that the major decisions about what of American music and musicians is to be recorded are made abroad, to satisfy commercial criteria, also determined abroad.

I suppose that the best place to wind up this dreary story is with the institutions and the patrons that make possible the existence and presentation of classical music in America. Classical music has always been a money-losing activity, requiring massive contributions, not to pay the stars but to support the intellectual and artistic infrastructure that has undergirded the Western tradition. Now, despite the massive sums being taken out of classical music by its most successful practitioners, this art is more than ever dependent on contributed income. It is contributed income that in large measure makes possible all the nonprofit institutions of classical music: these institutions include not only orchestras and opera companies, but also performing-arts centers, music schools, colleges and universities with music departments, and public television and radio.

What can be said about the present condition of these institutions, institutions devoted either wholly or in part to presenting music, or to training its practitioners? So far as the presenting of music is concerned, it might be helpful in this regard to look at what is going on in New York City, still, despite its present shaky social and financial condition, America's cultural capital. Here in New York one need do no more than look at Lincoln Center, the exemplar of all the attempts made in the 1960s and thereafter to centralize the performing arts in new buildings containing adequate and sometimes luxurious facilities and providing through their community status easy access to old and new funding sources both public and private.

As America's premier presenter of the performing arts, Lincoln Center houses the New York Philharmonic, the Metropolitan and New York City operas, and the Chamber Music Society of Lincoln Center, in addition to the New York City Ballet and the Vivian Beaumont Theater. I have discussed above the current state of the Philharmonic, and of the Metropolitan and New York City operas; it is significant that just this past May the City Opera publicly discussed the possibility of leaving the Lincoln Center umbrella and moving its performances at some point in the future to an old theater on West Forty-second Street. The City

Opera's reasons for such a revolutionary departure from the philosophy and practice of the way the musical arts are run in New York are many, and likely include competition from the vastly richer Metropolitan Opera,[3] scheduling pressure from the New York City Ballet, with which the City Opera shares the New York State Theater, and a mounting dissatisfaction with the facilities and acoustics of the State Theater itself. It must be mentioned also that the Chamber Music Society of Lincoln Center, directed for many years by the charming and musically gifted pianist Charles Wadsworth, was not long ago put under the direction of the cellist Fred Sherry. It was widely suspected that the reason for Wadsworth's replacement by Sherry was a desire for concerts that would appeal in style and repertory to the young rather than, as in the past, to the graybeards that form the backbone of the chamber-music public. Yet Sherry's tenure apparently failed to achieve its goals, and he too is now gone, leaving the Chamber Music Society rudderless.

But more important is the increased concentration of Lincoln Center on the independent production of public events. Though its constituent groups largely determine their own policies, Lincoln Center has always been something more than the sum of its constituents. In the past, it had mostly contented itself with the winter "Great Performers" concert series at Fisher Hall and with the highly successful summer "Mostly Mozart" series, also at Fisher. Of late, however, Lincoln Center, founded to be a showcase of the high performing arts, has begun to feel the hot breath of demands that it be socially and politically relevant to what is going on around it in New York City. High culture is not a very popular idea around the rhetorically populist administrations of Governor Cuomo and Mayor Dinkins. In this time of financial insecurity and raised taxes, the publicly funded arts must be seen to reach out to the entire public, not just to an elite suspected of being both undemocratic and rich. The implication is clearly that if the arts—and in this case classical music—cannot so reach out, then so much the worse for the arts and for classical music.

Thus Lincoln Center has set about a massive campaign to recast its image. Under the rubric of "Serious Fun!" it has introduced summer theatrical presentations, constituted (though as yet with little success) so as to reach the new-life-style public sympathetic to the spicy delights of the aesthetic avant-garde. With maximum fanfare, it has introduced jazz presentation as a Lincoln Center department, to the enthusiastic praise of the once staid *New York Times*. Indeed, a July full-page Lincoln Center ad in the *Times* said it all: out of the nine attractions featured, only three—"Mostly Mozart," "Live from Lincoln Center," and "Great Performers"—could be called classical attractions. Six of the presentations Lincoln Center chose to feature had nothing at all to do with high culture—"Midsummer Night Swing," recommended as a way to "Come dance with us beneath the summer stars"; "Serious Fun!" described in a quote from *New York Newsday* as "the most ambitious commissioning program in the history of Lincoln Center"; "Lincoln Center Out of Doors," described in a quote from the *New York Daily News* as "an outstanding array of events presented in the open air"; "Classical Jazz," described in a quote from the *New York Times* as "The most important jazz program in America"; "More Jazz," described, again in the *Times*, as "promis[ing] to give jazz its proper place in the American artistic pantheon"; and finally "Community Holiday Festival," described simply as "free performances [that] capture the holiday spirit." And as if to give teeth to the new Lincoln Center image, William Lockwood, the longtime head of programming for the "Mostly Mozart" and the "Great Performers" series, has now resigned; informed opinion has it that those responsible for Lincoln Center policy are requiring that Lockwood's replacement "be more than a classical-music person."

Public television and radio seem ever more concerned with the twin problems of money and ratings; unfortunately, money is not easily available for classical-music broadcasting, and the audience for classical music on television and radio, though perhaps sizable in absolute numbers, is only a small fraction of the audience of tens of millions that now constitutes the only acceptable criterion of media success. In this connection, the devoting by PBS of three prime-time evening slots this past winter to the Peter Sellars productions—or rather distortions—of *The Marriage of Figaro, Don Giovanni*, and *Così fan tutte*, was an ominous sign, in their unabashed appeal to a young, new, and classically unsophisticated audience. On radio, public broadcasting, for all the excellence of the work being done by small stations serving areas of low population density, seems to be giving up its attempt to present serious and extended classical-music concerts in metropolitan markets. Like public television (and like Lincoln Center), public radio appears to have decided to make its pitch to the new trends of gender, ethnic, and sexual multiculturalism; in this shift, classical music can hardly avoid being the loser.

In this discussion of today's musical institutions, it is hardly possible to ignore the problem of music education. College and university music departments across the country, along with music schools, are now turning out thousands upon thousands of graduates each year. As performers, these graduates are facing what is at best a bleak job market; in the better symphony orchestras, there are quite frequently hundreds of applications for each opening. Solo careers, especially for Americans, are practically nonexistent. The plain fact is that more musicians are being educated than can possibly find employment; the pressure to find positions for them is one of the major factors causing the proliferation of performing groups, all competing with each other for an ever less committed audience. It is also true that music schools are now drawing an increasing percentage of their students—often, I might add, the best ones—from the Orient. It remains unclear exactly what the motivation for this enormous influx of Asians into our music schools is. What is certain is that, given their limited acquaintance with Western culture, they have special educational needs, needs that are now being ignored. As for musicology graduates, they now find themselves thrown into a hiring world in which tenure-track positions in general are declining and which for white males hardly exist.

The last element in the current cultural situation of music to be considered is patronage—who pays for music, above and beyond what is taken in at the box office. This patronage has four components: government, corporations, foundations, and individuals. The lines between these components are not always clear, for each component exerts major influence on the other three, and contributions from one tend to draw contributions from the others.

Nevertheless, it is possible to make some general comments about the present state of these components. At the federal level, government support for music has peaked and is in all likelihood now dropping; by destroying the so-called "Good Housekeeping Seal of Approval" of NEA grants and by causing the Congress to shift funds from NEA to state disbursement, the recent scandals at the National Endowment for the Arts have hit serious music particularly hard. Furthermore, over the past few years the NEA itself has made increasingly stringent demands that its serious music grants be spent for "new," "exciting," "innovative," "cutting-edge" programs, all with increased attention to the encouragement of ethnic minorities and such formerly "underserved" areas as rural communities and inner cities. The states, suffering from severe budget crises, have taken advantage of the general loss of prestige for the arts produced by the NEA scandals to cut their own subsidies; the cuts in New Jersey and New York state, for example, have been draconian, not so much causing institutions to go out of business as forcing them to popularize their offerings in the hope of bringing in a larger paying public. Multiculturalism, too, is now being urged upon government funding sources, and this recommendation—I have mentioned above the ukase from the American Assembly—cannot but fall on political ears quite happy to appeal to organized gender, ethnic, and sexual constituencies.

One assumes—or rather one is repeatedly told—that corporate funding of music remains at much the same level as in the recent past. But it must always be remembered that corporate funding exists not for the sake of music (or the other arts) but for the sake of the image of the corporation. It will be remembered just how generous the oil companies were in supporting public television during the years of oil shortages and consequent high oil prices; though this support has largely disappeared with the decline of OPEC, we are still witnessing the presence of the cigarette industry in arts patronage as a way of ameliorating its very bad public-health reputation. Large corporate cultural grants go exclusively to high-image programs, a category that includes, in New York, both the Metropolitan Opera and the Next Wave Festival at the Brooklyn Academy of Music. Whatever the object of support, the requirement is not that the programs and institutions helped by corporations hold out the promise of being self-supporting; it is rather that they promise maximum publicity to the sponsor, and that the publicity be demonstrably targeted to politically, socially, and economically influential constituencies. In the case of small programs and institutions, corporate funding is low, and cannily calculated to spread the minimum amount of money around to the largest number of recipients.

Foundation patronage of music continues to be important, though it must be made clear that great foundations, despite their equivocations and denials, are no longer interested in ongoing support of classical music. Increasingly, foundations, if they concern themselves with music at all, are more interested in capital drives than in operating grants. A corollary of this policy is a disinclination to keep on supporting the same serious musical activities year after year: more than ever, variety is now the spice of foundation life.

And so the discussion naturally comes down to individual patrons. Gone are the days when such figures as Henry Lee Higginson at the Boston Symphony for several decades before World War I, Otto Kahn at the Metropolitan Opera in the 1920s, Clarence Mackay at the New York Philharmonic also during the 1920s, or, somewhat later, Mrs. Lytle Hull, again at the Philharmonic, would take major responsibility for the survival of institutions to which they had devoted their lives. Now musical boards are increasingly populated by people who represent either corporate funding sources or powerful community interests, or who are thought to be capable of raising money from others. There are in this matter no statistics available, so far as I am aware; but the widespread impression in the musical world is that, apart from the great institutions, individual gifts from board members are down, and that in order to get these gifts at all much more is required in the way of accurate balance-sheet projections than of musical excellence. Then, too, following the lead of colleges and universities in the past four or so decades, musical institutions are now seen by their boards as businesses, to be run with financial considerations first in mind and art second. It must be said, too, that hanging over this entire discussion of individual music patronage is the shift in the criterion for giving from the serious taste of the giver to the expectation of some popularity to be gained by the giver in the media and from the public recipients of his largesse.

Good news and bad news: an enormous human activity, performing much wonderful old music for great numbers of people, performing new music only under pressure and then to persistent failure, with everything done at great financial expense and with uncertain prospects both for the existence of sophisticated audiences and for financial survival. We should make no mistake: the issue before us is the survival, not of the classical music of the past (for great art can be preserved to come back another day), but of the place classical music has occupied in the cultural life of the West over the past two hundred years and perhaps more. During that time, classical music has been the transmitter, through its preternatural beauty, of some of the major values of the West. Some of these values, such as religion, truth, love, heroism, and honor, were communicated through a collaboration between great music and the extramusical words and symbols carried by and made more powerful through the music. Others of these values, such as order, clarity, complexity, rationality, and the worth of individual creation, were communicated more abstractly by the music in the very process of making its greatness manifest.

"All art constantly aspires towards the condition of music," Walter Pater wrote in the latter half of the century that believed art to be the successor to religion as the true salvation of human life. The classical music that we have celebrated has been for us the culmination of our civilization. Unrenewed, properly honored only in private, forced to justify itself to every demagogic politician, editorial-page writer, corporate mogul, and foundation executive, classical music now stands, for the first time in the modern world, on the periphery of culture. No matter how great the worldly success it may enjoy, no matter how high the hype that can be purchased, no matter how large the paying audience can be made to seem, classical music today is in deep trouble. It is not clear whether we can do more than bear witness.

(*The New Criterion*, 1991)

PART ONE

COMPOSERS

1

M U S I C A N D M A O

The subject of this book[1]—the penetration of music by politics—is not new. It has a disreputable history in our time as an example of the subjection of ideas to state power. What is new about Cornelius Cardew's approach is twofold: his god of action is Mao, not Stalin, and he is a willing, not an enslaved, transformer of art into propaganda. It is, one hopes, still noteworthy when a man offers himself into bondage.

Cardew is a well-known, even notorious, English experimental composer. Now approaching middle age, he was educated at the Royal Academy of Music, where he is currently professor of composition. In the late fifties he served as assistant to the German experimental composer Karlheinz Stockhausen; until the late sixties he was, by his own admission, a follower of both Stockhausen and the American John Cage. He was thus a part of the international musical avant-garde and, as such, essentially nonpolitical in his creative work, if not in his social ideas.

In 1969, along with two other English composers, Cardew founded (and himself became the driving force in) the Scratch Orchestra, a group of musicians and nonmusicians who come together for experimental performance activities. These activities included improvisation, performance of experimental compositions, performance of standard compositions in ways different from the intention of the composers and the tradition of past performances, and performances of Scratch Music.

Although it is difficult to define Scratch Music, because it did not ever achieve a settled form, Cardew's conception of it best conveys the flavor of his pre-Maoist approach to music. Scratch Music is a music of ideas-for-performance, not of sounds meant, as in traditional music, to be heard exactly as notated. It is a music of transient, changeable, impermanent qualities— its first practitioners conceived of it as being written in a scratch book. It is a set of directions for activities that may or may not involve music or even sounds. It is what anyone wants it to be.

The emphasis in the Scratch Orchestra, as can be seen from the idea of Scratch Music, was on voluntarism rather than on the discipline which is the sine qua non of traditional ensemble activities. This voluntarism led both to public scandal, consequent on the orchestra's concert behavior, and to internal disintegration amid factionalism and apathy. As of the beginning of 1975 the orchestra had temporarily been saved by several ideologically oriented Maoist participants, of whom Cardew is one. These militants have attempted to direct the orchestra away from aimless experiment and provocation and toward a conscious effort to serve the masses. On its surface, much of Cardew's book is about this attempt.

The book itself is composed of articles by others as well as by Cardew, although he has supplied all the introductory, explanatory, and connective material. The book begins with a short history of the Scratch Orchestra by Rod Eley, whom Cardew rather portentously describes as "the most educated of us." This is followed with attacks by Cardew on Cage and Stockhausen, an account of a "Critical Concert" in Berlin in 1973 at which Cardew performed avant-garde works and then flayed them on ideological grounds, and finally a chapter of self-criticism in which the composer repudiates his earlier work and attempts to map out a set of goals for a politically desirable music.

The political content of the book is a combination of Marx, Mao, and Marcuse, superficially digested and laboriously regurgitated. We are told endlessly that art and ideas reflect the class basis of the society in which they arise, that the bourgeoisie is decomposing in the face of the historically inevitable victory of the working class, and that the role of culture is to unite with the masses and hasten the revolution. Cardew and his collaborators see the avant-garde as a force attempting to escape the morbid clutches of the bourgeoisie; in their view, any support or toleration of avant-garde culture by the establishment is an exercise of repressive tolerance, a killing-by-kindness. The crime of Cage and Stockhausen is that they use their talents to produce music which, because it avoids direct involvement with politically revolutionary subjects and forces, is tolerated by the bourgeoisie even while being rejected as art. Thus the bourgeoisie wins the only victory still open to it—to delay the inevitable by co-opting the forces of change.

Cardew goes further. He attacks on ideological grounds some explicitly revolutionary compositions by two close sympathizers, Christian Wolff and Frederic Rzewski. Wolff's piece, *Accompaniments*, is set to a text taken from Jan Myrdal and Gun Kessle's *China: The Revolution Continued*. The text is a discussion by two Chinese, a veterinarian and a midwife, of the benefits to the people of the New China brought about by the improved sanitation and contraception developed in the light of Mao's thought. The music was written rapidly as a response to the text and consists of simple chords and rhythms to be applied, as is the vocal part, at the discretion of the participants. Cardew criticizes the piece on the grounds that the text is only seemingly about the revolution and its benefits; actually, he says, it is about "pollution and the population explosion, two of the great red herrings (secondary contradictions) that the bourgeoisie has brought out in the last few years to distract people's attention from the principal contradictions, capital and labor."

The two pieces of Frederic Rzewski that come in for political scrutiny are *Coming Together* and *Attica*. *Coming Together* is a setting of a letter written by Samuel Melville, a convicted radical bomber who died in the Attica rebellion, about the change in his attitudes and life caused by his imprisonment. The second piece, *Attica*, is based on a quotation of Richard X Clark, one of the leaders of the rebellion. Cardew criticizes these pieces for treating the texts musically in a subjective, fragmented, and repetitive way, so that the words become hypnotic and obsessive, rather than rationally clear. He further objects that the ideology underlying the Melville piece is anarchistic because Melville's consciousness is based on personal, rather than social, desires; therefore the piece appeals more to alienated youth than to the class-conscious proletariat.

In thus beating up on his closest comrades-in-arms, Cardew provides us with another example, and not yet the last, of the revolution devouring its children. Cardew also criticizes himself—for believing that in his compositions music and art could be autonomous, and that his music could provide a complete, self-enclosed world. He finds that this relic of bourgeois individualism as it separated him from the world also separated his music from the audience. Though he discusses fully the wrong motives musicians have had in the past as well as the motives they ought to have, nowhere does he discuss what an ideal music from his standpoint would mean in terms of notes and sounds—that is, in terms of music. Does he perhaps have in mind the Chinese anthem, *The East Is Red*? Or perhaps that product of collective composition, the *Yellow River Concerto*? Has any music been written that would satisfy his political criteria? Cardew seems able only to assist in the destruction of the past and the present, not to help in the construction even of his own future.

The problem, of course, is that he wishes to put culture at the service of politics. This desire, which surfaces at times of cultural and social crisis, remains eternally green in the face of the most shocking enormities perpetrated in its name. One need only point to the atrocities committed upon ideas—and what is worse, on people—whenever politics has taken command in our time. From the repression and liquidation of Soviet writers in the thirties, to the exile and murder of German writers by Hitler, to the extraordinary ravings of Mao's Cultural Revolution, the contemporary man of ideas has become a target for the exercise and abuse of arbitrary power. Ideas have suffered, and their holders have been killed. Cardew is selling a remedy nobody wants for himself. The record is clear; for culture, twentieth-century revolutions, whether of the left or of the right, have been a curse, not a blessing.

There is a further foolishness in Cardew's argument. He continually invokes the coming revolution of the working class. But where has it come: in the Soviet Union? Is Russia, that land without soviets and unions, controlled by the working class? China? Is not China controlled by yet another group of bureaucrats ruling under the self-proclaimed mandate of heaven? Where is the legitimacy of any of these revolutions? Perhaps Cardew sees the British working class, or the American, as a revolutionary force. But he has no evidence for this pipe dream, and the lack of evidence only makes his voice more isolated and shrill.

Music and Mao

Why, then, since this book is obviously meant as a political tract from beginning to end, does it seem to have so little to do with politics? Because its motivation is so strongly personal, and Cardew so strongly wants to be a musician. His tribute to the music of the nineteenth century must have been painful indeed to write:

> I believe I speak for the vast majority of music lovers when I say: let's face it, modern music . . . is not half as good as classical music. . . . What does good mean in that sentence? It means effective, wholesome, moving, satisfying, delightful, inspiring, stimulating. . . . By comparison with [what] we . . . derive from Beethoven, Brahms, and the rest, modern music (with very few exceptions) is footling, unwholesome, sensational, frustrating, offensive, and depressing.

It is no fun to be a child of such a parent. His rage and envy in the face of the past comes through clearly in his remarks on Wagner:

> I have never seen a Wagner opera. . . . I . . . know a piano duet version of the Prelude to Act III of Tristan and Isolde and once played in the fifth desk of cellos in a non-professional performance of the same piece. . . . I can hear someone saying, "My lad, if you've reached the ripe age of thirty-six without having learned anything about Wagner, you have only yourself to blame." Well, I think the reason is that virtually everything written and said about Wagner and his music is extremely boring and irrelevant to the present time, and reasonable musicians with a certain amount of work to do could not be expected to plough through it.

Is this a reason for not listening to the music? It seems much more like a rationalization of disappointment too deeply minded to be faced. Cardew laments his own lack of skills:

> I realize that I am not at all qualified to apply technical criteria because in my own period of training I had never mastered anything more than the rudiments. The rest had seemed irrelevant in view of my desire to break with the traditions of tonal music completely. The fact that I was able to pass exams and get diplomas despite my extremely limited compositional technique is due entirely to the fatally liberalistic attitude that permeates our education system.

One can only sympathize with his disappointed hopes and his frustrated ambitions.

It is clear that Cardew bitterly misses an audience for his works; he writes movingly of "the composer's bright dreams that wither up and die for lack of audience." The book discusses time and again the loss of audience and the resultant isolation of the artist; indeed, it seems to represent not so much a case of music supporting a political position as the case of a composer desiring to secure an audience even at the cost of submerging himself in it. It is clear, however, that this is a price Cardew will never be able to pay; not only does he cherish still (though unconsciously) his individuality, but there is also no large enveloping entity on the horizon with which he might negotiate the sale of his soul. Like the devil, revolution in Western society is a myth conjured up to deal with feelings of powerlessness; nobody believes in the revolution, Communists least of all. Cardew, alas, is condemned to freedom.

Cardew must be credited, though, with accurately describing the three most important elements in the musical crisis of the twentieth century. The achievement of the eighteenth and nineteenth centuries was overpoweringly strong; music education in our time has become academically fettered and musically slack; and the audience has died. The evidence is easily available. The musical repertory is not expanded by bringing in new or recently written pieces. It is expanded by finding "new" old pieces—forgotten operas of Donizetti or recently completed symphonies of Mahler. Music appreciation is increasingly confined to the dreary classes of our colleges, while music schools, in order to survive economically, try to make themselves relevant by training guitarists and giving courses in Far Eastern music and multimedia events. And the death of the audience is shown not only by the lack of interest in contemporary music, but even more tellingly by the fact, for instance, that both the New York Philharmonic and the Metropolitan Opera must advertise at enormous cost in order to recruit ticket buyers. The story is the same with the sale of classical records as with attendance at recitals.

The effect of all this on the creative musician has been disastrous. He cannot escape the shadow of the great masters; but his society will not allow him to rest content with being derivative. He does not starve: teaching jobs keep the wolf from the door. And there is the direct philanthropy of our governments and foundations, who will pay him if he does what they desire. But for whom does he write? Who listens? Who cares? Nobody. Not here in America, not in Europe, and not in Russia or

China, save when the masses are told they must. Writing music is like falling in love. One has to have someone to do it with.

The saving grace of this book, and of Cardew in general, is a certain wit, a faint suggestion of the sainted Stephen Potter, the renowned gamesman who taught us all how the athletically untalented might win at sports. Potter, behind the façade he so humorously presented of small-time cunning and bumbling trickery, was a spokesman for all those born against their will into a world of the taller and the more handsome, the richer and the quicker. This is an attractive and typically English attitude of resisting the big battalions of strength and talent by purity of desire, if not of motive. Cardew's political cause is not mine, but his musical cause may very well be. And in any case, how does one reject a man who can write, "Though Cage and Stockhausen have no hold on the working class, they did have a strong hold on me . . . "? Just think—all those millions of brawny workers and Cardew's tenderest feelings marching toward the sunrise as equals. Any gamesman will recognize the triumph.

(*Commentary*, 1975)

2

WHY KURT WEILL?

Suddenly, within the limited world of New York opera, Kurt Weill is all the rage. During the 1979–80 season, the Metropolitan Opera produced Weill's 1929 collaboration with Bertolt Brecht, *The Rise and Fall of the City of Mahagonny*, and also chose it for one of the company's valuable evenings on nationwide television. The New York City Opera has given similar exposure this past season to its revival of Weill's 1947 setting of Langston Hughes's adaptation of the Elmer Rice play *Street Scene*. The City Opera, furthermore, has just introduced an augmented adaptation of the Weill-Georg Kaiser play with music, *Silverlake* (1932); this new production, a kind of world premiere, was recorded shortly after the opening performance by Nonesuch for early release.

Not only have the stagings of Weill been seen and heard in New York opera houses and on television screens across the country. Reams of writing about Weill and his music are also becoming available to the interested reader. Journalists and music historians—building on the work of David Drew, an English critic and lonely laborer in the Weill vineyard for the past generation—have been emerging to tell the story of Weill's life and evaluate his pieces. Thus, beyond the flurry of newspaper and magazine coverage of the recent performances, there has just appeared a discursive and admiring biography of the composer, *The Days Grow Short*, by Ronald Sanders,[1] and the past year has also seen the publication of what reads like an expanded doctoral dissertation, *Kurt Weill in Europe*,[2] by Kim H. Kowalke.

Because Weill was highly successful twice while he lived—the first time after the 1928 premiere of *The Threepenny Opera* in Berlin, and the second as a composer of Broadway musicals just before and during World War II—and then again just after his death, with the New York production of *The Threepenny Opera* in 1954, the present interest cannot be understood simply as the discovery of a relatively unknown figure. It is rather a current manifestation of the appeal of a composer at once easy to grasp and difficult to categorize, and of a music at once off-putting and pleasing.

As a man, Kurt Weill was a product of the cultural flowering, under conditions of relative toleration, of German Jewry. He was born in 1900 in Dressau, also the birthplace of the most famous exemplar of the German-Jewish tension between particularism and universalism, Moses Mendelssohn. Whereas Mendelssohn was the son of a Torah scribe, Weill's father was a cantor and a composer of sacred music; as such he participated in the assimilation of traditional Jewish chanting to the then regnant oratorio style associated with German Protestantism.

Of three siblings Weill was the least inclined toward religion. Nevertheless, an outlet for his natural musicality was easily found in the rich secular musical life of Dessau—in particular an operatic theater strongly Wagnerian and patronized by the local nobility. In a minor way, Weill (who began composing at the age of ten or eleven) was the direct beneficiary of this patronage, as he was also of the contact with Jewish music lovers so often available then to the young and artistically gifted.

His first entry into a larger musical world came in 1918 with his matriculation at the famous Hochschule für Musik in Berlin. During his single semester there he studied composition with Engelbert Humperdinck, the disciple of Wagner and the composer of *Hansel and Gretel*. In the difficult economic conditions following the German defeat in World War I, he made an attempt at supporting himself through minor conducting jobs in provincial opera houses. Meanwhile he continued to compose—a string quartet, a cello sonata, two one-act operas, and an oratorio based on the Song of Songs (all still unpublished and in some cases lost). Then, in December 1920, Weill was accepted as a student at the Prussian Academy of Arts in the master class of Ferruccio Busoni, the

Italo-German composer whose greatest fame was as a legendary piano virtuoso. Before his encounter with Busoni, Weill had been under the spell of the German romantics; under the influence of Busoni's idiosyncratic combination of modernism and classicism, Weill's music began to reflect the stirrings of the avant-garde and the concomitant rejection of the nineteenth century.

An early document of this turn to the present may be found in Weill's First Symphony, begun in 1920 but drastically altered upon its completion in the first months of his association with Busoni. As the symphony stands now, it is a piece of absolute music in the sense that it employs only instruments and sets no words, but it was in fact written under the inspiration of a socialist-pacifist play by Johannes Becher. Becher was soon to discover the Marxism which allowed him to end his life as a culture bureaucrat in East Germany after World War II; prophetically enough, the play which inspired Weill was called *Workers, Peasants, and Soldiers: The Awakening of a People to God*. In its final form, Weill's First Symphony owes something to the harsh expressionism of early-modern Schoenberg, and something also to the melodic ethos of Mahler.

But after a few other pieces, including the Violin Concerto of 1924 with its Stravinsky-like timbre, Weill stopped writing purely instrumental music (and would only make one further essay in that area, the Second Symphony of 1934) in favor of music utilizing the power of words. This turn no doubt owed something to Weill's background, which combined the worlds of synagogue music and the provincial opera theater. But a more important cause must have been the impulse that has so often driven composers toward opera: the desire to find a wider audience. The audience Weill had in mind was not the kind which had in the past supported what he called "socially exclusive, 'aristocratic' art"; instead he envisioned a public composed of "simple, naive, unassuming and traditionless listeners, who, trained by work, sport, and technical skill, bring along their healthy sense of fun and seriousness, good and bad, old and new." It may be questioned whether Weill ever made a serious attempt to find this pot of artistic gold at the end of the proletarian rainbow. It is, however, clear that the very act of looking for a broad audience meant a drastic change from the sophisticated and relatively inaccessible world of musical modernism to which Weill was in other ways sympathetic; in fact the rest of Weill's compositional career was to be marked by pre-cisely the search for effect which lies at the heart of nineteenth-century romanticism.

Weill's first mature attempt at opera was the nondescript—though ini-tially successful—*Der Protagonist* (1924–25), a collaboration with the German expressionist playwright Georg Kaiser. Heard today in an obvi-ously poor tape of an Italian radio broadcast, the music seems heavy for all its dryness of texture; one excerpt, a pantomime for both instruments and voices, has been recorded but possesses little distinct musical char-acter.

Another 1925 work makes a more attractive impression. *Der neue Or-pheus*, a cantata for soprano, violin, and orchestra written to a text by the poet Iwan Goll, is a retelling of the famous Greek legend in the setting of modern Berlin. The work marked an important way station on Weill's road to a more accessible style, employing suggestions of popular music drawn from the burgeoning cabaret world. This tendency became more pronounced in the 1925–26 *Royal Palace*, again to a text by Goll, which incorporated such popular dance forms as the tango and the foxtrot, and was marked by the sharp, insistent rhythms later so characteristic of Weill. One more work of these years closed out Weill's searchings: *Der Zar lässt sich photographieren* ("The Czar Has His Picture Taken"), a 1927 collaboration with Kaiser, in which Weill again used popular dance forms. Clearly for his breakthrough only one thing was lacking—a li-brettist with his finger on the pulse of the times.

That librettist, of course, turned out to be Bertolt Brecht. The partisans of Weill and Brecht differ as to the relative importance of each in their joint efforts. Neither Sanders in his Weill biography nor Kowalke in his musicological study is immune to this kind of special pleading for Weill. And on Brecht's behalf, Eric Bentley goes so far as to claim basic author-ship for some of Weill's most famous music. Whoever influenced whom must remain a moot question; Weill and Brecht were both overflowing with theories about what they thought they were doing and what others should be doing.

Much critical writing has been devoted to these theories—in particular Brecht's idea of epic theater and alienation, and Weill's conception of "gestic" music and opera as a return to the dramatic musical theater of Mozart. Though the precise application of these notions seemed vague, their general drift was clear enough: the world of individual and private concerns was to be transvalued through a simplified and schematic presentation of generalized symbols and mass emotions. In art similar movements were involving the replacement of the easel painting by the poster; in the theater it produced the rise of the agitprop play. But whatever the artform, the artist's goal was to find and merge with the audience of the democratized future—the people.

In theory this new audience was located in the working class, but where Brecht and Weill actually found it was in the same middle class which had for so long supported high culture. This once proud social alignment had, however, been mortally weakened by military defeat and economic disintegration, and in its weakened condition it was open to the fatal allure of two creations of its enemies—radical politics and popular culture. Brecht, who was soon to become an out-and-out Marxist and, some highly trumpeted divagations notwithstanding, would remain a Communist hero for the rest of his life, recognized the implications of all this more clearly than Weill. Yet despite the fact that Weill seems to have shunned organizational affiliations and loyalties, and that according to his wife and exponent, Lotte Lenya, he was (at this time in Berlin) "a liberal like everyone else," it is obvious from the work he did with Brecht just how closely their views coincided.

Their first collaboration, in 1927, involved a setting by Weill of several poems from Brecht's *Die Hauspostille* ("Domestic Breviary") about life in Mahagonny, an imaginary American boom town where the possession of money is the only virtue, opportunism the only standard of conduct, and alcohol the universal solvent. Weill's musical parody of a cantata, called the *Mahagonny Songspiel*, contained one of his greatest hits, the "Alabama Song," a sinuous melody fairly dripping with sexual insinuation and languorous eroticism. Elsewhere the music is prevailingly light, tuneful, and attractive. The style is unabashedly popular, and the influence of American jazz—Weill was a great admirer of Louis Armstrong—everywhere apparent. Gone altogether are the clotted sonorities and the free tonality of Weill's earlier music.

The *Mahagonny Songspiel* was first staged at the Baden-Baden Festival, at that time the shrine of contemporary music, in the summer of 1927. The work was a sensation, both for the music and for the production, which placed Lotte Lenya in the middle of a boxing ring and employed actors wearing overalls to troop around with placards bearing left-wing slogans. The réclame was sufficient to inspire Brecht and Weill to enlarge the short work into a full-length opera, portentously called *Aufstieg und Fall der Stadt Mahagonny* (The Rise and Fall of the City of Mahagonny).

Before completing this task, however, they took the time to produce a work that more than anything else was to make their fame. *Die Dreigroschenoper*—in its English version *The Threepenny Opera*—was written for a young Berlin producer who was looking for a modern play with a musical score. The idea of updating John Gay's *Beggar's Opera* (1728) had come to Brecht from one of his assistants, and it immediately impressed the producer as "smelling of theater." The story is, as can quickly be seen, at heart the same as that of Brecht's *Mahagonny* poems. Morality is reversed: the hero is a highwayman, beggars are millionaires, and true aristocracy comes from success in crime.

In his score Weill now continued the procedure he had followed in the *Mahagonny* suite—a succession of musical numbers, each constituent song being complete in itself. In *The Threepenny Opera*, as in so much of what he was to write from then on, the musical momentum, insofar as it existed at all, was interrupted at regular intervals for spoken dialogue and stage action. For Weill this was a personal discovery linking his work to Mozart and to *Der Freischütz* of Weber; for those who had come to expect music to absorb the drama, all Weill had managed was to write incidental music for the theater.

These niceties aside, the *Dreigroschenoper* was a phenomenal success. The combination of the gutter cynicism so beloved of Brecht and the jazzy tunefulness of Weill scored instantly; eventually the biggest hit was the opening "Ballad of Mack the Knife," inserted at the last moment to please an actor who wished to show off his fancy clothes (though it was later given to someone with a less pleasant voice). Just how broad was the appeal of this recital of the hero's evil deeds may be gathered from its fourth stanza (the words written, it must be remembered, by a supporter of proletarian internationalism and set by a Jewish composer):

Und Schmul Meier bleibt verschwunden
Und so mancher reiche Mann
Und sein Geld hat Mackie Messer
Dem man nichts beweisen kann.[3]

[And Samuel Meier disappeared for good,
As well as many a rich man,
And Mack the Knife has all his money
Though you cannot prove a thing.]

How percipient to have found, in the Berlin of 1928, a sentiment on which left and right could both agree!

Barely hidden beneath the nihilism and the romanticizing of violence was a vein of maudlin sentimentality informing both Brecht's dramatic conception and Weill's music. To the themes of true love among the fallen and the romantic pirate of legend Brecht added the happiest of happy endings—reprieve from the gallows combined with instant accession to the aristocracy—while Weill's music alternated honky-tonk melodies with jazzy ostinatos and an occasional parody of a religious chorale. This mockery of middle-class conventions could only profit from middle-class self-hatred and from the persistent attachment of the audience to the sentiments being parodied.

Neither Weill nor Brecht could have been altogether happy with the reputation for frivolity they so quickly gained from the *Dreigroschenoper* and they made several ineffectual attempts at thoroughgoing seriousness; notably, the *Berliner Requiem* of 1928, written on commission from the German Radio to commemorate the tenth anniversary of the Spartacist uprising, and a "didactic cantata" on the subject of Lindbergh's transatlantic solo flight, *Der Lindberghflug* of 1929—high-minded, mostly solemn, and dull.

The full-length operatic version of *Mahagonny* possesses more interest. As the recent Metropolitan Opera production makes clear, Brecht's book is immensely powerful and fascinatingly perverse in its presentation of man as a beast. Weill's music, however, again cast in the form of conventional song numbers and orchestral interludes, with most of the action carried by spoken dialogue, is thinner in content than the score of *Dreigroschenoper*, and overall there is an air of repetition.

His score for the next collaboration with Brecht, *Happy End* (1929), the story of a Salvation Army effort to save some gangsters, was replete with what had by now become his familiar banalities—marches, hymns, ballads. In the case of this work, Brecht's book was no better than Weill's music. The explicit social message here overwhelmed the sentimentality, and not surprisingly the price was lack of popular success.

So too, and even more clearly, with *Der Jasager* (The Yes-sayer), of 1930. Intended for performance by high-school students, it concerns a boy's desire to obtain medicine from a distant place for his sick mother, his inability to sustain the pace of those with whom he is traveling to that place, and his agreeing to being killed in order to allow the others to proceed safely. The twin themes of totalitarian acquiescence and the subordination of the individual to the group were to occupy Brecht for much of his creative life. Indeed, the similarity of *Der Jasager* to Brecht's notorious *Die Massnahme* (The Measures Taken)—written in collaboration with the composer Hanns Eisler the same year and asserting the need for revolutionaries to liquidate those who even unwittingly betray them—only confirms his ultimate moral decision to come down on the side of tyranny.[4]

Weill's music for the parable of Leninist virtue Brecht produced in *Der Jasager* is plain, plodding, and repetitious, though in its treatment of the relationship between mother and son it is not without its mawkish aspects. Indeed, given the means to which Weill restricted himself in order to make the work performable by young and untrained students, such a musical outcome was no doubt inevitable. And yet the very plainness and repetition of Weill's music seem to reinforce the idea of obedience to a simple, clear, and efficient authority.

On several grounds—his progressivism, his work with Brecht, his use of mockery, and above all his Jewish origin—Weill was anathema to the coming Hitler regime. The premiere of *Mahagonny* had been greeted by a popular disturbance in which the Nazis may well have had a hand; a subsequent performance in Oldenburg was canceled under Nazi pressure. Still more ominous was the reaction to Weill's final large work of his German period, *Der Silbersee* (The Silverlake) of 1932, a collaboration with Georg Kaiser. Though ideological radicalism here went by the boards, as Weill's musical radicalism had gone sometime before, the Nazis disrupted a performance in Magdeburg and soon made performance anywhere in Germany impossible.

In *Silbersee* Weill wrote a score remarkable, even for him, in its indulgence of pastiche: parody and sincerity, conventional opera and cabaret, waltz and tango—all are thrown into the pot. Just how little the effort succeeded in arousing the audience may be gathered from the wholesale changes and additions the New York City Opera has found it necessary to make in its current production. Uniquely in the case of what we are told is a major work by a composer deserving serious attention, the published credits for the production read:

Silverlake, opera in two acts by Kurt Weill. Libretto by Hugh Wheeler, based on the original libretto by Georg Kaiser. Lyrics by Lys Symonette. Additional music from Weill's incidental music to Strindberg's "Gustaf III" and Leo Lania's "Konjunktur" integrated by Miss Symonette.

Like so many artists of his time and place, Weill was now to be on the run. His first stop was France where, in addition to composing some trifles *à la française*, he wrote the music to his final work with Brecht, the ballet with singing *Die sieben Todsünden* (The Seven Deadly Sins), a title Brecht later made more explicit by adding *der Kleinbürger* (of the Petit Bourgeoisie). This tale of two sisters, one speaking for respectable virtue, the other indulging instinct and desire, ends with virtue cynically rewarded as they retire from their wanderings to a small house purchased by the licentious one's earnings. What could earlier in Weill's music career have been construed as, at least on one level, hostile parody, here became mere entertainment, for with *Die sieben Todsünden* Weill was in fact well on the way to his later American career as a composer of Broadway musicals.

Further evidence of this trend can be adduced from Weill's Second Symphony (1934), his last purely instrumental composition. Written in Paris, it represented an unambiguous rejection of the modernism of its

1921 predecessor; unhappily, like so many artistic retreats, it issued in vapidity.

In emigrating to America in 1935, Weill joined a flood of refugee intellectuals who were about to establish the first resident cosmopolitanism this culture had ever known. Viewed from the vantage point of today's hardheaded cultural internationalism, some of the early stirrings of this new sophistication are embarrassing. Such was the case with Weill's first major American project, a grandiose scheme hatched in the fertile brain of Meyer Weisgal, the fabled Zionist fund-raiser. Weisgal aimed at nothing less than staging the entire history of the Jewish people, written by Franz Werfel and directed by Max Reinhardt. The size of the undertaking—it was found necessary to gut and then restructure a large Manhattan theater—guaranteed both endless delays and eventual financial failure. Weill's score has almost totally disappeared, along with the hopes of everyone involved.

His next major project was an antiwar musical, with a text by the mildly left-wing writer Paul Green. *Johnny Johnson*, which was revived and recorded in the 1950s by an excellent cast, seems now merely puerile in its sentimental pacifism, looking backward as it does to World War I rather than to the looming menace of Hitler. Artistically the effect is one of an incongruous linkage between a music that still retains European elements and a libretto exuding the comfortable certainties of American provincialism.

Everything changed for Weill, however, with his first real American success, *Knickerbocker Holiday*, written in 1938 to an antifascist (but also anti-Roosevelt) book by Maxwell Anderson. Heard today, the show seems an unintentionally funny mixture of piety and oafish humor surrounding the wistful "September Song."

Success beckoned again in 1941, with Weill's score for *Lady in the Dark*, in which Moss Hart brought to Broadway the emergent cultural interest in psychoanalysis. No greater contrast to the showy social nihilism of Weill's Brecht years could have been found. The use of fantasy to enable a successful career woman to accept the reality of her life—and the implicit celebration of the American values of success and prosperity—are telling evidence both of the power of this country to absorb its immigrants and of Weill's essential adaptability to the winds of ideological change. Nothing now appears especially memorable about Weill's music, and it seems a safe bet to say that the work was carried, on the stage, as it is on a surviving recording, by Gertrude Lawrence's brilliant performance in the title role.

Now that the war was on, Weill devoted much attention to providing entertainment for workers in defense plants. This project, perhaps not altogether happily named the "Lunch Time Follies," pleased him greatly, for it was an opportunity to reach a different and even less sophisticated audience than his Broadway successes allowed. He returned to Broadway, however, in 1943, with *One Touch of Venus*, to an S. J. Perelman story with lyrics by Ogden Nash. Once again the moral is one of acceptance: a man falls in love with a statue of Venus he has inadvertently summoned to life, but eventually settles willingly for her homey, real-life lookalike. As with his other American scores, most of what remains to be heard today is only the oily polish of Broadway, rather than any real musical or dramatic penetration.

Much less commercially successful was his 1945 musical, *The Firebrand of Florence*, a collaboration with Ira Gershwin; what little of the score has been recorded sounds like an artificial combination of would-be seriousness and uninspired patter. Two years later Weill attempted a full-fledged Broadway opera, *Street Scene*, adapted from Elmer Rice's 1929 play and supplied with lyrics by the Negro poet Langston Hughes. Rice was here expressing the disgust felt by intellectuals at the end of the 1920s as they viewed American life; Hughes's adaptation after World War II was backward-looking rather than pertinent to its moment, and Weill's music played on this inherent character of dated sentimentality. What he wrote has been called by a historian of the American musical theater "thoughtful and appropriate," but it might more accurately be described as tear-jerking without being memorable.

Now Weill became involved in yet another school opera, though one a world away from the *Jasager* of his Brechtian days, with its heavy moral message and its essentially colorless, neutral music. In *Down in the Valley* (1948) Weill used Arnold Sundgaard's story of a man who is to be hanged for killing the tormentor of his true love as the basis for an American folk opera, employing actual folk songs as melodic material. The work has been widely performed in colleges and universities; it has served many young people as their first introduction to opera. Unfortunately, the whole is again marked by musical thinness and the practiced exploitation of audience sympathy.

Weill's last completed work was the Broadway musical *Lost in the Stars* (1949), based on Alan Paton's then bestselling novel about racial oppression in South Africa, *Cry, the Beloved Country.* It was only fitting that Weill's American career, which had gotten off the ground with Maxwell Anderson in *Knickerbocker Holiday,* should have ended in collaboration with Anderson on this congenial subject, so presciently reflecting the rise of the color problem in the United States itself. Weill's music eschews any serious attempt at African folk realism and, like all his Broadway efforts, now seems the very model of glossy, high-minded commercialism. He died on April 3, 1950, during the musical's moderately successful run.

For all the talk about Kurt Weill's contribution to our native musical style, his American career is difficult to take seriously in artistic terms. Four musicals, a Broadway opera, a host of projects large and small: all this has left behind only a few songs beloved by aficionados of the genre.

Some of this disappointing record is implicit in the nature of popular culture in general and the Broadway musical in particular. Because popular culture is fleeting and ephemeral, its specific manifestations are necessarily short-lived; the very intensity of success bears within itself the seeds of obsolescence and replacement. As for Broadway, it represents at best an uneasy marriage between musicians of generally serious background and the lure of show-business fame. Yet even among Broadway composers, it is hardly self-evident that Weill stands apart from his rivals, among whom may be counted (in ascending order of musical talent) Richard Rodgers, Leonard Bernstein, and—on the level of real if flawed genius—George Gershwin. Certainly nothing Weill wrote can compare musically with *Porgy and Bess.*

Weill was, it is true, remarkably malleable in his ability to echo national styles. Harold Clurman, for example, has written of him: "If he had landed among the Hottentots, he would have become the outstanding Hottentot composer of the Hottentot theater." Yet how far Weill was from penetrating the American psyche is obvious from comparing his *Down in the Valley* with such an authentic piece of Americana as Douglas Moore's *The Ballad of Baby Doe* (1956). Moore's melodies bear the stamp of the American past; his musical architecture seems particularly attuned to the place of the frontier in our history; most of all, his well-made music, though ultimately minor, gives an impression of depth and richness. In the final analysis, where Moore evokes America, Weill evokes Broadway.

There are, to be sure, important features common to Weill's American and European careers. Chief among these similarities is the use at important moments of easily comprehensible tunes made up of repeated fragments at once short and lush. The element of motoric excitement, which often seems in Weill rattle for rattle's sake, tended to diminish as he selected subjects more reflective of conventional pieties. He usually set words so that they could be clearly heard; much of this clarity was, however, a result of the sparseness of the musical texture surrounding them. And further easing the problems of performance, most of his music is comfortably singable by nonoperatic vocalists.

Weill's reliance on relatively untrained singers is deeply related to the essential nature of his musical aims. The kinds of performers for whom he wrote are more at home in the communication of words than in music per se; his wife and greatest interpreter, Lotte Lenya, has been a prime example of what his work needs to be most effective. But such performers are not really musicians; they are actors and entertainers who happen to sing. So it is hardly surprising to find that, for all of Weill's statements in the 1920s about the power of music and its properly independent role in opera, his work marks a retreat from the high ambition and accomplishment of the nineteenth century. For Wagner as for Beethoven, music was in practice as well as in theory a universal language with an all-inclusive vocabulary describing every human emotion, thought, and activity. In Weill, on the other hand, music was at its best restricted to heightening mood and feeling, to fixing a moment in the audience's mind, to being attractive even when what was happening on the stage was not.

Weill thus remains a composer of music for the theater rather than a composer of opera. The audience for which he wrote, after all, was not primarily a musical one. It was not interested in a permanent musical creation meant to be heard and reheard, but rather in a one-time theatrical experience. In Berlin his audience came from the cabaret; in America its home was the Great White Way.

This is why Weill was at his best where the theater to which his music was incidental was at its best—in the *Dreigroschenoper* and, to a lesser extent, *Mahagonny*. When Brecht was not at his best, as in *Happy End* and *Die sieben Todsünden*, Weill slipped from sentimentality into banality. And when Weill's collaborators were drawn from Broadway, there his music remained.

Just how little Weill's music stands on its own, how superficial and pallid it is when deprived of staging and words, becomes obvious from his own instrumental arrangement of the score for *The Threepenny Opera* (*Kleine Dreigroschenmusik*). And yet it would be a mistake to underestimate Weill's contribution to the *Dreigroschenoper* and *Mahagonny*. That contribution was to provide the open, unashamed emotion needed to make palatable and even to cloak Brecht's cynicism and nihilism. Weill was the sugar coating on Brecht's bitter pill; it was he who sensed that in maudlin tunefulness lay the key to a successful attack on the bastions both of bourgeois respectability and of high culture.

By now, of course, we have been vaccinated a thousand times against Weill-Brecht and against Weill-Broadway. What once was shocking in the one and brightly new in the other is now merely pleasant and beguiling, melody and lyrics for a night on the town. Perhaps the most important meaning of the current interest in Weill, then, is that New York's two opera companies—one of them among the leading houses in the world—have chosen to cater so prominently to just such a taste.

(*Commentary*, 1980)

3

AMERICAN MUSIC

The Years of Hope

On one of the accreditation visits that European guardians of cultural life periodically pay us, the polyglot literary critic George Steiner has measured America and found it, as ever, wanting. Writing in the quarterly *Salmagundi* (Fall 1980/Winter 1981), he rejects the creative significance of our entire society, accusing us of having produced nothing, save some literature, of original importance. What virtues we have, in his view, are either importations from the old country or applications of wealth and energy to the conserving of otherwise alien artifacts.

In his strictures Steiner says a great deal about our musical life as well, and ventures a broad characterization of American efforts in composition. The passage is worth quoting at some length:

Roger Sessions [and] Elliott Carter are composers of undoubted stature. Charles Ives is a most intriguing "original." Up to this point in its history, however, American music has been of an essentially provincial character. The great symphony of "the new world" is by Dvořák. It is Varèse's *Amériques* which comes nearest to a musical transposition of its spacious subject. Again, limiting oneself to the 20th century—a limitation inherently weighted in America's favor—it is obvious that there are in American music no names to set beside those of Stravinsky, of Schoenberg, of Bartók, of Alban Berg and Anton von Webern, that the *oeuvre* of a Prokofiev, of a Shostakovich, perhaps even of a Benjamin Britten represents an executive "density" and imaginative continuity strikingly absent from the work of American composers. And even if the Stockhausen-Boulez era is now passing, its role, its formal and substantive logic in the history of Western music, are on a level which, until now, American composers have rarely challenged, let alone matched.

To answer this comprehensive charge in Steiner's terms is to deal with it on the ground staked out by his admirably skillful use of language. Although he limits his consideration to this century—a frame of reference he finds weighted in our favor—in fact all the figures he mentions, with the exception of Shostakovich and Britten, were formed musically well before World War I, that great watershed in high musical culture. And even here he hedges a bit, speaking only of the oeuvres of Prokofiev, Shostakovich, and Britten. Similarly, although he does not praise Boulez and Stockhausen explicitly, by mentioning their "formal and substantive logic" he manages to avoid giving the proper devil's due to John Cage.

Perhaps we ought to be inured to this sort of thing; Steiner's cultural diagnosis, after all, only carries on in the spirit of his predecessors, going all the way back to Mrs. Trollope. And yet—can it be denied that what he says about our music finds an extraordinary resonance in our own attitude toward ourselves? For what Steiner has done is only to echo, pointedly it is true, the verdict of our own musical institutions, large and small, rich and poor, superior and inferior; among these institutions I give, as is only proper, pride of place to our audience.

It takes no great perspicacity to observe that we are at this time securely a musical colony of Europe and of the musicians Europe has trained. Our great orchestras are, as if by right, in the hands of foreign maestri; even the aspiring ensembles of sunbelt and badlands feel the need to employ these missionaries to the heathen. As with conductors, so with soloists and singers. And since commercial developments do in fact mirror the expression of cultivated taste, we can hardly be surprised at the virtually complete withdrawal of major American companies from the domestic recording of serious music.

In the world of American composition, the situation is the same. The recent tenure of Pierre Boulez at the New York Philharmonic, intellectually and musically the most interesting such period in the domestic musical life of the past quarter century, was marked by expressed disdain for almost all our native products. Elsewhere new American works have been and are being played, but these performances arise out of a sense of duty and a consciousness of external pressure; it is not too much to say that each premiere has about it the palpable air of a final performance. The recent Kennedy Center American music competition, in which the works of even the most respected and best-known American composers were submitted, seems tacit confirmation of the general predicament of our creative situation. The meager result of the musical components of our 1976 Bicentennial celebration is, alas, another.

Was it always so? One piece of evidence suggests that things were once better, that American music in another day was marked both by hope and by a sense of fulfillment. The piece of evidence is the spate of birthdays of our grand old composers which we have been celebrating in the past few years. In 1980 Aaron Copland—a child of the century— was eighty; William Schuman and Samuel Barber were seventy; Virgil Thomson, at eighty-four, was given the accolade of a PBS special. And to round out our recent observances, three years ago Elliott Carter was seventy, and five years ago Roger Sessions was eighty.

The attention devoted to the birthday of Copland in particular suggests, as such events always do, that history is preferred to actuality. Yet the enjoyment with which today's audiences listen to Copland's music is undeniable; a Copland concert even does well at the box office. And public reaction to the now frequently played music of Barber and Schuman, though perhaps less full-blooded than in the case of Copland, carries the same message: this is our music, our sound, and our pleasure.

Let us then, for the moment, leave behind George Steiner's negative conclusions. Let us rather try to answer a valuable question posed in the headline of a recent article by Peter Davis in the *New York Times*: "America's Senior Composers—Why Was Their Impact Profound?" Davis's own answer stresses the relative simplicity and unity of the music scene of the 1930s and 1940s, as contrasted with today's fragmentation, and the fact that such men as Copland were the first American composers who were sufficiently free of the prior taint of Eurocentric academicism to use national materials and speak with a national voice.

Any attempt to expand and broaden Davis's answer, and to draw con-

clusions from it, should properly begin with a consideration of the remarkable confluence of creative talent born in the two decades centered
on 1900. If we perform the unfashionable task of looking up birth dates,
we shall find that these years produced no fewer than eleven major
American composers, each of whom has written a body of interesting,
significant, and affecting music. Merely to name them in the order of
their birth dates is to appreciate their riches. In 1893 Douglas Moore was
born, and in 1894 Walter Piston; in 1896, Virgil Thomson, Howard
Hanson, and Roger Sessions; in 1897 Henry Cowell, and in 1898 Roy
Harris; in 1900 Aaron Copland; in 1908 Elliott Carter, and in 1910
Samuel Barber and William Schuman. Though none of these men is unknown—and a few of them have been the object of national attention—
the music of several is today almost forgotten, and the music of others is
honored more in the breach than in the hearing. For that reason it may be
worthwhile to sketch, in however rudimentary a fashion, the achievement of these eleven composers.

To begin with Douglas Moore is to make clear the ground of American
consciousness on which so many of these composers have stood.
Moore's first mature work was the 1924 *Pageant of P. T. Barnum*. Some
years after his innocent and happy treatment of America's favorite show-
man, he went on in 1938 to set Stephen Vincent Benét's *The Devil and
Daniel Webster*. His last opera, the 1966 *Carry Nation*, is another example
of his preoccupation with the American past. In the finest work of his
career, the 1956 *The Ballad of Baby Doe*, Moore wrote an American classic, capturing in high art for years to come the frontier sadness of failed
dreams and opportunities, of personal disaster in a world of speculative
uncertainty. Here is not America as viewed by Europeans; here is the
real thing, the colors right and the balances finely tuned.

By contrast, the achievement of Walter Piston has nothing of overt
nationalism about it at all. It is the achievement of an absolute musician,
wide, solid, and full of musical beauty. Piston is best known for a lighter
work, *The Incredible Flutist*, a ballet suite premiered in 1938 by the Boston
Pops Orchestra and by no less famous an American conductor than
Arthur Fiedler. More importantly, he wrote eight symphonies spanning
the years 1937 to 1965, more than a half-dozen works for solo instru-

ments and orchestra, and a wealth of chamber music. It is in his string quartets in particular that Piston's richness and profundity can be experienced; both the Second Quartet of 1935 and the Fifth Quartet of 1962 are complex works of pure music-making, and nothing short of masterly.

With Howard Hanson we come to one of the most distinguished all-around careers in the history of American music. By turns composer, music-school administrator, and tireless conductor of his own and his colleagues' works, Hanson is a romantic symphonist able to domesticate in his own music the influence of Sibelius and also of Rachmaninoff. In such an extraordinary work as his 1938 Third Symphony he has combined a rich Slavic-Nordic harmonic palette with open, long-lined, characteristically American-sounding melodies.

Little need be said here of Virgil Thomson, now rich in years and honors. His film scores from the mid-thirties, *The Plough That Broke the Plains* and *The River*, are classics of that descriptive genre. On a more elevated level, he is perhaps the most accomplished setter of American speech rhythms ever to write serious music. He has managed in his two Gertrude Stein operas, the 1927–28 *Four Saints in Three Acts* and the 1947 *The Mother of Us All*, to make clear that which no amount of literary criticism seems yet to have found possible: the connection between the sophisticated expatriate modernism of the 1920s and its roots in plain American life.

As can be gathered even from George Steiner's limited praise, Roger Sessions has indeed been one of our most important composers. It can be said of him that in his quiet, self-effacing, and self-respecting way he has been our musical conscience. Open to influence but never an imitator, he made his name with *The Black Maskers* of 1923. In his long career he has written nine symphonies, many of them in the years after 1958. The first of these later works—another of the numerous Third Symphonies of high quality which American composers have produced—is serene and uncompromising, a lesson in how musical dryness can be rich in feeling, and how dissonance need not rob harmonic structure of recognizable shape. His chamber music, too, including the string quartets of 1936 and 1951 and a 1958 string quintet, commands deep respect and enduring affection. His 1970 setting of Whitman's *When Lilacs Last in the*

Dooryard Bloom'd is an altogether more penetrating and authentic work than Hindemith's 1946 treatment of the same words. Given Sessions's stature, it is a particular disgrace of an already shame-ridden industry that not one of his works is currently available in an up-to-date recording on a major commercial label.

Henry Cowell is, in the way which later came to full flower (and perhaps even went to seed) in the person of John Cage, a difficult and varied phenomenon to encompass. At one and the same time highly serious in his commitment to music and seemingly aimless in his unceasing experimentalism, Cowell was a lifelong propagandist for "New Musical Resources," as the title of his 1930 book put it. At first these new resources lay for him in unorthodox sounds—which included playing the keys of the piano with fists and elbows and plucking the strings inside in the fashion of a harp; but he was also an early innovator in complex rhythms and the serial ordering of composition. Cowell was deeply interested in music from cultures other than Western, and he was an early innovator in methods of musical indeterminacy, paving the way for post–World War II developments. At last he seemed to come to a kind of rest in his American past, utilizing the spirit of old tunes and forms in a music purged of the avant-garde. But even when we take into account the relative quietude of his later music, his entire career suggests not the arrival but the quest.

The reputation of Roy Harris can be described as a brilliant high followed by a slow descent into a kind of obsolescence. Of all the American Third Symphonies, his was the most successful; indeed, it may well be our most frequently performed native symphony. His First Symphony, commissioned in 1933 and premiered the next year by Koussevitzky in Boston, combines rhythmic disjunctions and jerkiness with the beginnings of an identifiable melodic style. It was his particular brand of melody which was to make Harris's fame in 1937 with the Third Symphony. On occasion his reliance on the folk ethos—in, for example, the 1940 *Folksong* Symphony—makes it difficult to accept some of his work as belonging to an altogether serious genre. In his chamber music, however, the musical impulse seems refined, elegant, and moving. Harris's prolific output is another casualty of the current American recording scene.

In contrast to the desuetude which has befallen so many American composers, Aaron Copland has become something of a legend in his own time. By melodic shape he has conquered, so fusing his style with the materials on which he has drawn that it remains a matter of fine speculation whether he has created the American sound or the American sound has created him. He has written always with effort and care, producing finely crafted scores never a minute too long and containing never a note too many. It is our loss that he stopped composing, or so it is believed, in the middle 1960s. Through his performing career, and especially through his genial personality, he has been a clear witness to the proposition that there can be an American music both serious and successful, both native and universal.

With Elliott Carter we arrive at an achievement—and a problem— very close to the heart of the contemporary composer's relation to his audience. That problem, simply put, involves the degree of complexity and heterogeneity which even educated listeners can reasonably be expected to comprehend. From beginnings not uninfluenced by Copland, if his 1939–43 *Elegy* is any evidence, Carter has taken a path of increasing severity and complexity, reaching in his music of the last three decades an intellectual density fascinating to performers and, as yet, bewildering to audiences. Still, at least as late as the 1965 Piano Concerto, the by now classic American sound of wide-spaced melodies is audible in Carter's music; all that impedes an appreciation of this quality is the multiplicity of the notes, the sophistication of the rhythms which accompany them, and the formidable thickness of the texture in which they are embedded. Were the musical value of Carter's building blocks not so self-evident, no one would even make the attempt to understand his work; as it is, we are locked into trying.

Samuel Barber, whose recent death removed a figure of special distinction in our national music life, was vastly successful as a composer of instrumental music. His 1949 Piano Sonata is the most recent piece to have entered the international virtuoso repertory. His 1941 Violin Concerto and 1962 Piano Concerto are widely and successfully performed. As an orchestral composer he possessed the grand line, as his works demonstrate from the 1936 First Symphony on. His melodies and harmonies linger in the ear; once heard, the famous *Adagio for Strings*, also written in

1936, can never be forgotten. His vocal music, too, has a special prominence. Not one but two of his operas were performed by the Metropolitan Opera, itself hardly a recent booster of native efforts. While *Vanessa* (1958) had a promising start with the critics and public, it did not enter the repertory. *Antony and Cleopatra* (1966), written for the opening of the new Metropolitan Opera house at Lincoln Center, proved an initial disappointment. Still, listening to a tape of the original performance strongly suggests that here, too, Barber's music will last, and that his vocal music may well represent his finest achievement.

It is fitting to bring these thumbnail appreciations to a close with William Schuman, who is not only still composing but also still serving as spokesman and goad for an American music. Early in his writing career, his music seemed a combination of motor energy and a melodic line—if not an accompanying atmosphere—drawn from popular American music. These qualities are exemplified in the unjustly neglected 1942 Piano Concerto. Increasingly, however, a tragic, tightly dark-hued mood has become prominent in his music. In *To Thee, Old Cause* and the Ninth Symphony, both of 1968, this note is particularly pronounced; in the latter work, inspired by the monument in Rome to the Jews and Christians killed by the Nazis in the Ardeatine Caves, there is evident a new, almost demonic, quality developing out of his earlier rhythmic nervousness. Overall, he seems to be accepting with some nobility a downturn in the American fortunes he would rather have celebrated. His is a talent and a music as yet undervalued, even during his seventieth birthday year.

It is plain from even a cursory glance at these composers and their work that we have found no single, uniform style, no overarching similarity of musical approach, no consistently identifiable American character. Rather we have found conservatives and modernists, romantics and intellectuals, nationalists and cosmopolitans, the self-willed and the eclectic. What, then, links these diverse creators? Perhaps the unifying element is to be found not in output but in input, not in effect but in cause. Instead of trying to unify their music, it might be better to try to understand the world into which they were born and the world in which they wrote.

From the point of view of today's mood of apathy, cultural pessimism, and anomie, the turn of the century in this country seems a time of enthusiasm, optimism, and even integration. The frontier had been won; the domestic economy, though still subject to bubbles and panics, was expanding at a historically unparalleled rate; immigrants by the millions were being easily absorbed; science and technology were prolonging life and making it easier; in extending its borders in both the Caribbean and the Orient, America was claiming its manifest destiny. At home, a call was also being heard to cultural greatness. The system of higher education was being modernized and professionalized; American painting was restless with the call of modernism, and museums and private collections all over the country were enlarging apace; in music, American orchestras—and the Metropolitan Opera—were in the process of becoming the equals of any in the world. For the first time in our history, an independent, broadly based artistic culture was seen as an inevitable and desirable development.

Some of this momentum undoubtedly continued into the years before World War I. Nonetheless, the period of the 1910s and the early 1920s seem like the plague years. Our intervention in Mexico, labor unrest at home, our backdoor entry into World War I, the demeaning peace negotiations at Versailles, the farce of Prohibition, the stench of corruption in national politics—in a few years our national self-image, especially as perceived by our culture-creating classes, had gone from Parsifal to something approaching an impotent rotter. Thus it was that, immediately after the war that America had fought to save democracy, Europe became the refuge of our best and brightest. For both Copland and Thomson, Paris in particular was the home of music, of art, of life. Nor were they alone; of our eleven composers, ten were in Europe for extended periods between the wars, most to study, some to live. Only William Schuman stayed home.

But this mass departure did not last. Most of our composers began coming home even during the 1920s. Copland's case is typical. By 1925 he had decided to return home to write a consciously American music. Virgil Thomson had been back in this country in 1923 and 1924 and returned periodically thereafter until the outbreak of World War II. By

1927 he was working with Gertrude Stein on *Four Saints*. Similarly, Moore had left Paris in 1921; Hanson had left Rome in 1924; Harris had left Paris (and his teacher Nadia Boulanger) in 1929.

The idea of America was in the air. Ernest Bloch, an American resident since 1916, wrote in 1926 a giant symphonic poem entitled simply *America;* based on traditional and folk sources, it ended with something very close to a national anthem. On a less exalted level, Douglas Moore had written his evocation of P. T. Barnum in 1924. In the 1930s this explicitly nationalist movement in music gathered steam; among the many examples of the trend are Randall Thompson's 1932 choral work, *Americana,* and Henry Cowell's 1937 *American Melting Pot* and the *Old American Country Set.*

The concern of American artists with their homeland was undoubtedly increased after 1929 by the worldwide depression, which hit America with particular force. Family allowances and fellowships shrank, and for reasons both moral and economic the expatriate life no longer seemed supportable as it once had. The America these artists came home to was vastly different from what it had been just a few years before. The crash, far from being a cause of disorganization or revolution, had produced the powerful political reaction of the New Deal. Along with the effort to reconstruct the economy came a desire to build a new society, a confidence in our national toughness under adversity, and a belief in the future of native culture. World conditions furthered this American mood, not least among intellectuals; for many of them, the Popular Front, born of Stalin's desire for allies against Hitler, inspired respect both for the attractiveness of the masses and the goodness and power of the United States.

For musicians, the teeming America of the 1930s was no longer a simple extension of the Europe which had earlier enthralled them. Everywhere in America there was new musical life, as demonstrated by a large increase in orchestras and concerts (the majority of them privately financed), in music education all the way down to the elementary-school level, and, above all, in radio broadcasting both national and local. And, most gratifying to composers, audiences across the country were newly willing to listen to native products in a manner neither patronizing nor dutiful, but rather out of a desire for art as the shared experience of the community.

Americans had become more receptive not only to their own culture, but to musical culture in general. With the rise of Nazism, émigrés came at first from Hitler's Germany, then from Austria, and finally from all of Europe for shelter and employment. This exodus included the most distinguished composers and performers of the age, who brought to American musical life a new energy and sophistication; their contribution was made on the basis of permanent residence, not, in the manner of today, as an incidental benefit scattered during concert tours.

It seems reasonable to speculate that our new national musical strength, though most prominently displayed in the rise of explicitly nationalist compositions, also must have deeply affected those artists who had no desire to write specifically "American" works. The music flowed from many composers in a hitherto unexampled (for America) richness, variety, and depth. Such diverse composers as Hanson, Piston, Sessions, and Barber, with all their various feelings about America and Europe, nonetheless partook with the nationalists of an enthusiasm for the creative possibilities here at home and exemplified in their music the high seriousness of the national mood.

The first years of the 1940s saw a continuation of this momentum. The buildup to World War II concentrated the minds of the American people; the Japanese attack that finally brought us into the war completed the process of unification which had begun back in the late 1920s. So beguiling was this atmosphere that composers not infrequently succumbed to a kind of grandiosity which, as in the case of Randall Thompson's 1943 *The Testament of Freedom*, a musical setting of the words of Jefferson, quickly became its own punishment.

Victory, when it came, produced an unavoidable feeling of let-down, and the unstable peace that followed the war blurred the lines between good guys and bad guys that had been so clear in the 1930s. Then, too, travel once again became possible and even easy, exposing Americans once again to the blandishments of our musical mother countries, where the wine was better and artists were truly respected.

Looming over all these factors was an overriding loss of national confidence. Slowest to appear in the economic arena, it was manifest first in politics. By 1947 it became clear that elements of both the right and the left had deserted the center of the grand American wartime coalition, the one to support a new isolationism and the other to advocate sympathy for Soviet policies. In ideas, the prevailing tone of discussion was set by the rise of the existentialist philosophy associated with Heidegger and Sartre. Only in painting and to some extent in dance did American culture remain a world pacesetter.

In music the American retreat was shown in various ways both public and private. A minigeneration of European artists, blocked from world careers by war, now toured the United States in force. The fact of cheaper wages abroad, aided by a union ban on domestic recording here, spurred the takeover of the American recording market by European labels and artists. The most gifted American music students, performers and composers alike, began once again to go to Europe in droves to study; in this they were aided by imaginative federal government subsidies.

In composition the late 1940s saw the initial triumph of what has been called the Second Viennese School, but which might with equal justice be called the First School of Paris. René Leibowitz and Olivier Messiaen became the gurus of many of our younger composers. Boulez and Stockhausen soon followed, and the era of Darmstadt was upon us. It was soon to be the age of integral serialism and later of aleatorics, of the signal generator and the tape recorder. Yet first-class music continued to be written here, not only by the composers I have described above but also by their followers and successors. Some continued on their own paths, independent of international trends; others, as time passed, seemed to compose less and less.

But whatever happened to individual composers, what was missing was the sense of a distinctly American music, of distinctly American developments in composition. Indeed, by the time the New York intellectuals clustered around *Partisan Review* rediscovered America in 1952 (in the famous symposium "Our Country and Our Culture"), American music speaking of and to our own situation was gone, and with it the atmosphere of hope that had marked earlier decades.

Is such a collective atmosphere indeed necessary for music-making? Can great music not be produced by socially isolated artists writing out of the experience of their isolation? There can be no ready answer to this question: individuals can individually do just about anything. But artistic movements, broad trends informing and informed by a whole society, do seem to be deeply related to social optimism—even when such optimism, as in nineteenth-century Germany, may be less than solidly based.

A warning, however, is in order here. Because such positive social attitudes may be vital to the creation of art does not mean that they—or the art itself—can be elicited by the conscious actions of those who hold the reins of politics and society. Above all, optimism, like happiness, can never be the planned result of governmental fiat or bureaucratic direction. No lasting art issued from the exhortations to joy of Hitler and Goebbels; Stalin's policy of socialist realism resulted not in the enlivening of music but in the persecution of musicians. Any similar attempt in our vegetarian American context would bring about something vastly more benign but equally lifeless.

Since I began with George Steiner, it would not be fair to end without attempting to answer his strictures about American music. Are any of the composers I have discussed here, from Moore to Schuman, the equal of the European names he cites?

At this moment in the history of musical taste, the reputations of such as Schoenberg and Bartók plainly stand by themselves. The problem, however, is that if we persist in judging all musical activity as Steiner does, by the received standards of the masterpiece and the immortal oeuvre, we will forever remain what he has accused us of being—conservators of someone else's far greater past. Such a judgment might be fair and even constructive if elsewhere in the world there were at this time vibrant musical health and glorious creative activity. But the great musical cultures of Europe seem no better off—except, of course, for their history—than do we.

Whatever value Europe may have had for us as a model in the past, it does not seem to be a viable model today. If we are to revivify our musical life, it is to our own past that we must look for both inspiration and confidence. What I have tried to suggest is that we do indeed possess a musical past of which we can be proud. How we will use that pride is a matter of creative invention, not of imitation. It is for composers to provide the invention; perhaps it is for society to provide the context.

(*Commentary*, 1981)

4

LENNY ON OUR MINDS

Sunday afternoon, November 14, 1943, was fairly quiet, as wartime Sunday afternoons go. The Russians, then our allies, were pressing the Germans back from Zhitomir; American submarines had just sunk several Japanese ships in the South Pacific; Allied forces, both British and American, were making limited gains on the Italian front.

At home, cultural activities went on much as always. The Sunday crowd of music lovers had assembled in Carnegie Hall for the New York Philharmonic Symphony Orchestra concert, scheduled to be led by the venerable émigré conductor Bruno Walter. But in that age of radio, the concert's impact was no longer restricted to the audience in the hall: across the country the orchestra's immense broadcast public was lined up in front of its sets, awaiting the beginning of what must have been for many an experience comparable to attendance at church.

The concert began (as was the custom in wartime) with the "Star-Spangled Banner," smartly played by the Philharmonic and sung by the audience with a vocal accuracy and splendor few trained choruses today could better.[1] Even before the national anthem, the CBS radio listeners found out something the ticket buyers had been told only a few moments earlier: the concert was not after all to be conducted by Bruno Walter, for the beloved maestro had been taken ill. In his place, appearing without the benefit of a rehearsal, would be the orchestra's Massachusetts-born, Harvard-educated, Serge Koussevitzky and Curtis

Institute-trained assistant conductor. The name of this untried twenty-five-year-old musician was Leonard Bernstein.

Veni, vidi, vici, Lenny: the rest is history. The program he conducted, typical of so many the young genius would do in the years to come, included the *Manfred* Overture by Robert Schumann, *Theme, Variations, and Finale* by the Hungarian Miklós Rózsa (later to make a name in Hollywood for the musical scores to *Quo vadis?* and *Ben-Hur*), and *Don Quixote* by Richard Strauss. At this point the broadcast ended with a reading of war news bulletins, and Bernstein finished the concert in Carnegie Hall with the Prelude to Wagner's *Die Meistersinger.* The performances were brilliant, the audience cheered, and next morning both the *New York Times* and the *Herald Tribune* carried enthusiastic front-page stories. Musically Leonard Bernstein was launched, and so—it must have seemed—were we.

What the *Times* called "a dramatic musical event" was nothing less than the cometlike appearance of a great musical hope, the native-born star performer whose high talent and public acceptance would demonstrate once and for all that greatness on the concert stage need not be imported and European, but could be recognizably, uniquely, and wonderfully American.

This performing triumph—Bernstein was to conduct the Philharmonic ten more times in the 1943–44 season—was soon followed by an equally great success in composition. On April 18, 1944, just five months after Bernstein's Philharmonic debut, the Metropolitan Opera House witnessed the premiere of *Fancy Free* by the Ballet Theatre (now the American Ballet Theatre). *Fancy Free* was Bernstein's first collaboration with the dancer Jerome Robbins, whose choreography greatly assisted him in telling the exuberant story of three sailors at liberty on a twenty-four-hour spree in New York. Bernstein's music mixed jazz and "serious" elements in a brash and immediately compelling manner. The public and the critics swooned. Everything finally had come together: in Leonard Bernstein American music now had its Columbus and its Barnum all rolled into one.

Today, forty-one years later, the sixty-seven-year-old erstwhile prodigy is still in the news and on our minds. The great public occasion this time is a plush, operatic performance of Bernstein's 1957 Broadway hit *West Side Story*, immortalized in the composer's own conducting not just on black vinyl, audiocassettes, and compact discs[2] but also in a May 17 PBS Great Performances documentary devoted in large part to the musical's recording sessions and in toto, as always, to Lenny. And on July 4 he will again sound a symbolically American note when he conducts the National Symphony of Washington in a concert of his own music and that of John Philip Sousa. The concert will be televised across the country from the West Lawn of the Capitol.

The years between the start of Bernstein's career and his present status as America's most famous homegrown classical music figure have been filled with a bewildering profusion of activities, some of them serious and most of them in some way successful. To describe Bernstein's musical life over what is now approaching a half-century is to provide a chronicle not just of his triumphs but also of the hopes and failures of American music itself.

Leonard Bernstein, the callow American youth whose career as a conductor had begun in Carnegie Hall as a last-minute replacement for a famous European sage, went on to become, from 1958 to 1969, the most popular, though perhaps not the most respected, music director of the Philharmonic since Arturo Toscanini. Bernstein's exciting performances, in a repertory notable for its easy combination of classical masterpieces, certified crowd-pleasers, and little-known but major American works, galvanized audiences despite the opposition of purists discomfited by his wild gyrations on the podium and evident lack of interest in perfect orchestral ensemble. The box office told the story: in contrast to the easy availability of tickets under his immediate predecessors (and his successors), when Bernstein was the orchestra's leader there was talk of a waiting list for subscriptions, and single admissions were just about impossible to come by. Similarly, in contrast to the current absence of an exclusive recording contract for the Philharmonic, Bernstein's numerous CBS recordings with the orchestra sold like the proverbial hotcakes (and still sell well today), bringing in substantial royalty checks vital not just to the financial health of the orchestra but even more to the pocketbooks and the morale of the players.

This glamorous career as leader of one of America's establishment orchestras, publicized and remunerative as it certainly was, hardly constitutes Bernstein's only claim to musical fame. He spent the fifteen or so years between his conducting debut and his accession to the Philharmonic post learning his craft with the Boston Symphony as Koussevitzky's hoped-for successor, with the New York City Orchestra as its director from 1945 to 1948, and through numerous guest appearances the world over. Even more sensationally, he made a stunning career on Broadway as a composer of musicals, three of them long-running hits and one other—*Candide* (1956)—perhaps the most frequently discussed and highly praised "miss" in the history of the American musical theater.

Bernstein's Broadway hits had begun only thirteen months after he substituted for Walter and just eight months after the first performance of *Fancy Free*. *On the Town*, which opened at the Adelphi Theater in New York on December 28, 1944, was a dramatic adaptation and expansion of *Fancy Free*. It kept Robbins's dances and Bernstein's music, and added brassy lyrics (and stage performances) by the composer's long-time friends and associates Betty Comden and Adolph Green. The result was captivating, and *On the Town* ran for 463 performances on Broadway. MGM bought the movie rights for more than $100,000 and made the film a starring vehicle for Gene Kelly and Frank Sinatra. In a curious throw of the moviemaking dice, only four of Bernstein's original musical numbers (including, at least, the still classic "New York, New York") were used; to fill out the movie, producer Arthur Freed commissioned an altogether humdrum score by the now forgotten Hollywood composer Roger Edens.

Broadway lightning struck for Bernstein a second time in 1953, when *Wonderful Town*, an adaptation (starring Rosalind Russell) of Ruth McKenney's famous *New Yorker* magazine series "My Sister Eileen," began a run of more than five hundred performances. Just three years later, in 1956, Bernstein suffered a failure that paradoxically only heightened his reputation as a creative force in American show music. *Candide*, written to a book by Lillian Hellman and lyrics by John Latouche, Richard Wilbur, and Dorothy Parker, ran for a mere 73 performances. But Bernstein's score emerged triumphant from all the clumsiness onstage, and revivals of the work (in altered dramatic form) were hits on Broadway in 1973 and at the New York City Opera in 1982.

Bernstein's greatest Broadway triumph was the 1957 musical *West Side Story*. This setting of the stock Romeo-and-Juliet situation of young lovers fated to suffer because of the incompatibility of their social origins was first conceived by Bernstein (and Robbins) as arising out of urban tensions between Jews and Catholics; with a certain prescience, in its final form the work dramatized the conflict between rival "American" and Puerto Rican street gangs. The show, with lyrics by the then youthful Stephen Sondheim, contained the hit songs "Maria" and "Tonight," and dances again choreographed by Robbins. It ran 981 times on Broadway, and a remarkable 1,040 times in London. As a movie it won an Oscar as Best Picture of 1961. Despite the music's tendency (less evident on the vibrant original-cast recording[3] than on the composer's new, electronically gilded version) to substitute sentimentality for sentiment, one hardly had to be a Pangloss at the time to view Bernstein, still under fifty, as the heir to Irving Berlin, Jerome Kern, and Richard Rodgers— and perhaps even to George Gershwin.

Bernstein's success on Broadway was now so great it was easy to forget that many of his artistic roots lay not in commercial music but in large-scale "classical" music meant for performance in the concert hall. He had completed the *Jeremiah* Symphony, still one of his most impressive efforts, as early as 1942; based on Hebraic cantillation but nonetheless recognizably American in its jazzy timbre and rhythms, *Jeremiah* seemed to amalgamate the composer's proud Jewish heritage with his equally proud American artistic consciousness.

Bernstein's next symphony, subtitled (after W. H. Auden's poem) *The Age of Anxiety*, appeared seven years later. Though admirably written for the orchestra and the solo piano (and brilliantly played in performance and on two recordings by Bernstein's longtime friend Lukas Foss), this work, like the even more rhetorical and trendy 1961–63 Symphony No. 3 (*Kaddish*, dedicated "To the Beloved Memory of John F. Kennedy"), seems today vastly less authentic and straightforward than *Jeremiah*, a composition written before the appurtenances of success and the ensuing self-indulgence had become a part of the composer's modus operandi.

No account of Bernstein's achievements in the first three decades or so of his career would be complete without an account of his activities as a pianist, most often playing the works of others. A student at Curtis of the great Russian taskmistress Isabelle Vengerova, Bernstein was long able to integrate a strict technical training with his own inborn digital facility and exciting rhythmic sense. The result has been scintillating performance of works as different as the Beethoven C-major and the Ravel G-major concertos. A still more remarkable example of Bernstein's playing, because it is of material which rarely engages the attention of the greatest pianists of the day, is a 1947 recording of his friend and mentor Aaron Copland's Piano Sonata (1941). Now reissued by New World Records,[4] it provides a much needed object lesson in how apparently dry and "intellectual" music can be ennobled through commanding and dedicated performance.

A word, too, must be spared for Bernstein's impressive facility as an accompanist of singers in both serious and what can only be called "patter" material. His collaborations with his great friend mezzo-soprano Jennie Tourel in French and Russian songs have now become mythical. His playing of popular cabaret material is equally stunning; that this particular accomplishment was his at a young age can be heard today in private recordings[5] made in 1939 with Judy Holliday (then still Judith Tuvim) and Comden and Green.

While Bernstein is often seen as a musical triple threat—he was called "Triple-Note Man of the Music World" in a psychologically perceptive 1945 *New York Times Magazine* article by Mark Schubart—he actually has four strings to his artistic bow: conducting, composing, playing the piano, and teaching.

Bernstein did some conventional teaching in the late 1940s under Koussevitzky at Tanglewood, and in the 1950s at Brandeis University. But his great services to music education have not been rendered in the studio or in the classroom. His gift in teaching, as in performance, has been for warm, humanly persuasive communication via the electronic media and, in particular, on television. In the 1950s on the Ford Foundation–CBS (later ABC) series "Omnibus," and in the 1960s on the New York Philharmonic–CBS Young People's Concerts, Bernstein was the force for music appreciation that Walter Damrosch and Ernest Schelling had been a generation earlier. To remark this is not to damn with faint praise: Damrosch on the radio and Schelling in live concerts were central in training the musically literate audience of a bygone and simpler era. Bernstein, for his part, through his broadcasts and their publication in *The Joy of Music* (1959) and *The Infinite Variety of Music* (1966), has been responsible for the last intellectually sophisticated and successful attempt made to interest and educate today's vast public in the great masterpieces of the Western musical tradition.

The lives of some great musicians—Bach's is a case in point—appear almost seamless; for them creation is a continuous outpouring, a straight-line development of their genius. In the lives of others, there are great watersheds. For Beethoven the turning point was the onset of deafness, redirecting his musical thoughts from the public display of the virtuoso to the tortured self-examination of the lonely creator. For Wagner, it was the revolution of 1848, when he decided that only in a radically new world could he achieve his operatic goals. Though surely lacking Beethoven's and Wagner's terrifying singlemindedness of artistic purpose, Leonard Bernstein, too, has been dramatically affected by extramusical pressures: the late 1960s, those difficult years for creators oversensitive to the social turmoil around them, seem to have changed the manner in which he does his art and engages his public.

When Bernstein announced in November 1966 that he would leave as music director of the Philharmonic upon the expiration of his contract in 1969, the *Times*, as it had done upon his debut, ran a front-page story with the news. Bernstein's own words, important enough to be quoted once more in Howard Shanet's standard 1975 history of the orchestra, made his reason for leaving clear enough: "A time is arriving in my life," he said, "when I must concentrate maximally on composing, and this cannot be done while retaining the great responsibilities inherent in the Philharmonic post, which is a full-time commitment, and indeed, more than that."

Alas, matters hardly seem to have worked out the way Bernstein planned. To adapt Dean Acheson's trenchant words about England having lost an empire and not yet found a role, when he left the Philharmonic Bernstein gave up a great orchestra without seeming to be able to compose very much in the bargain. The real change in his new life has not been from conductor to composer, but from resident conductor in New York to guest conductor the world over.

In New York, Bernstein is now a kind of permanent visitor with the Philharmonic, holding the newly created title of Laureate Conductor. Though he has not appeared with the orchestra every year—this past season, for example, he did not conduct the Philharmonic at all—his appearances with the orchestra have been frequent enough to demonstrate conclusively that he still retains his standing with the New York musical public. But the Philharmonic audience now sees only a limited side of their hero's musical personality. When he has appeared with the orchestra in recent years, he has tended—as the Canadian critic and broadcaster Paul Robinson pointed out in a 1982 study of Bernstein as conductor[6]—to favor contemporary music; in Paris, by contrast, where he has conducted often in recent years, he has emphasized French music.

If Bernstein as a conductor has a spot where he feels at home today, it is neither New York nor Paris, but rather Austria. Paul Robinson put the case well for what many see as the conductor's present apotheosis: "from the early 1970s on, Bernstein began to inherit the mantle of Furtwängler and Bruno Walter, conductors who had had long associations with the Vienna Philharmonic. Bernstein was no longer an American phenomenon; he was now a great conductor in the European mainstream." In concert and in opera, the Viennese public has taken Bernstein to its bosom; on records, his lush readings with the Vienna Philharmonic of the complete Beethoven and Brahms symphonies, no less than his spacious and even languid Vienna *Rosenkavalier* and his Bavarian Radio *Tristan und Isolde*, have gone a long way toward changing the image of Bernstein in this country as well as abroad from one of a hard-driving, motorically exciting, and ever youthful American conductor to that of a relaxed, expansive European wise man of music.

But even the greatest conductors come and go, while composers can remain forever. What of the compositions, for the writing of which Bernstein left the New York Philharmonic? Here the record is dismaying. It has now been sixteen years since Bernstein conducted his last concerts as music director in New York; in that time he has written scarcely more than a handful of reasonably large-scale compositions: *Mass* (theater piece, 1971), *Dybbuk* (ballet, 1974), *1600 Pennsylvania Avenue* (musical, 1976), *Songfest* (song cycle, 1977), *Divertimento* (orchestral suite, 1980), *Halil* (Nocturne for Solo Flute, String Orchestra and Percussion, 1981), and *A Quiet Place* (opera, 1983).

Except for *Mass*, a succès de scandale at its premiere, most of these works now seem no more than highly visible *Gebrauchsmusik*, compositions written for specific purposes and hardly memorable beyond the initial uses to which they were put. All their outward intensity of feeling, melodic attractiveness, and high craftsmanship have not altered the impression that their greatest virtue has been a negative one: an absence of the ugliness and even inept writing widely associated nowadays with new music.

Dybbuk, for example, was written for Jerome Robbins to choreograph; on its own, even in the composer's concert version, the music lacks the capacity to transcend its origin as a ballet. The determinedly eclectic *Songfest*, written to mark the Bicentennial, draws from so many poetic and artistic sources that it appears to lack any single integrating, individual voice.

Divertimento, written to celebrate the hundredth anniversary of the Boston Symphony Orchestra, is suffused by Bernstein's touching nostalgia for the Boston Symphony, whose director he never became; as music the composition is no more than a congeries of forms and styles, ranging from the waltz and the mazurka to the blues and a Sousa march, all characterized with the elegance and grace of a born pasticheur. By contrast, the emotional world of *Halil*, a tribute to an Israeli flutist-soldier killed in the 1973 war with Egypt, does invoke the affecting image of an oriental shepherd boy piping at night in a desert by turns peaceful and war-torn. The result, though both melodic and dramatic, still seems to suffer from a conceptual flaw: the composer's inability to make an artistic choice between his sadness over lost young manhood and his recognition of a warrior's—and a country's—need to fight for survival.

It would be kinder to pass quickly over Bernstein's two tries, since he left the Philharmonic, at writing traditionally staged works for voice. *1600 Pennsylvania Avenue* was the composer's attempt, with the collaboration of Alan Jay Lerner, to write a Broadway musical on the occasion of the Bicentennial. What Broadway historian Gerald Bordman described as a "servant's-eye view of the White House from Washington to Teddy Roosevelt" turned out to be, again in Bordman's words, "a one-week fiasco." The composer himself must agree: *1600 Pennsylvania Avenue* is not included in the list of compositions appended to *Findings*, his most recent (1982) collection of writings.

A Quiet Place, the sequel to *Trouble in Tahiti*, Bernstein's 1952 opera of suburban life, was jointly commissioned by the Houston Grand Opera, the John F. Kennedy Center for the Performing Arts in Washington, and the Teatro alla Scala in Milan. The composer's score seems a kind of neo-Puccinian attempt at melodic writing, unfortunately accomplished without Puccini's emotional force. The effect of the Houston premiere on the *Times*'s Donal Henahan was crushingly clear: "To call the result a pretentious failure," Henahan wrote, "is putting it kindly."

Whatever the ultimate rank of *Mass*, the earliest of his major post-Philharmonic works, there can be no doubt that it did make an impression upon its first appearance, though perhaps not the impression the composer had intended. Commissioned (at the suggestion of Jaqueline Kennedy Onassis) for the opening of the Kennedy Center in Washington, the work represented a late stage in Bernstein's lifelong career as an enthusiastic leveler of cultural barriers and distinctions. Following in the footsteps of such musical-theater successes as *Hair* (1968) and *Godspell* (1971), *Mass* was based on the Roman Catholic liturgy, but also included additional texts by Stephen Schwartz (composer and lyricist of *Godspell*) and Bernstein himself.

As might have been expected, Bernstein and his collaborator did not leave the Roman service unaltered. A notable change was the repetition, in the original Hebrew words, of the Latin

Sanctus, Sanctus, Sanctus
Dominus Deus Sabaoth.
Pleni sunt coeli et terra
Gloria tuae.
Benedictus qui venit in nomine Domini

[Holy Holy Holy
Lord God of Hosts.

Heaven and earth are full of
Thy glory.
Blessed is he who comes in the name of the Lord.]

Nor was this merging of Catholic and Jewish religious observance the only syncretism *Mass* essayed in its attempt to be all things to all men. Throughout the work passages of traditional prayer were made to alternate with lines redolent of the 1960s in the Haight-Ashbury world:

PREACHER:	God made us the boss
	God gave us the cross
	We turned it into a sword
	To spread the Word of the Lord
	We use His holy decrees
	To do whatever we please.
CHORUS:	Yeah!
PREACHER:	And it was good!
CHORUS:	Yeah!
ALL:	And it was good, Yeah!
	And it was goddam good!

The cast of this extravaganza of quasi-religious universal brotherhood includes street people and dancers. The pit orchestra consists of a concert organ and a "rock" organ, in addition to the usual strings and percussion; the costumed stage orchestra includes brass, woodwinds, electric guitars, and keyboards. The musical itself is a hodgepodge of classical and jazz, serious and pop, folk and rock, opera and Broadway. The whole effect is one of sentimentality and fuzzy thinking run amok. Most charitably put, it all sounds like an artifact of its troubled time, a zany *Parsifal* produced by The Living Theater.

Mass, in all its florid display of feeling, is an authentic reflection of the caring, sharing Bernstein public persona that intimates swear is the real Lenny. The persona was described at its most fragrant, and wittily impaled, by Tom Wolfe in his now historic *New York* magazine article "Radical Chic." This merciless dissection of a 1970 fund-raising party the conductor and his late wife, actress Felicia Montealegre, gave in their Park Avenue apartment for the Black Panthers stressed Bernstein's political naïveté, the happy indulgence of a media star's ability to support the claims of the enraged spokesmen for the poor while at the same time living like a millionaire.

The verdict on Bernstein's one major attempt at music education in the 1970s has also been unfavorable. In giving the 1973 Charles Eliot Norton Lectures at Harvard (telecast on PBS, issued on records by CBS, and published three years later in book form as *The Unanswered Question*), Bernstein was speaking from a platform that had previously been graced by, among others, Igor Stravinsky, Paul Hindemith, and Aaron Copland. As his contribution Bernstein chose to base a defense of tonality in music (as against the twelve-tone system of Arnold Schoenberg) on the transformational grammar of Noam Chomsky, the noted linguistician then at the height of his reputation as a radical opponent of the Vietnam War. As always, Bernstein's delivery of both works and musical examples was earnest and persuasive, though perhaps even more marked than in the past by a tendency to wallow in his own glamour; the problem lay not simply in the presentation but also in the basing of eminently plausible conclusions on so difficult and perhaps tangential a foundation as the work of Chomsky, thus enraging people who knew more about Chomsky and linguistics than Bernstein did, while at the same time bewildering the music-loving audience he was addressing.

Throughout his long career, Leonard Bernstein has been criticized by friend and foe alike for his seeming inability to concentrate on just one of his several musical talents. These critics have been responding to a well-nigh universal perception that this remarkably gifted individual has achieved in no one area what his genius seemed to promise in several. Now, as Bernstein approaches the eighth decade of his life—and his sixth decade of musical creativity—it is difficult not to feel that his fulfillment as a great artist seems even farther from him than it did twenty years ago.

His claim to be our true American combiner of traditional symphonic greatness with authentic Broadway melody and appeal, so brilliantly staked out with the *Jeremiah* Symphony, *Fancy Free*, and *On the Town*, seems to have bogged down in bathetic ideology, facile wit, and mere commercialism. His promise as the first homegrown conductor to perform European masterpieces in our own American way seems to have become a kind of outdoing the great Austro-German baton wielders at their own game. His magnificent abilities as a pianist have spurred him neither to write an important body of works for the keyboard nor even to exert a major influence on his performing colleagues. Finally, his heaven-sent gifts for the electronic communication of high musical art have foundered on the twin shoals of overintellectualization and exaggerated self-promotion.

It is difficult to know whether what we now see as Bernstein's disappointing achievement is due to an excess of disparate talents, or, conversely, to some ultimate flaw in their basic constitution. Not being a psychologist, the critic is surely more comfortable discussing what is, not what might have been. In any case, the best refutation of any speculative approach to understanding Bernstein's creative fate is proffered by his associate Jack Gottlieb as the conclusion to the composer's entry in the 1971 *Dictionary of Contemporary Music*: "Critics . . . have said he would become a better musician if he concentrated on only one musical discipline to the exclusion of others. The fact is that had he followed their advice, he would have ceased to be himself."

Two things, however, are abundantly clear about Leonard Bernstein. He is the most generously gifted artist in American musical history; his achievement, whatever it eventually may prove to be, will always be judged not in its own terms but in those of the extravagant hopes his great artistic endowment has engendered. Because he is still very much an active artist, because he is so talented, because he is so unpredictable, he continues to be the stuff of which our musical dreams are made. That is why, just as he was almost forty-two years ago, Lenny is still on our minds.

(*The New Criterion*, 1985)

5

Hugo Weisgall's

Six Characters

*Please do not be surprised when a reality is born, formed and invoked by
the magic of the stage itself—. Do you not believe in the creative power of
your own profession?*

—The Father, in *Six Characters in Search of an Author*

A momentous event in American opera took place in Chicago at the
Lyric Opera Center for American Artists (the junior company of the
Lyric Opera of Chicago) this past June. This event was almost unher-
alded; it was only noticed locally, and (save for an enthusiastic review
by *The New Yorker*'s Andrew Porter) it was ignored afterward by a national press interested on the one hand in star singers and on the other in
the latest "cutting-edge" atrocities. Nevertheless, Hugo Weisgall's *Six
Characters in Search of an Author* (1956), with a libretto by the Irish playwright Denis Johnston, showed itself, in the September National Public
Radio broadcast of the Chicago performances, to be a masterpiece, and
perhaps indeed *the* masterpiece, of American opera. At the very least, it is
now plain that *Six Characters* deserves to be placed on the level of such
vastly important works as Virgil Thomson's *Four Saints in Three Acts*
(1927–28), Douglas Moore's *The Ballad of Baby Doe* (1956), and Samuel
Barber's *Antony and Cleopatra* (1966).

It cannot be said that *Six Characters* was absolutely unknown prior to its Chicago performance. Commissioned in the mid-1950s by the Ditson Fund at Columbia University and produced at the New York City Opera in the 1958–59 and 1959–60 seasons with funding from the Ford Foundation, the opera was a great success on its premiere, and won admirers notable both for their sophistication and for their enthusiasm. But these days success among the cultivated does not a place in the operatic repertory make, and *Six Characters* did not receive a professional production in all the years from the beginning of the 1960s until its rescue five months ago by the good taste and high courage of Ardis Krainik, the Lyric Opera's general director.

Before we can understand why this miscarriage of artistic justice should have taken place, it is necessary to examine the nature of *Six Characters* as a work of art. This examination must begin with the remarkable 1921 play by the Italian author Luigi Pirandello on which the opera is based. The play immediately established itself as one of the monuments of the modern European theater, a reputation that it has not lost to this day; it has been available since the 1920s in various English translations.

As a whole, Pirandello's plays—including the recently often performed *Henry IV*—were founded upon a rejection, at once principled and emotional, of so-called ordinary reality, and its supersession by the created reality Pirandello attempted to put on the stage. *Six Characters* presents simultaneously a group of actors and the characters (in real life, so to speak) they hope to portray. The characters are not content to be at the mercy of the actors and wish to find an author to tell their own, as yet unwritten, story. What Pirandello means to accomplish is thus first to destroy the illusionism of the stage and its practitioners, and then, by artistic sleight-of-hand, to claim that the creations of art can replace life.

Weisgall and his librettist had the brilliant idea of turning the Pirandello play-within-a-play into an opera-within-an-opera. Thus Pirandello's actors now become opera singers, and his stage characters operatic characters. The intermediary between professionals and the uncooperative personages they hope to portray remains the Director, transformed from genus theatrical to genus operatic. The six characters turn out to be six members of a troubled family—the very voluble Father, Mother, Son, and Stepdaughter, a silent young boy, and an equally silent young girl whose unrelated and unmotivated drowning provides the denouement of the story; the Stepdaughter and the two children are the illegitimate offspring of the Mother by another man, now dead. There is one additional character, at once peripheral and central: Madame Pace, a dressmaker doubling as the keeper of a brothel. The main body of the plot recounts the Father's attempt, in Madame Pace's brothel, to seduce the Stepdaughter, whom he fails to recognize.

The characters attempt to persuade the singers and the Director to let them play themselves. Led by the Director, the professional singers at first resist, claiming that only they have that one necessity for performing opera: union cards. But as *Six Characters* goes on, the superior reality of the characters pushes their would-be representatives into the background. At the end, as both characters and singers abandon the stage, it is clear that it is the characters who have won the day, for they will be remembered, while the singers—and the Director too—will never be more than faceless performers.

It goes without saying that the recriminations, guilt, and hatreds that suffuse the opera are the very stuff of twentieth-century *angst*; not surprisingly, they are the very stuff of opera itself. It is by no means the smallest achievement of *Six Characters* as a work for the lyric stage that it manages so completely to link the historical preoccupations of opera with the abiding psychological atmosphere of contemporary life and culture. On the philosophical level, the opera takes over, and deepens, Pirandello's lifelong concern with the inescapably nihilistic questioning of the metaphysical nature of reality.

It is true that for *Six Characters* to have succeeded as it has it was necessary that its creators, and in particular its composer, be fully aware of the civilized culture that has gone into the making of the art of our century. Of all twentieth-century composers, Weisgall is one of the most intellectually and musically sophisticated. The son of a well-known Jewish cantor, he was born in 1912 in Czechoslovakia and came to the United States in 1920. He has a Ph.D. in German literature from Johns Hopkins and thereafter graduated from the Curtis Institute of Music. He served in World War II as assistant military attaché to governments-in-exile in London, and after the war was cultural attaché in Prague. He has taught at Juilliard and at Queens College and for many years has been on the faculty of the Jewish Theological Seminary. In a fitting recognition of the respect in which he is held in our intellectual life, he is now president of the American Academy and Institute of Arts and Letters.

One must not overlook for a moment that it is music, and only music, that has made *Six Characters* the artistic miracle that it undoubtedly is. First and foremost, Hugo Weisgall is an extraordinary musician, with an easy command of all the literature and materials of music. As a musician, he is known primarily for his operas, a long string of which constitute the largest single contribution in the history of American opera. His works before *Six Characters* include *The Tenor*, written in 1949–50 to a libretto based upon Wedekind, and *The Stronger*, written in 1952 to a libretto based upon Strindberg. His later works include *Purgatory* (1958, after Yeats), *Athaliah* (1963, after Racine), *Nine Rivers from Jordan* (1968, with Denis Johnston), *Jenny, or The Hundred Nights* (1976, John Hollander, after Mishima), and *Gardens of Adonis* (1959–81, John Olon-Scrymgeour, after André Obey and Shakespeare).

Most recently, Weisgall has been composing *Esther*, based on the biblical story. This opera was originally commissioned by the San Francisco Opera and its then general director, Terence McEwen. *Esther*'s production in San Francisco has now been canceled by the new general director, Lotfi Mansouri, on the grounds that the work was too ambitious for San Francisco's resources.

While the rejection of *Esther* was publicly explained in terms of its casting requirements, there can be little doubt that the real cause of the San Francisco withdrawal were the *musical* demands Weisgall makes on performers and audience alike. He has always written—and *Six Characters* is certainly no exception—in a difficult style, harmonically knotty even though always clearly scored. His writing has often seemed post-Bergian, in its combination of a high level of chromaticism and what might be called the avoidance of the avoidance of tonality. What is so remarkable about Weisgall as an operatic composer is his ability to write music that both impresses solely as music and at the same time mirrors the stage in a consistently uncanny way.

It is this combination of musical independence and dramatic relevance that so distinguishes *Six Characters*. In composing the opera,

Weisgall drew on many sources: updated Gregorian chant, the nineteenth-century Italian *verismo*, and Schoenbergian expressionism. Like Pirandello himself, whose original play has its roots in the life of the playwright's native Sicily, Weisgall draws on his entire artistic and human background to create his work.

The stature of the musical outcome of *Six Characters* is proven by one simple fact: unlike most American operas, and unlike almost all operas written since World War II, it contains vocal material—notably, the arias for the Coloratura and the Stepdaughter in act 1—that can be excerpted from the opera and performed independently in concert. What gives these arias their precious attribute of autonomous existence is sheer songfulness—extended, ripe, and memorable. Much the same thing can be said, too, about the immense power of the opera's end, with its gathering intensity of melody. Indeed, it is the profusion of melody, pleasurable to sing, play, and hear, that marks the entire score of *Six Characters* and earns it its distinguished place among American operas.

For some years we have been hearing a great deal about "music-theater," a supposedly new fusion of song, word, and stage action that will replace opera as a creative force. The candidates for the successful achievement of this fusion have run the gamut from the 1976 Philip Glass/Robert Wilson *Einstein on the Beach* through the 1987 John Adams/ Peter Sellars *Nixon in China*; hardier souls have even modeled their expectations—if not realizations—on the ineffably tacky David Byrne and his Talking Heads.

But for all the provocations, genteel and often otherwise, that these supposed achievements have offered, their lack of musical value had doomed them to be no more than *pièces d'occasion*, works of no artistic value devised to exploit a particular moment in the chaotic history of the avant-garde and its life-styles. For a real achievement in true music-theater, we must look to Weisgall's *Six Characters*, which manages at one and the same time to be a masterpiece in its independently existing music and a masterpiece in its unity of sound and stage.

If Weisgall's work, by virtue of its excellence, does not belong to the present idea of music-theater, where, then, does it belong? The answer is simple: it belongs to the history of opera in general, and to the history of Italian opera in particular. I have earlier mentioned Weisgall's use of *verismo*—the unfettered musical and dramatic expression of the most bloody happenings of daily life—a kind of opera associated with, among others, Puccini, Leoncavallo, and Mascagni. Weisgall is also to be seen, surprisingly enough, in the tradition of Gian Carlo Menotti, whose *Amelia Goes to the Ball* (1937) was written when both Menotti and Weisgall were at Curtis. In his later *The Old Maid and The Thief* (1939), *The Medium* (1946), *The Telephone* (1947), and *The Consul* (1950), Menotti attempted exactly the linking of music and theater that has so inspired Weisgall; indeed, it is not too much to say that Weisgall, in his direct communication with the audience through musicodramatic means, is the thinking man's Menotti. Above all, Weisgall, like Menotti, represents a hopeful development within the tradition beyond the operatic cul-de-sac symbolized by the vacant lushness of Puccini's *Turandot* (completed by Alfano after Puccini's death in 1924 and first produced in 1926) and by the huge scale of Berg's *Lulu* (1937).

The Chicago performance of *Six Characters*, judged by the broadcast, was replete with excellences. First-class young singers—in particular, baritone Robert Orth as the Father and soprano Elizabeth Byrne as the Stepdaughter—seemed comfortable with the challenging vocal lines. Rarity of rarities, the singers' English diction was uniformly excellent, something attested to by the quick response of the audience to the work's many subtle literary and musical witticisms. In the small orchestra, the wind and brass playing was splendid, though the strings, too few in number, seemed ill at ease, as did the conductor, Lee Schaenen. But any carping about the orchestra aside, the whole performance breathed a spirit of ensemble, of a company whose members were used to making opera performances together.

So far as Weisgall and his works are concerned, there are now two tasks urgently facing the world of American opera. The first, and perhaps the easier of the two to accomplish, is a New York production of *Six Characters* staged by the New York City Opera, with all the resources that this talented company, so sadly underemployed in the recent past, can muster. Such a New York production would at the very least have the advantage of being able to provide a more representative sound in the vital string parts; it would also have the advantage of being able to draw on the pioneering experience of the Chicago production.

The second task facing American opera, hardly less important than a New York production of *Six Characters*, is a major company production of *Esther*, to take place as soon as possible after its now imminent completion. Despite what has been said officially in San Francisco about *Esther* and its difficulty, its musical requirements are no greater than those of, say, Berg's *Wozzeck* and *Lulu*; its production requirements are similarly within reach of any large opera house. To ask this much for Hugo Weisgall is not only to pay a debt of honor to this imperfectly appreciated master, it is to begin to attempt to fill in the historical record of American opera and of American music. We have the idea in this country that only Europe has great artistic traditions. We have the idea, too, that great art is no longer being created. *Six Characters in Search of an Author* shows that we have art in our past. It also shows us that we have a great artist living in our present. It is high time that those responsible for our operatic life recognize these facts, and act upon them.

(*The New Criterion*, 1990)

6

A NEW LOOK AT PROKOFIEV

There have been three great modern Russian composers: Igor Stravinsky (1882–1971), Dmitri Shostakovich (1906–75), and Sergei Prokofiev (1891–1953).[1] In an important sense, each member of this trio is musically defined by his physical relation to the land of his birth. Stravinsky, resident in France at the time of World War I, chose not to return to Russia after the October Revolution of 1917; he was to go back only once, for a short and not entirely satisfactory visit in 1962. As for Shostakovich, he was Stravinsky's opposite in the matter of residence as in so much else; he remained in Russia his entire life, save for a number of visits abroad carefully calculated by his Soviet masters to enhance the prestige of Soviet art. Prokofiev, finally, lived as an adult both in his own country and abroad, spending the 1920s and much of the 1930s in Europe and America, then returning home as the Great Purge reached its height, and remaining there until his death less than one hour before that of the infamous Josef Stalin.

As the world saw them, these three composers were publicly very different. Stravinsky, born of upper-class stock and long associated with the equally upper-class balletomane Serge Diaghilev, was resolutely anti-Bolshevik. Shostakovich, dubbed by many an artistic child of the Revolution, seemed almost until the very end of his life a loyal and cooperative Bolshevik, even in the face of withering criticism of his music by Stalin's multitudinous cultural henchmen before and after World War II. Prokofiev, in contrast to both Stravinsky and Shostakovich, took no interest or part in politics. Like Shostakovich, he was forced to toe the Communist aesthetic line, not only in order to continue working but in order to continue living; also like Shostakovich, he saw his associates imprisoned and in some cases executed. Unlike Shostakovich, Prokofiev was personally touched by the terror, when his estranged wife, the mother of his two sons, was arrested in 1948 and taken off to a camp from which she was not released until 1956.

Musically, as far as Stravinsky is concerned, the verdict of history is clear: three great ballets for Diaghilev, culminating in the primitivist *The Rite of Spring* (1913); a group of hauntingly lovely neoclassic works, the best of which are the oratorio *Oedipus Rex* (1927) and the ballet *Apollo* (1928); a number of astringent works written in American exile, ending with the opera *The Rake's Progress* (1951); and finally, in the last two decades of his life, a startling appropriation of twelve-tone technique, resulting in some very dry music and much flattering critical discussion. Overall, thanks to Robert Craft and others, Stravinsky remains in death what he was in life: the most written-about composer of the twentieth century.

With Shostakovich the verdict, though only recently arrived at, is also reasonably clear: fifteen important and public symphonies, most of them projected on a very large canvas, divided—after the youthfully shocking First Symphony (1924–25)—between bathetic but popular pro-Soviet works like the Fifth (1937) and the Seventh (1941), on the one hand, and courageous moral outbursts like the Thirteenth ("Babi Yar," 1962) and the Fourteenth (1969), on the other; fifteen beautiful and intensely private string quartets written between 1935 and 1974; a large number of other chamber works; several concertos; many film scores; and a brutally realistic opera, *Lady Macbeth of the Mtsensk District* (1934), known in the version revised after much political pressure as *Katerina Ismaylova* (1962). Overall, Shostakovich has managed, through the posthumous publication of seemingly authentic memoirs, to transform his image in death from what had appeared to be that of a Soviet hero to that of a martyr equaled in dissidence perhaps only by Solzhenitsyn.

There is no such clear verdict on Sergei Prokofiev. He began his career at the end of the first decade of this century as a shocking pianist performing his own shocking compositions. The enfant terrible first of the Saint Petersburg Conservatory and then of Russian musical life in general, with his dissonantal, rigidly motoric music and similarly hard-edged pianism, he divided sophisticated concert audiences into violent supporters and equally violent detractors. When he began his exile from the Bolshevik Revolution in 1918, he continued abroad the reputation for provocation he had done so much to earn at home. But by the end of his life in 1953, Prokofiev, sick and increasingly feeble, had become a Soviet composer, finally forgiven for the crime of having lived abroad and, despite a crushing 1948 attack on him for formalism—i.e., placing private considerations of style and structure ahead of easy accessibility to a mass audience—honored with several much coveted Stalin Prizes.

Prokofiev's work may be divided into three periods: Russian, exilic, and Soviet. Always facile, he composed a huge amount of music, of which perhaps half was written prior to his return to the Soviet Union in the mid-1930s; of this first half, half again was written in his self-imposed exile after the Revolution. Altogether, in a compositional career stretching over a half-century, he completed seven symphonies, seven operas, seven ballets, four scores for dramatic productions, six film scores, five piano concertos, two violin concertos, two cello concertos, two string quartets, nine piano sonatas, two violin sonatas, a cello sonata, a host of songs, much solo piano music, and assorted orchestral, choral, and instrumental works.

Not surprisingly, the piano works of Prokofiev's Russian period, which were responsible for his early reputation, are no longer shocking. Instead, they now seem by turns flippant and sentimental. Two short dissonantal works, *Suggestion diabolique* (1908–12) and *Toccata* (1912), have become virtuoso showpieces beloved of hard-driving pianists; they were especially popular a generation ago, at least in this country, with young pianists anxious to profit from the public regard for Vladimir Horowitz's clangorous tone.[2] *Visions fugitives* (1915–17), twenty wistful and spicy keyboard miniatures, are very much more tuneful and refined, though hardly more memorable as musical thought. The four piano sonatas that date from this period do no more than replicate the mixture of cynicism and emotionality on a larger scale; the best of them, and the only one heard often today, is the Sonata No. 3 (composed 1907, revised 1917): short, sweet, and brilliant, it smacks of a greatly talented conservatory student showing off all his tricks upon graduation. The composer's first two piano concertos, the earlier written in 1911–12 and the latter in 1912–13 but revised in 1923, make the same impression with still greater presumption; indeed, it was through his playing of the Concerto No. I in a public contest that Prokofiev beat his fellow students and emerged in 1914 as the best pianist at the Saint Petersburg Conservatory.

Prokofiev's orchestral compositions during this time, though much talked about in their day, now seem hardly more consequential. The *Scythian Suite* (1914–15), drawn from an unproduced ballet written at the suggestion of Diaghilev, bears a too close resemblance to Stravinsky's *Rite of Spring*, while *The Buffoon* (composed for Diaghilev as a ballet in 1915 but now known in its 1922 orchestral version) openly reverts in style and mood to Stravinsky's preceding triumph, *Petrushka* (1911). The Symphony No. I (1916–17), subtitled "Classical," stems from a then common desire to abandon the lushness of nineteenth-century romanticism in favor of eighteenth-century clarity; but in contrast to the gravity of Richard Strauss's earlier *Ariadne auf Naxos* (1911) and Stravinsky's later *Pulcinella* (1920), Prokofiev's classicizing can easily strike a listener today as mere fussiness. One work of this period, the Violin Concerto No. I (1916-17), seems less trivial and, in parts, genuinely melodic; but though very much in the soloist's repertory today, it too makes an overall impression of scrappiness.[3]

Prokofiev's first important work outside Russia, though conceived there, was the opera *The Love for Three Oranges* (1918–21). This setting (with the composer's own libretto) of Gozzi's eighteenth-century parody of Chari and Goldoni was a venture into the vein of the *commedia dell'arte* so clear to Strauss and Stravinsky; more successful on its first performance in Chicago than elsewhere thereafter, it has won some popularity in the post-1945 Western operatic repertory, and in this country the famous March from act 2 even became (in supposedly McCarthyite America!) the theme music of the smash radio program "The FBI in Peace and War."

For Prokofiev, exile after 1918 meant not just composing but earning a living by giving regular piano concerts. For an appearance with Frederick Stock and the Chicago Symphony at the time of the premiere of *The Love for Three Oranges*, he completed his Piano Concerto No. 3 (1917–21). This was to prove his finest work to date, and to become one of the most popular twentieth-century piano concertos. Though the many extended fast sections still suffer from Prokofiev's tendency to athletic bustle in the place of inner vitality, each of the work's three movements contains passages of long-lined lyricism; the concluding movement in particular is marked by perhaps the first appearance of what was to become a typical Prokofiev grand melody, chaste and pure, rich in timbre but lean in harmonization.[4]

We learn from Harlow Robinson's recent biography of the composer[5] that in 1924 the increasingly successful émigré conductor Serge Koussevitzky, about to take over the Boston Symphony Orchestra, suggested that Prokofiev make a "hit" of the symphony he was then writing. But Prokofiev's Symphony No. 2, premiered by Koussevitzky in Paris the next year, was a meandering and harsh work, lightened only by the lovely, Ravel-like opening of its second (and final) movement. The work did not please the modernist cognoscenti, but it was well received in the Soviet Union, where the first signs were beginning to appear of what was later to become a beguiling welcome mat for Prokofiev.

There were other portents as well of artistic rapprochement with Russia's new masters. The formerly arch-anti-Bolshevik Diaghilev commissioned from Prokofiev a "Soviet" ballet, *Le Pas d'acier* (1925–26); the title is usually translated as "The Steel Step." This dry and unappealing work is a Paris-hatched evocation of Communist mechanization and industrialization. Initially the work was successful in Paris but was ill-received in the Soviet Union, where Prokofiev, Robinson tells us, was accused of a "distorted view of Soviet reality"; evidently the commissars did not relish praise from the effete Diaghilev and his coterie.

Another of Prokofiev's misfires at this time was *The Flaming Angel* (1919–27), an opera about female sexual obsession, based on a novel by the Russian symbolist Valery Bryusov. In this tense and brittle work, Prokofiev was so concerned with setting speech to musical accompaniment that he seems to have minimized any melodic expression for the voices. Despite his best efforts, the opera was not staged until 1955, and then only in Venice. In a valuable article on Prokofiev's operas,[6] George Martin asserts that *The Flaming Angel* demonstrates "much the same kind of power" as Strauss's *Elektra* (1906–8). Yet such a comparison surely understates the power of the extended outbursts of onrushing song which mark the latter part of *Elektra*; all of Strauss's dissonances—and here they are indeed more daring than those of Prokofiev—are integrated and redeemed by an even more daring lyrical passion. It was precisely this ultimate balancing of cacophony with melody, of harmonic disorder with order, which the Strauss of *Elektra* accomplished, and which the Prokofiev of *The Flaming Angel*, despite an attempt at song toward the end, could not manage.

Prokofiev did use much material from *The Flaming Angel* in his Symphony No. 3 (1928). Here the prevailing sound is harsh and heavy, and the symphony is rarely played today. But in fact Prokofiev's aesthetic was now beginning to change; the lyrical and combative elements that made up his musical personality were coming into equilibrium. An important token of this development was the tuneful and sometimes even romantic *L'Enfant prodigue* (1929), Diaghilev's last production before his death the same year. Material from this new, more relaxed Prokofiev forms the basis of the Symphony No. 4 (1930). This very beautiful work has had a checkered history and unfortunately has been known mainly in the composer's very much expanded 1947 revision, but in its original, highly concentrated form it seems the first fully realized example of the mature romantic classicism we associate with the best music of Prokofiev's Soviet period.

Another important work in these years when Prokofiev was going back and forth among the Soviet Union, Western Europe, and America is the Piano Concerto No. 4 (1931), written as a commission from the one-armed pianist Paul Wittgenstein, brother of the famous philosopher. This four-movement work for the left hand alone, immensely hard and even unrewarding to play, was spurned by its dedicatee because of its difficulty, and then frowned upon in the Soviet Union, perhaps for its lack of programmatic content. As a result it lay unperformed until 1956, and is rarely played even today. Nevertheless, the work combines two brilliant outer movements with a chastely beautiful slow movement and a dramatic third movement; the slow movement in particular marks another step on the road to the fully mature Prokofiev. The same can hardly be said of the bright and beady—and more frequently played—Concerto No. 5 (1932), a work that in retrospect seems a last reversion to Prokofiev's early hyperathletic manner.

As the decade of the 1930s progressed, Prokofiev was to spend more and more time in the land of his birth. Harlow Robinson makes it clear that despite the worsening political situation the Soviet Union had much to offer the now middle-aged composer. In the West, he had had to support himself and his family with constant piano appearances; in Russia he would be supported, as a composer, by the state. In the West he felt at the mercy of a small, inconstant, and complexity-loving audience captivated by the always fashionable Stravinsky, a musical figure who both fascinated and repelled him; in Russia, he thought he had found a vast and eager public ready, because of its roots in prerevolutionary Russian musical tradition, to support his newfound lyrical clarity. Robinson sums up the matter well: "Ultimately, it was [Prokofiev's] desire to compose in a more simple style that led him to return to the USSR."

Despite the horror of what was happening in Russia in the period after Prokofiev's return, it cannot be denied, I think, that he began to write his best music then. Thus in 1933, while in the Soviet Union, he composed the whimsically satirical score for the film *Lieutenant Kijé*, a work that has found a secure place in the orchestral repertory; in 1935 he wrote the very beautiful Violin Concerto No. 2, whose melodies grow more ravishing as each year passes; in 1936 he wrote the charming *Peter and the Wolf*, entrancing children all over the world while educating them about the instruments of the orchestra.

Finally, in 1935–38 he produced one of his most important scores, the ballet *Romeo and Juliet*; in a bow to his own past, he included in this new work the well-known Gavotte from the "Classical" Symphony. The long score of *Romeo and Juliet*, powerful in its evocation of both communal conflict and the pathos of young love, is today known not just as a ballet but, perhaps even better, in the three orchestral suites that have been extracted from it.[7] Here, for the first time, Prokofiev was neither an enfant terrible nor a troubled genius struggling to find his own consistent voice; instead, he had become a master whose best works to come—and they were to be many—would bear the stamp of icy passion and refined athleticism.

Yet this time of artistic transcendence for Prokofiev—the time, also, when he decided to reside permanently in the Soviet Union—was marked as well by the terror and exterminations of Stalin's purges. The murderous attention which this tyrant had been paying to the Russian peasantry was now extended to the army, the bureaucracy, and society as a whole. It was also extended to the arts. In music, the ax fell on Shostakovich in 1936 for his opera *Lady Macbeth*, successful on its premiere two year earlier, but now suddenly choked off because of Stalin's detestation of the licentious story and the frank musical treatment. Shostakovich's Symphony No. 4 (1935–36) was withdrawn, and only the appearance of the Symphony No. 5 (1937), subtitled "A Soviet Artist's Practical, Creative Reply to Just Criticism," restored him to the Stalinist book of life.

The dictator's chosen enemies were not simply particular pieces of music but any tendencies still remaining in Soviet society to look elsewhere than to the current definition of political orthodoxy for cultural nourishment and guidance. In practice, this meant a demand for musical happy endings and a ban on any form of modernism and any contemporary foreign influences.

The implications of such an artistic straitjacket for Prokofiev's music, and even for his physical survival, gradually became clear. He made public political statements, and he began to write what can only be called political nonceworks, starting off with a wretched *Cantata for the Twentieth Anniversary of the October Revolution* (1936–37); ironically, this piece of bombast did not do the job its creator intended, for it was not performed until 1966.[8] In the years before his death, Prokofiev was to write several such compositions, including the drinking song *Zdravitsa* (1939), usually translated as "Hail to Stalin"; the oratorio *On Guard for Peace* (1950); and the *Festive Poem—The Meeting of the Volga and the Don* (1951), written to celebrate the completion of yet another slave-labor project.

But the real Prokofiev, happily, is not to be found in any of these extorted potboilers. He is to be found, for example, in the Piano Sonatas

Nos. 6 through 8 that he began to sketch in 1939. All of them have gone into the international piano repertory, perhaps the last solo works—with the exception of the Sonata Op. 26 (1949) by the American Samuel Barber—to do so. Of these three vital compositions, the most brilliant, the most moving, and curiously the shortest is the Sonata No. 7, completed in 1942.[9] This titanic work resounds in its outer movements with the sounds of the coming war, but contains in the glorious slow movement a manly tenderness that ennobles the surrounding struggle.

Prokofiev also continued to write for orchestra and the ballet. His Symphony No. 5 (1944), though very much a public work, now seems more authentic than Shostakovich's Symphony No. 7 (1941), subtitled "Leningrad." The ballet *Cinderella* (1940–44), still today very much in the shadow of *Romeo and Juliet*, is even finer than the earlier score in the purity and intensity of its melodic expression. Mention must be made, too, of the two massive film scores, *Alexander Nevsky* (1938) and *Ivan the Terrible* (1942–46), both written in close collaboration with the great director Sergei Eisenstein. Gripping as film accompaniment, these works maintain their life in the concert hall, though in both cases Prokofiev's own musical style is subordinated to the attempt to accommodate the historical, not to say mythic, Russian subject matter; in any event, this music is the high-water mark of the composer's achievement as a Soviet patriot.

Throughout his life, Prokofiev was committed to operatic composition. As an aspect of his accommodation to the political climate at the end of the 1930s he wrote *Semyon Kotko* (1940), based on a story combining post-1917 events in the Ukraine with a traditional boy-meets-girl, boy-wins-girl plot; although the political libretto could not have been more orthodox, or the musical treatment more lyrical, the conflicted political atmosphere of the Hitler-Stalin Pact seems to have doomed the work on its premiere, and it remains neglected.

Prokofiev made one further operatic attempt to please his masters: the *Story of a Real Man* (1948), based on the best-selling novel of Boris Polevoi about a wounded Russian flyer who returns to combat after his legs are amputated. In the music for this, his last opera, Prokofiev combined cinematic techniques of short scenes and rapid alternations of mood with traditional operatic forms of aria and duet, and even introduced evocations of popular dance music. Once again, however, he failed to please his masters, and the work was not performed for the first time until 1960; since then it has become a regular part of the repertory in Moscow.

More important by far, however, is *War and Peace*, which the composer worked on from 1941 until the year before his death, in spite of illness and the firestorm of Andrei Zhdanov's 1948 onslaught on musical life. In *War and Peace*, Prokofiev rests not on the quicksand of Soviet attitudes to current events but on the very core of Russian history, made into immortal literature by Tolstoy. From so immense a historical canvas, Prokofiev fashioned an enormous opera that in its original version threatened to require two evenings for its performance.

After a hugely successful 1946 production in Leningrad of the first half of the opera, Prokofiev made both extensive revisions and many—evidently too many—cuts. After the cuts were restored, the revised *War and Peace*, now brimming with expansive melodies and striding rhythms, was finally staged in Moscow in 1959. The work has never been produced in the United States by a major opera company; given the fact that *War and Peace* very possibly contains the strongest music, qua music, of any opera written since Strauss, such a staging by one of our repertory-starved operatic behemoths is long overdue.[10]

Prokofiev's compositional career—and his life—was rounded out by his final two symphonies and a remarkable work for cello and orchestra. The Symphony No. 6 (1945–47) was evidently to be more severe and introspective than its very outgoing predecessor; the late musicologist Boris Schwarz (in the 1983 second edition of his indispensable *Music and Musical Life in Soviet Russia*) correctly found "the orchestral sound . . . harsh and metallic . . . the low brass instruments . . . often snarling . . . the high woodwinds shrill. . . . " But even here, the lovely slow movement, with its perhaps unintended reference to a theme from the American Howard Hanson's "Nordic" Symphony (1923), musically justifies the surrounding density. The quite different Symphony No. 7 (1951–52) seems to evoke the gentle and nostalgic sides of Paris in the 1920s; listening to the soaring opening movement of this work, one can only marvel at the capacity of the artist to find warmth in his imagination at a time when real life was unbearably bleak.

The same must be said of the *Sinfonia Concertante* (1950–52), a work brilliantly played the world over by Mstislav Rostropovich, for whom it was written. Here, in a tightly packed piece of less than twenty minutes' duration, Prokofiev sums up the entire melodic and virtuoso tradition of the Russian solo concerto, a genre made famous by Tchaikovsky and Rachmaninoff, and to which Prokofiev himself contributed so much.

The ironies of Prokofiev's life are startling. A composer of genius grows up under conditions of relative artistic freedom; he leaves his revolution-ridden homeland to work in total freedom—but then writes his best music after intentionally deciding to incarcerate himself in the land of his birth, one of the most bloodthirsty tyrannies the world has ever known. Did Prokofiev behave in some sense culpably in writing music—beautiful and great music—under a dictator? Can it be true that despotism, rather than freedom, is peculiarly conducive to great art?

These are difficult questions to answer, for they go to the heart of the spiritual life of the twentieth century. In the particular case of Prokofiev, it is essential to realize that we have little record of his politics, or of his wider activities outside music. Though he left behind a fascinating memoir of childhood and student days at the Saint Petersburg Conservatory,[11] he wrote very little of a personal nature about his adult life; as Harlow Robinson has convincingly demonstrated, Prokofiev was a man of abrasive utterance but few explanations. Moreover, of those colleagues who may have known him intimately, few can have survived into happier times with their memories and energies intact.

In any case, unlike his younger colleague Shostakovich, who early on supported the Bolshevik Revolution and who served (under duress) as a Stalinist spokesman on well-publicized propaganda visits to Europe and the United States after World War II, Prokofiev confined his political acts to perfunctory statements and obligatory ceremonial compositions that were in no case successful. Given the conditions of the last years of Stalin's reign, Prokofiev's stubborn insistence on writing abstract symphonies in addition to the required program music speaks for his artistic courage, not for any craven capitulation.

It is also clear that Prokofiev's artistic turn away from the stridency and flippancy associated with the hypertrophy of musical modernism occurred well before his return to the USSR, and that the roots of his best music lay in works he wrote while still in the West. In going back, was Prokofiev beguiled by the prospect of an adoring and receptive audience? Of course he was. But it is hardly peculiar to want to write for an approving audience. Furthermore, it would be wrong to overlook the close attachment of composers to their homelands; in general, it is difficult to separate the greatest music from the national circumstances under which it was written. The idea of Mother Russia, as important to Prokofiev as it is to Solzhenitsyn, was hardly invented by Stalin, exploit it though the dictator did in order to mobilize political sentiment.

So far as the creation of art under tyranny is concerned, we can hardly believe that any domination of man by man is so complete as to destroy all autonomous human experience, the nonpolitical as well as the political, the artistic as well as the social. Even under totalitarianism some kind of private experience persists, and so too, by implication, does the life of the artistic imagination. Boris Pasternak conceived and wrote his novel *Doctor Zhivago* under the worst conditions of repression; in the more abstract and therefore more enclosed area of music, the individual expression of genius remained similarly possible.

Today, in our present era of perhaps exaggerated hopes for *glasnost* and *perestroika*, is there a risk that in praising works of art created under Stalin we may be offering an apology for, or even a defense of, past or future evil? There can be little doubt that present and future Soviet governments—and present and future Stalinists—will attempt to use Russian art and creativity to justify past actions and future plans. It is, after all, the fate of great art to be enlisted in every cause, good or bad. All the more necessary, then, to insist on the distance that separates art created by individuals working within the matrix of a great people from the crimes of sanguinary usurpers. Clearly the point is not that despotism is good for music, any more than the fate of the musical avant-garde in the West after World War II proves that political freedom is bad. The point, rather, is that any attempt to extract apodictic lessons about the creation of art from our knowledge of the political circumstances that surround it is to reduce artistic creativity to the level of a recipe, as if writing a symphony were like baking a cake. This, indeed, was Stalin's position; it need hardly be ours.

With Sergei Prokofiev, what we know is that there occurred in him that most fecund conjunction of an original artistic genius with an artistic tradition still alive in a large population. It is the business of critics, among others, to maintain such traditions; the genius comes from elsewhere and above.

(*Commentary*, 1989)

PART TWO

PIANISTS

7

RUBINSTEIN

THE GREAT ENTERTAINER

When Arthur Rubinstein died last December at the age of ninety-five, there was remarkably little feeling of loss in the musical community. As had been the case with his life, Rubinstein's death, too, seemed natural, another fulfillment of the kind which appeared (at least to onlookers) always to have been his lot.

Rubinstein enjoyed a long and splendid career. Born in 1887, he was before the public from the 1890s to the 1970s, a period beginning with the vigorous manhood of Claude Debussy and ending with the old age of John Cage. Despite this almost unparalleled longevity as a performer, Rubinstein was never, even during the years of his phenomenal success, perceived as the world's greatest pianist. During the 1920s, for example, this title was shared by Josef Hofmann and Sergei Rachmaninoff; from the mid-1930s to the present day, the undisputed champion has been Vladimir Horowitz. And if the applicable title were to be not the world's greatest pianist but the world's greatest musician-pianist, the names of Artur Schnabel, Alfred Cortot, and Edwin Fischer would seem, for most music lovers, beyond compare.

Hofmann, Rachmaninoff, and Horowitz all belong to the class of virtuosi, those who astound by feats of dexterity, lightness, and elegantly applied force. Schnabel, Cortot, and Fischer are regarded as thinkers, those whose musical ideas are always prior to, and more interesting than, mere mechanical execution. Rubinstein, by contrast, did not astonish with his fingers, and he did not inspire with his mind. He did both less and more: he gave pleasure, he made his listeners happy—in a word, he entertained. Not only was this his claim to fame and riches, it is now his claim to our admiration.

The story of Rubinstein's life is to be found, no doubt often highly embroidered, in two marvelous volumes of memoirs, written in the 1970s when his failing eyesight and strength made further piano-playing difficult.[1] These more than one thousand pages tell of a Jewish prodigy from Poland who managed, at the age of three, to impress the great violinist Joachim, friend and adviser to Brahms. From the age of ten, Rubinstein (under Joachim's guidance) studied in Berlin: piano with Heinrich Barth and theory with Max Bruch. He worked a bit with Paderewski, and, perhaps more important, received a notable *éducation sentimentale* from numerous women who were only too charmed by his extreme youth and passionate eagerness to please.

Almost out of his teens, Rubinstein began to concertize extensively, though not yet profitably. In 1906 he toured the United States, giving seventy-five concerts, not very successful, under the sponsorship of the Knabe Piano Company. Residence in Paris brought him into contact with the *jeunesse dorée*, and some of its aristocratic elders as well. Great names of society and music whizzed in and out of his life; he dined out much more often and more regularly than he practiced the piano. When he visited Poland, he hardly saw his family, choosing instead to pass the time in the great world of Warsaw. And wherever he lived, he was on a kind of dole.

Such a state of affairs was hardly tenable. In 1908, this creature, who had so clearly been born to gladden hearts, attempted suicide in Berlin, the scene of his dreary student days. The attempt itself—at least as he himself describes it—was farcical, but in his memoirs he adds bathos to farce as he tells what happened next:

Then, half-consciously, I staggered to the piano and cried myself out in music. Music, my beloved music, the dear companion of all my emotions, who can stir us to fight, who can inflame in us love and passion, and who can soothe our pains and bring peace to our hearts—you are the one who, on that ignominious day, brought me back to life.

Beyond the self-indulgence, something important had happened. From this day forward, Rubinstein was the man we have always known: "I discovered the secret of happiness and I still cherish it: Love life for better or worse, without conditions."

Although worldly success was still a few years off, Rubinstein was now ready to receive it. His musical reputation grew, as did his contacts with such famous artists as Leopold Godowsky, Pablo Casals, and Eugène Ysaÿe. In London, just before and during World War I, he laid the foundation for his later English triumphs. Indeed, it was in London in 1915 that Rubinstein received a concert offer which was to mark the beginning of fame and fortune: an invitation to play the Brahms D Minor Concerto in San Sebastián.

Rubinstein came to Spain and conquered. In his memoirs he is characteristically frank in describing what happened in San Sebastián: "The concert was not well attended; the theater was only half-filled. But my personal success, after this monumental and sober work, was absolutely sensational. No Saint-Saëns, no Liszt, no Chopin, had ever excited a public to that extent." During the 1916–17 season he gave more than a hundred concerts in Spain. With this kind of success, it was hardly surprising that he soon received an invitation to Argentina. There, and in the rest of South America, he scored a success even greater than in Spain.

For Rubinstein, the 1920s marked an extraordinary period in which he combined the life of an artist with that of a *boulevardier*. He immersed himself in the currents of modern art; he was a friend of the French *Les Six* and of Jean Cocteau, the major influence upon that group. He associated with, and played the music of, Karol Szymanowski, Poland's greatest twentieth-century composer. He performed widely a piano transcription of Stravinsky's *Petrushka* which the composer himself had written for him. He became close to Manuel de Falla in Spain and to Heitor Villa-Lobos in Brazil, and he played their works all over the world. De Falla's "Ritual Fire Dance" from *El amor brujo* and, to a lesser extent, Villa-Lobos's short *Polichinelle* became Rubinstein's ubiquitous musical signature.

The 1920s also saw the beginnings of Rubinstein's prolific career as a maker of phonograph records.[2] In a remarkable display of constancy in this age of shifting commercial arrangements, the pianist spent more than a half-century with just two recording companies: first His Master's Voice in England, then its affiliate RCA when he became an American resident in the 1940s. It was his work in the recording studio, combined with the advent of Vladimir Horowitz as a virtuoso technician, which convinced Rubinstein that in performance he needed to do more than just give the spirit of a composition, letting the exact notes fall (as he always had) where they might.

In his personal life, too, Rubinstein was now ready to settle down. In 1932, this confirmed bachelor married a woman half his age. Aniela Mlynarska was the daughter of Emil Mlynarski, the foremost Polish conductor of the day. She provided Rubinstein with a family—they eventually had four children—and the kind of social stability he craved. The ensuing fifty years were a whirlwind of concerts and tours, of elegant homes on both coasts of the United States and in Paris, of endless supplies of wine, song, and lobster, if not (as before) women.

Rubinstein continued to play almost into his nineties. Indeed, it seemed that his appetite for playing, and his strength to indulge the appetite, grew as he himself grew older. In the mid-1950s, for instance, in a series of five concerts repeated in Paris, London, and New York, he played again seventeen of the concertos he had performed over the years: works by Beethoven, Brahms, Chopin, Schumann, Mozart, Liszt, Saint-Saëns, Rachmaninoff, Franck, Grieg, and de Falla. In just a single concert he would do both Brahms concertos or three Beethoven concertos. In 1961, he gave a series of ten solo recitals in New York, playing different pieces on each program.

His last concert was a benefit at Wigmore Hall in London in April 1976. Once again, his memoirs sum up both the moment and his retrospective feelings about it:

As for myself, it was a symbolic gesture; it was in this hall that I had given my first recital in London [in 1912] and playing there for the last time in my life made me think of my whole career in the form of a sonata. The first movement represented the struggles of my youth, the following andante [stood] for the beginning of a more serious aspect of my talent, a scherzo represented well the unexpected great success, and the finale turned out to be a wonderful moving end.

Now that Rubinstein is dead, it is at last possible to assess his achievement as an artist. No one will dispute that his audiences enjoyed his concerts. But there is a deeper question to be answered: just how well did Rubinstein play?

Perhaps the best place to begin is with some of the numerous and widely available stereo LP recordings Rubinstein made for RCA during the 1950s, 1960s, and 1970s. There are something like one hundred of them, and they cover, with few exceptions, the repertory he played during his lifetime. Here are most of the great romantic concertos and many of the classical works for piano and orchestra; here too are almost all the solo works of Chopin, several of the most popular Beethoven sonatas, some of the most important solo works of Schumann, and a smattering of the earlier twentieth-century music Rubinstein played not out of duty but out of liking. And there are numerous examples here of chamber music for piano and strings, a genre which Rubinstein cultivated even at the times of his busiest concert activity.

Listening to these records en masse does make clear just what—in addition to Rubinstein's infectiously ebullient stage personality—gave his audiences so much pleasure. In his records, one always hears clearly articulated melodies, proudly carried high above their pianistic background. Yet these records also bear out Rubinstein's reputation among musicians: rarely do the performances seem unique documents either of pure piano-playing or of compelling cerebration.

The records are at their weakest, it seems to me, in performances of preromantic music. Rubinstein's approach to Mozart, as demonstrated in his concerto recordings, is heavy, often wayward in articulation, and immensely dutiful. It is of some significance, too, that the orchestral background (most likely at Rubinstein's choice) is romantically sweet and overly full of feeling, rather than classically energetic and astringent, as is required if the solo part is to be heard in proper context.

As for Rubinstein's recordings of the Beethoven concertos, of which the 1960s set with Erich Leinsdorf and the Boston Symphony and the 1970s set with Daniel Barenboim and the London Philharmonic are both currently available, they offer clear examples of how far a pianist can go by knowing how the music ought to sound, even if the physical ability necessary to implement this conception is rapidly waning. Not surprisingly, the earlier set, made when the pianist was "only" in his mid-seventies, seems somewhat fresher and less tenuous; the latter, made more than a decade later, suggests the "shipwreck" that Charles de Gaulle called old age. These are painful documents, not least because of the listener's constant awareness of an intensely captivating personality here defeated by infirmity.

On records as in concert, Rubinstein shied away from the late Beethoven sonatas (though in his much younger days he played the Sonata in B-flat Major, Op. 106, the "Hammerklavier"). But he did often play such earlier works as the "Pathétique" (C Minor, Op. 13) and the "Appassionata" (F Minor, Op. 57). His early 1960s recordings of these works, though technically adequate, seem cautious by comparison both with his reputation as a firebrand and with his 1950s recordings of the same works. For those used to the performances of Beethoven specialists, Rubinstein's approach will inevitably seem decorative, as if he were bemused by the local beauties of the music rather than concerned to communicate the strong bones of Beethoven's structures.

Rubinstein was renowned during his American heyday as a Brahms interpreter, and those fortunate enough to have heard him play the B-flat Concerto in concert as late as 1960 will recall the magisterial approach he brought to this work. A 1959 recording with Josef Krips and the RCA Symphony Orchestra and a 1960 concert recording with Witold Rowicki and the Warsaw Philharmonic demonstrate not only how completely Rubinstein identified with this style, at once knotty and luxuriantly romantic, but also how well its technical problems were under his control even as he grew older. By contrast, his last recording of the piece, with Eugene Ormandy and the Philadelphia Orchestra about 1970, though pianistically vastly superior to his final Beethoven concerto efforts, can be no more than a souvenir for those who remember the artist in earlier and better days.

One of the most attractive features of Rubinstein's Brahms playing was his characteristically rich, deep tone, simultaneously tender and strong. In his concerts, this tone was always in the forefront; though it did not always survive in reproduction on modern records, it can be heard in the numerous short solo pieces of Brahms recorded by Rubinstein in the early days of stereo. The same tone remains in evidence in the pianist's discs of Schumann, which include the famous A Minor Concerto (with Carlo Maria Giulini and the Chicago Symphony) and such solo pieces as the *Carnaval*, the *Fantasiestücke* Op. 12, and the *Etudes symphoniques*. Here, on 1960s stereo issues, there is much to admire in the sensitivity and sheer ability to make melodies and harmonies easily discernible by the listener; yet these performances, too, seem to suffer from a certain digital lethargy, as if the pianist were having trouble getting his fingers and hands up from the keys quickly enough to provide the necessary space between the notes.

Throughout his American career, Rubinstein was most famous as a Chopinist. His Chopin repertory was enormous, and he drew on it often in his recitals. He recorded Chopin in quantity three times: first on 78-RPM for HMV in England during the 1930s, then for RCA on mono LP in the 1950s, and then finally on stereo LP (again for RCA) in the late 1950s and early 1960s. Many of these last records, including the Barcarolle, the Ballades, both concertos, the Mazurkas, the Nocturnes, the Polonaises, both major sonatas, and the Waltzes, are still easily available; together they give a coherent picture of Rubinstein's Chopin playing at the end of his career.

That picture is essentially ruminative, gentle, often introverted, and also often backward in rhythmic impetus. The Chopin presented by the later Rubinstein is a poet rather than a virtuoso, a self-reflecting musician rather than the heroic lion of the keyboard. This essentially miniaturist approach, in Rubinstein's hands, is capable of producing many felicities; on occasion, as in the Impromptus and the Berceuse, or in the quieter Mazurkas and Nocturnes, it is decidedly effective. But when the music itself is on a larger canvas, as in the Barcarolle and the Polonaises, we are reminded all too often that what we are hearing is an old man's Chopin, a musical suit cut to fit the cloth of necessary caution.

Even where Rubinstein evidently decides to gamble, to push his fingers beyond their comfortable competence, as in the later recordings of the two Chopin concertos, the result is forced and artificially brilliant; the whole somehow suggests those reproductions of paintings in which

special care has been taken to make the colors seem bright and compelling. There is a great difference between this kind of straining after survival and the true art of concerto playing, which properly consists in the
soloist's constantly shaping the entire performance, including that of often unresponsive orchestras and conductors. To do this requires a kind
of forcefulness Rubinstein clearly no longer possessed.

Enough has been said here to paint the essential outlines of the Rubinstein we can now hear in stereo. His recordings of later music, including
the Rachmaninoff C Minor Concerto, the Paganini Rhapsody, and the
Tchaikovsky B-flat Major Concerto, are still in the catalogues. The late
recording of the Rachmaninoff C Minor with Eugene Ormandy and the
Philadelphia is notey and tame, altogether inferior to the earlier stereo
version (still available) with Fritz Reiner and the Chicago. The Paganini
Rhapsody (again with Reiner and the Chicago) is a not very satisfactory
account of a score Rubinstein learned relatively late in his life and with
which he always had technical trouble. The Tchaikovsky, with Erich
Leinsdorf and the Boston, is a routine account of a work that Rubinstein's arch-rival Vladimir Horowitz made peculiarly his own (in recordings with Toscanini).

If the 1960 performance of the Brahms B-flat Concerto is a magisterial
document, then one side of a disc containing excerpts from the ten-
concert series in New York in 1961 is a document both of the intimate
Rubinstein and of Rubinstein the performer of twentieth-century music.
On this record, no longer available, the pianist plays twelve *Visions fugitives* (from Op. 22) of Prokofiev and the *Próle do Bébé* Suite (1918) by
Villa-Lobos. His playing treats every note with seriousness, commitment, and, above all, a plentiful fancy; the result is delectable, and sad,
too, in its way: still more evidence, if more were needed, of the funda-
mentally wrong road taken by piano music sometime after the 1920s.

It goes without saying that in the last two decades of his life Arthur
Rubinstein played magnificently for a man of his age; it also goes without saying that his audiences, to the very end, were conscious of receiving full value. If such factors were all that were relevant in the making of
musical judgments, then Rubinstein's career could now be seen as having reached its greatest triumph at its close.

But more is involved than an audience memory of Arthur Rubinstein, even though that memory is one of pleasure. Although there once was a time when all that was left of an artist's reputation after his death lay secreted in the fading and inaccurate memories of concert-goers, now everything is different. Proof of that difference has been the very fact that I have been able to examine Rubinstein's playing not just memory by memory, but by listening to note after note. It is the phenomenon of sound recording which has made this difference; and it is the enormously prestigious Rubinstein recorded archive which requires us to take his playing seriously.

For these recordings are now widely taken as imperishable documents of an authentic tradition; as such, they will continue to shape the expectations and perceptions of audiences. Because this is the way such music is supposed to sound, this is the way audiences will want it to sound. As far as young performers (and their teachers) are concerned, it can be put crassly: here is what succeeded. With this model as a guide, others too may find fame and fortune at the keyboard.

Lest this seem cynical, consider the extent to which today's pianists, regardless of age, sound old; indeed, the present generation of musicians has turned the adage "wise beyond one's years" into anything but a compliment. Among pianists, outbursts of brilliance are too often seen as proof of immaturity and unmusicality; every fast tempo and forceful dynamic scheme is taken as a sign of insensitivity. What is the antidote to these artistic shortcomings? Listen to the great, students are told.

Given the synthetic character of creative musical life today, it would be quixotic to ask that audiences and musicians cease listening to recordings. And as for music criticism, whatever else it might or might not be able to do, it can hardly be expected to inspire originality. Critics have little choice but to make distinctions, to point out better and worse. Fortunately, such an act of discrimination is possible in the case of Arthur Rubinstein, for in addition to the records I have been discussing, there is another kind of playing to be heard from this pianist.

I refer to Rubinstein's earlier recordings. By earlier I do not, for the most part, mean his mono LP discs, or even the many 78s he made in this country during the 1940s. Despite the presence among those recordings of several excellent performances—in particular, chamber music with

Heifetz and Feuermann (later Piatigorsky) and both the *Symphonie Concertante* and the first four Mazurkas of Szymanowski—Rubinstein's playing on them often sounds hard and brittle, as if he were attempting to give a perfect performance for the microphone.

Such, indeed, may well have been the case. Much has been made, correctly, of the chilling effect that the meteoric rise of Vladimir Horowitz had on Rubinstein's perception of his own technical abilities; too little has been said in this connection of the pianist's own thoughts on the impact of the phenomenon of recording. In the second volume of his memoirs, describing his life in Paris just before the outbreak of World War II, Rubinstein wrote:

My readers will certainly be astonished that now I seem to barely mention my music making and my concerts, but to describe long tours, concert by concert with detailed programs, is utterly impossible. All I can say now is that my playing improved considerably, mainly due to the fact that the American public was more demanding than any other, and also to my recordings, which had to be note-perfect and inspired. The result was that I learned to love practicing and to discover new meanings in the works I performed.

But *did* Rubinstein's playing improve? The answer—coming, as it can only come, from recordings of this period—must be no. For a reasonably large body exists of Rubinstein recordings made at a still earlier time, on European if not on American labels; and this body of recordings from before the late 1930s provides eloquent testimony that Arthur Rubinstein was once a supremely great pianist, with a supremely interesting and exciting personal approach to music.

Perhaps the earliest of Rubinstein's HMV records was a disc he made in 1928 of the Schubert Impromptu in A-flat Major (D. 899, 4) and the Chopin Waltz, again in A-flat Major, Op. 34, No. 1.[3] The Schubert is searchingly musical and pianistically magnificent; comparison with the later and now standard recordings of Fischer and Schnabel suggests that only Schnabel was in Rubinstein's league as a Schubert player. The Chopin is by turns tender, gay, and brilliant; the technical mastery Rubinstein possessed at this time is made startlingly clear in his ability to play difficult decorative figures at extreme speed and with exemplary clarity.

The next record in the HMV numbering series is the Chopin Barcarolle.[4] Not only is this performance distinguished by a piano tone beautiful even for Rubinstein (in his memoirs, we are told that it was done on a Blüthner rather than the more likely Steinway or Bechstein); it also brings together, on a large scale, the same combination of insight and virtuosity the pianist shows in the Schubert and Chopin "miniatures." Here, in the grandest romantic music, is freedom elevated to the rank of order. And on a purely mechanical level, informed ears will hear on this disc remarkable trills, octaves, and runs.

The next year Rubinstein made a record of his—and his audience's—beloved Spanish music.[5] *Navarra* and *Sevilla* of Albéniz are authentic crowd pleasers, and they are also tests both of a pianist's rhythmic sense and of his ability to play dense chordal masses at great speed without heaviness. Rubinstein succeeds magnificently, and one's pleasure in the gorgeous color and ease he brings to this music is hardly diminished by the liberties he takes in the *Navarra* with the exact text Albéniz prescribed.

On the next record of Rubinstein issued by HMV at this time,[6] we find an unlikely combination: the Brahms Capriccio in B Minor, Op. 76, No. 2, and the Debussy Prelude from Book I, *La Cathédrale engloutie*. Each performance is completely in the character of the music it presents, and one scarcely knows which to admire more, the yoking of a serious approach with a light piano tone in the Brahms or the bell-like clarity of the sonorities in the Debussy.

Because Rubinstein had made no prior recordings with orchestra, perhaps the greatest interest attaches to his discs of the Brahms B-flat Concerto made in 1929 (or 1930: the memoirs are unclear on the matter).[7] He seems to have been uncomfortable during the recording sessions because he was physically separated from the conductor, Albert Coates, with whom in any case he had had no chance to rehearse. Rubinstein wanted the takes destroyed, and one can understand his reasons: he plays wrong notes galore, and the orchestra (the London Symphony) is hardly first-class. But the performance is still extraordinary; Rubinstein plays without caution, as if in full confidence of his ability to get the keys down properly without taking individual aim at each one. There is no point in looking to this recording for the ultimate in realized perfection; there is every reason to cite it as an example of that pianistic attitude of risk and force which must underlie concerto playing.

Much has been written about Rubinstein's 1931 recording of the Chopin F Minor Concerto with John Barbirolli and the London Symphony Orchestra;[8] it is enough here to remark that, for those fortunate to own the original 78s or to have access to the LP reissue, it still sets the standard for richness of tone and intimate force of conception. The recording, probably made the next year, of the Brahms Sonata in D Minor for Violin and Piano, in which Rubinstein appears with his Polish compatriot Paul Kochanski,[9] is an extraordinary example of chamber-music playing. Kochanski, sadly an underrecorded violinist, plays beautifully; Rubinstein is able to make soft piano phrases clear without drowning his partner out.

Rubinstein's recording of the *Triana* of Albéniz (again, as with the *Navarra*, in his own version)[10] maintains the caliber of his achievement in Spanish music; three Villa-Lobos pieces on the other side of this disc document not just wonderfully attractive music, but also the incredible hand coordination Rubinstein deployed at this time. It is difficult to praise too highly his 1932 recording of all the Chopin Scherzos[11] and the 1934–35 discs of the complete Polonaises.[12] In their combination of power and beauty they are unrivaled. Exceptional among these performances are those of the B Minor Scherzo and the two famous Polonaises, the so-called "Military" in A major and the "Heroic" in A-flat major. Whether one fastens upon the passage work, the repeated chords, the rapid left-hand octaves, or just the sustained cantilena, here is a summit of Chopin playing and of piano playing altogether.

One recording from this period remains to be mentioned. As I suggested earlier, we have grown to associate the Tchaikovsky Concerto in B-flat Minor with the name of Horowitz; his supercharged performances with Toscanini seem about as far as human capacities can go in the direction of icy brilliance, breakneck excitement, and the extremes of strength and speed. Rubinstein, however, made a recording of this work almost a decade before Horowitz;[13] done with Barbirolli and the London

Symphony, it was a great seller before (though not after) the first Horowitz album appeared in 1941.

Rubinstein's performance of the Tchaikovsky on this early recording is lighter than Horowitz's. Only a little, if at all, slower, it is not so relentlessly driven, and it is a good deal more "romantic." Indeed, instead of the Horowitz excitement, Rubinstein supplies sentiment. Today, after a generation of pianistic attempts to imitate Horowitz's daggerlike fingers, it would seem that Rubinstein's more luxuriant approach wears rather better.

These early records, taken together, go a long way toward explaining Rubinstein's success in the concert hall. He provided technique, daring, emotion, tenderness, power, all in about equal measure. Fortunately, evidence of just what he did supply in concert (rather than in the studio) can be found on recordings made live without subsequent editing. In this regard, two performances from the 1940s stand out. They are both of concertos: one, from 1944, of the Beethoven C Minor with Toscanini and the NBC Symphony,[14] and the other, from 1947, of the Chopin E Minor with Bruno Walter and the New York Philharmonic.[15]

Here, collaborating with great conductors and orchestras, Rubinstein does indeed prove himself the supreme entertainer among pianists—not because he was a show-off in the manner of a Pavarotti, but because he brought the culture of a great musician to the pleasurable re-creation of the greatest art. Though he gladly accepted the love and homage of the audience, he gave in return an authentic experience of the highest culture of the nineteenth century. That he did this for so many, and for so many years, is proof enough that in calling him an entertainer one is not denigrating him, but rather raising him far above the pack of applause-mongers whom music lovers today know as "stars."

(*Commentary*, 1983)

8

BARTÓK AT THE PIANO

Composers of serious music in the twentieth century have often complained about the mixture of incompetence and self-regard with which performers have allegedly played their works. The champion at this kind of complaint was Igor Stravinsky, who disliked the performances of such of his works as *The Rite of Spring* even when they elicited enthusiastic responses from the audience. Arnold Schoenberg, too, was at times unhappy about the way his works were played. In my own experience, Darius Milhaud was frequently caustic about performances of his music and that of his colleagues. And numerous lesser-known figures have oscillated wildly between trying to get their pieces programmed and then ascribing the inevitable failures to how these pieces were performed.

Composers, one must assume, have always been persnickety about performances; one can hardly imagine a performer having gone with a light heart to play Beethoven's music for the master. Until recent times, however, there was a way to deal with the performance problem: the composer could execute the work himself. Composers like Gustav Mahler and Richard Strauss were famous conductors, and Richard Wagner was by most accounts a great interpreter of the Beethoven symphonies as well as of his own music. Indeed, Stravinsky himself recorded, often more than once, the great majority of his orchestral pieces.

But while some major composers have been conductors, the most significant medium for the composer-performer has been the piano or its predecessor instruments, the harpsichord and the organ. Much of the greatest music from Bach onward has been written for these keyboard instruments: and many of the composers responsible for this flowering have also been performing virtuosos. Among them were Bach himself, Mozart, Beethoven, Chopin, and Brahms. Closer to our own time, Debussy, Scriabin, Rachmaninoff, and Prokofiev were recognized as great pianists. Even Stravinsky, though hardly in the virtuoso class, often played his own piano works in the 1920s and 1930s.

Considering that the phonograph has existed throughout this century, there are surprisingly few distinguished documents of the contemporary composer as pianist. On records, Debussy can dimly be heard as he plays accompaniments in 1904 for soprano Mary Garden. He can also be heard, more strongly, in piano-roll recordings of moderate sonic authenticity. Prokofiev is represented on a number of discs of his own music made in Europe in 1932 and 1935. Unfortunately, only one large-scale work—the Third Piano Concerto (1921)—is in this collection.[1] Rachmaninoff, as one of the two greatest pianists of his age (Josef Hofmann being the other), did make a substantial number of records, including all his piano concertos, the Paganini Rhapsody, and some of his smaller pieces as well. He also made recordings of music by other composers; two of these, one of the Chopin B-flat Minor Piano Sonata and the other of the Beethoven Sonata in G Major, Op. 30, No. 3, for Piano and Violin (with Fritz Kreisler as his partner), are among the classics of the phonograph.[2] Of Stravinsky's playing, only one large-scale example is available: a somewhat aimless performance of his Capriccio, made in Paris in 1930;[3] another interesting but flawed recording, of the Concerto for Two Solo Pianos, made (again in Paris) in 1938 with his son Soulima, can be heard only on a tape copy at the New York Public Library at Lincoln Center.

Given this relative paucity of material by composers demonstrating how they think their music should go, the appearance in 1981 of some thirteen LPs containing all the known piano playing of Béla Bartók—and a limited amount of spoken material as well—was an event of great interest in the musical community.[4]

Incontestably great as Rachmaninoff's playing was, he was hardly a modern composer; even Prokofiev now seems increasingly a phenomenon of the older romantic music rather than of the age of the avantgarde. Bartók, by contrast, was a wholly *modern* composer—perhaps the only one who also happened to be a pianist of renown.

During his lifetime, Bartók was esteemed, not just for his performances of his own works, but also for the way he played the classics, from Bach and Scarlatti to Chopin and Brahms. In 1905, at the age of twenty-four, he entered the Paris competition for the (Anton) Rubinstein Prize; his losing there to Wilhelm Backhaus could hardly be called an indignity. Shortly thereafter, in 1907, he received an appointment to the Academy of Music in Budapest, where he taught piano. During the next few years, he played in Spain, Portugal, and England, in addition to France. He also edited, in a pedagogical format, keyboard music by Bach, Couperin, Scarlatti, Mozart, Haydn, Beethoven, Schubert, and Chopin; in addition, he made piano transcriptions of harpsichord and organ pieces by Italian masters of the seventeenth and eighteenth centuries.

After World War I Bartók undertook a purposeful expansion of his performing career. In 1922 he played in London and Paris; thereafter, he made frequent tours of Czechoslovakia, England, Germany, Italy, the Netherlands, Romania, and Switzerland. He played as a soloist and also gave duo recitals with such famous Hungarian violinists as Joseph Szigeti and Zoltán Székely (later the first violinist of the much admired Hungarian Quartet).

In the 1927–28 season Bartók made a tour of the United States where, playing programs largely of his own music, he impressed more as a pianist than as a composer. After his American tour, he went to the Soviet Union, appearing in Moscow, Leningrad, Odessa, Kharkov, and Kiev. He continued to play in the 1930s, and toward the end of the decade began to give concerts at two pianos with his second wife (and student), Ditta Pásztory Bartók. Following his decision to leave Nazi Europe in 1940, he gave an important recital at the Library of Congress in Washington with Szigeti; the solid program for this concert included the Beethoven "Kreutzer" Sonata, the Debussy Sonata, and the composer's own Second Sonata and First Rhapsody. Bartók went on playing the piano (and teaching) until close to his death in New York in 1945.

It was perhaps in part to provide for all this activity that Bartók wrote so much for the piano. In 1926, these works included the folk-derived *Out of Doors* Suite, the harsh and motoric Piano Sonata, and the propulsive First Piano Concerto; the concerto received its first performance at a contemporary music festival the next year with Bartók at the piano and Wilhelm Furtwängler conducting.

At this time, too, he started on an extended set of piano pieces called *Mikrokosmos*. This collection, eventually to number some 153 separate works, constitutes the most thoroughgoing attempt in our century to write music of progressive difficulty that can be used to introduce the student pianist not just to the piano or to music but to *contemporary* piano music.

In 1930–31 Bartók wrote his Second Piano Concerto, another percussive and driving work, which he first performed in 1933 in Frankfurt am Main with the great conductor of modern music Hans Rosbaud. His late career as duo-pianist with his wife was responsible for the writing of one of his most important works, the Sonata for Two Pianos and Percussion (1937); when Bartók orchestrated this piece in 1940, it became the Concerto for Two Pianos, and in this form the couple played it for the first time with Fritz Reiner and the New York Philharmonic in 1943. His wife, too, was responsible for what must be considered Bartók's last (almost) fully completed work, the Third Piano Concerto (1945). His hope in writing it, destined to be unrealized, was that, as a performance vehicle for her, it would be a source of income after his death.

Matched against this impressive list of large works, the Bartók recorded legacy seems always tantalizing, never conclusive. There are two problems to be faced here: the first is the sadly limited number of his own pieces that Bartók recorded, either commercially or privately; the second problem, more interesting than sad, goes to the very nature of the distinction between composition and performance.

The Bartók recorded material is divided into four parts: phonograph recordings made for commercial purposes; privately made recordings (surviving in often drastically incomplete form) of live performances; piano-roll transcriptions; and a few almost inaudible home cylinders dating back as far as 1912, when Bartók was thirty-one. Of these four categories, only the first—the commercial recordings—is consistently satisfying.

Some of these recordings have been widely available before. They include the *Contrasts* (1938) with clarinetist Benny Goodman and Szigeti; the First Rhapsody for Violin and Piano (1928), also with Szigeti; and thirty-two pieces from the later sections of the *Mikrokosmos* (all made in 1940 for Columbia in America). Relatively unknown, and welcome in this excellent LP transfer, are the 78-RPM discs of his own music Bartók made in 1928 and 1929 for HMV in Budapest, in 1930 for Columbia in London, in 1936 for Patria in Budapest, and in 1937, again for Columbia in London. In addition to these (which were not, except for the three English Columbia discs, issued in the United States), the present set contains hitherto unreleased test pressings, made about 1929 in Budapest, of four sonatas of Scarlatti.

The second category of recorded material, that of live performances, includes the previously available 1940 Library of Congress concert with Szigeti and the Bartók husband-and-wife broadcast performance (with the services of two very overburdened percussionists) of the Sonata for Two Pianos and Percussion. Important because of their previous unavailability, though only ranging in sonic quality from merely acceptable to almost unlistenable, are radio broadcasts of Bartók as both soloist and ensemble player. While many of these primitively made recordings contain only small bits of movements and pieces, three large works are fortunately preserved here in their entirety. They are the Brahms Sonata in F Minor for Two Pianos, played by Bartók and his wife in 1939; the Liszt *Concerto pathétique*, also for two pianos, played the same year by Bartók and the Hungarian composer and pianist Ernö Dohnányi; and Bartók's own First Rhapsody for Violin and Piano performed (also in 1939) by Bartók with the now forgotten Hungarian violinist Ede Zathureczky. One short solo work, the Brahms Capriccio in B Minor, Op. 76, No. 2, is also here in complete form.

The many fragments presented in this compilation of live performances show Bartók playing alone, with his wife, and with orchestra. The composers represented are Bach, Mozart, Beethoven, Chopin, Liszt, Debussy, and Bartók himself. While there is much important music here—in particular Bartók's Second Piano Concerto conducted by

Ernest Ansermet and the Liszt Variations on a Theme of Bach ("*Weinen, Klagen*")—so limited are the excerpts in duration and in sound quality that (except for an almost complete performance of the Chopin Nocturne in C-sharp Minor, Op. 27, No. 1) one can only gain hints as to what the real performances must have sounded like.

The piano-roll recordings in this collection are of two kinds, both transferred to disc via rerecording from the original rolls. The first batch, consisting of short pieces by Bartók including the *Romanian Folk Dances* (1915), was recorded on Welte-Mignon rolls, probably in Berlin in 1920. The Welte process was relatively (though not very) successful in reproducing a pianist's individual tone color and nuances; as transcribed in the 1960s on a Steinway concert grand belonging to Arthur Rubinstein, the performances seem authentic enough. Somewhat less believable are the transcriptions, evidently put on disc some years ago, of a few Pleyel rolls Bartók seems to have made in Paris in 1923; this set of performances includes the driving *Allegro barbaro* (1911). When taken all together, the piano-roll recordings (no doubt because of the rigidities of the process) are musically inferior to both the commercial recordings and the off-the-air dubbings.

The private cylinders, the final category of recorded material in this collection, were sonically poor to begin with, and have been wretchedly handled by their owners and by the passage of time. Certainly in their fits and starts, their blasts and disappearances, they cannot alter the melancholy verdict on the relationship of Bartók to the phonograph: during his lifetime he was badly treated and often ignored both as composer and as pianist. Some of the fault belongs to the inadequacies of the then available technology; some, too, must belong to the shortsightedness of the recording companies and, it goes without saying, the record-buying public. Some responsibility also must have been the composer's own: he was a loner who seemed to possess little gift for pursuing a career.

And yet, incomplete as the Bartók recorded corpus is, it does throw a great deal of light on musical matters both pianistic and compositional. Since these Hungaroton records have appeared, there has emerged a veritable chorus of critical opinion proclaiming Bartók one of the greatest pianists of the age. That this opinion should be widespread in the composer's native Hungary is no surprise, since reasons of pride and politics combine to make every small country assiduous in honoring its own musical prophets; true as this observation is across the world, it has special relevance to socialist governments painfully searching for every possible shred of legitimacy.

But in the West, too, the huzzahs have been loud. The English critic Max Harrison, writing in the January 1982 *Gramophone*, found in these records "the profound musicality of the playing of one of the greatest musicians of our century." And here in America, *New York* magazine's Peter Davis wrote about what he called "Bartók's . . . warmly inflected, rhythmically expansive yet always very precisely articulated style . . . the subtle rubato effects, liquid phrasing, and gradual stoking of emotional fire [that] mesmerize the ear."

Yet well as Bartók undoubtedly played, and interesting as these records are, they do not support the conclusion that he was one of the immortals of pianism. Even in the very best of his solo playing—the small pieces of his own which he recorded for HMV in 1929—one finds a certain wayward quality, sometimes appearing as "charm," sometimes as an almost vulgar taste, and sometimes as a lack of involvement in the structure of the music.

Thus, at the beginning of the very first LP record of this entire two-volume set, in the alternately gay and moody "Evening in Transylvania" (No. 5 of the *Ten Easy Pieces* of 1908), what impresses the listener at first as a real delicacy of feeling soon begins to seem an arbitrary dislocation of the natural rhythmic flow; in slow passages, the hands are, in a predictable way, not together; after a properly debonair execution of the first spirited syncopations, the return to the soulful beginning is marred by a harsh attack on the opening note of the section; overall, strange as it is to say, pianist Bartók seems disinclined to observe the scrupulous markings of composer Bartók.

In the next piece on the first record, the "Bear Dance" (No. 10 of *Ten Easy Pieces*), one is immediately seized by the virtuosity of Bartók's fast left-hand repeated notes, but here too the pleasure palls as the pianist's right hand, playing the chordal melody, makes a habit of rushing to the downbeat. The result seems perverse, as if a mannerism repeated often enough could thus justify its employment.

In the *Allegro barbaro*, a Prokofiev-like work demanding the utmost in steely wrists and easy coordination between the hands, Bartók is at the beginning fleet and effortless: as the short work gathers momentum, however, what had initially appeared easy turns out to be by turns slightly rushed and slightly labored. In seven of the *Fifteen Hungarian Peasant Songs* (1914–18), recorded about 1936 in Budapest, Bartók often loses control of the balance between the hands, allowing the left to drown out the right; at the end, in the enormously difficult section marked *quasi cornemuse*—like a bagpipe—the sixteenth-note ornamentation is indistinct, the whole effect becoming a rushed jumble. The first piece from *Three Rondos on Folk Tunes* (1916) finds Bartók laconic rather than simple in the affecting slow sections, and somehow frivolous in the fast ones—the performer again not taking seriously what the composer has written.

All these impressions are confirmed by the unreleased test pressings of four Scarlatti sonatas played by Bartók about 1929. The usually complete notes accompanying these LPs are not very helpful in this case, but it would seem that two sonatas were meant to go on each side of what must have been a 10-inch 78-RPM record. There thus may well have been time pressure on Bartók, forcing him to play very fast indeed in order not to exceed the limit of approximately three minutes per side. In any event, the playing is fast, often beyond what the listener can hear; the fingers race, and the music rushes. It is as if Bartók thought that getting everything over with quickly were a solid artistic virtue.[5]

Also demanding consideration are the 1940 Columbia discs of Bartók as soloist in numerous pieces from the *Mikrokosmos*, and as the partner of Benny Goodman and Szigeti in the *Contrasts* and of Szigeti in the First Rhapsody for Violin and Piano. Bartók's playing of the *Mikrokosmos* pieces seems didactic, perhaps expressing his own view of the works as educational in function; be that as it may, his performance is joyless in execution of the many peasant rhythms, and often clumsy even in the midst of some formidable keyboard feats of lightness and velocity. The by now fabled recording of the *Contrasts* displays a "cool" piece in a "cool" performance, with both Goodman and Szigeti cautious and Bartók's impact diminished by a combination of the subsidiary piano part and muffled recording of the instrument's characteristic clang. The recording with Szigeti of the Rhapsody, by now considered a classic too, seems excessively straight; the performance as a whole is driven and tense, mechanical rather than exciting. None of these three recordings communicates a sense of Bartók as a performing personality.

The Library of Congress performance with Szigeti is Bartók's major recorded achievement as a chamber musician. Szigeti was a thoroughly serious violinist, whose playing of the great repertory was altogether free of the simpering cuteness so characteristic of today's encounters between international celebrity violinists and profound music. In the Beethoven "Kreutzer" Sonata, a work in which the pianist must usually demonstrate his artistry by considerately staying out of the violinist's way, Bartók is especially strong and forthright; there is nothing here of the slightly mannered and withal routine approach that marks so much of his other playing. The performance of the Sonata for Two Pianos and Percussion, already disfigured by the incompetent playing of the percussionists, does not show excellent ensemble between the two pianists, and Bartók's playing in particular (he took the first part) seems almost fragile.

The newly available broadcast transcriptions do little to change the impression made by the more familiar Bartók performances. The Brahms F Minor Sonata, without doubt the chief behemoth of the nineteenth-century two-piano literature, fails to achieve clarity in this performance by the Bartóks. The composer, not surprisingly, was a stronger pianist than his wife; in order to keep from drowning her out, he positioned his piano so that its tone was blocked by the raised lid of his wife's piano. As a result, she comes to the fore, while he remains tinkling in the background. When to this acoustical imbalance are added the brisk tempos and the somewhat rootless approach so frequent in Bartók's playing in general, the outcome is something of a muddle. In the case of several fragments from the Mozart Sonata in D Major (K. 448), the same approach produces a jerky, hard-driven performance.

With the Bartók and Dohnányi performance of the Liszt *Concerto pathétique*—an unfamiliar warhorse indeed—Bartók's piano is again placed in an unfavorable position, and his tone is accordingly thin and distant. But even apart from the placement of their pianos, compared to

Dohnányi's luxuriant but disciplined playing, Bartók's is nervous and febrile, suggesting on occasion that he (quite understandably) did not believe in the music's fustian rhetoric.

There is one performance here, that of the First Rhapsody for Violin and Piano, which provides a major discovery. The discovery is not Bartók's playing, but rather that of his colleague, the violinist Ede Zathureczky. Employing a big, lush tone, Zathureczky infuses Bartók's work with a strong emotional content solidly based on firm rhythm and an instinct for the harmonic and structural form of the music. Though the record notes explicitly state that "Zathureczky's performance of the First Rhapsody, when compared with Szigeti's concert and studio recordings of the same work, show how little another's personality could assert itself at Bartók's side," the evidence here is very much to the contrary. In addition to the palpably different mood coming from the Zathureczky performance—the work of a major violinist—the timing for his collaboration with Bartók is almost a full minute longer (in a piece lasting about ten minutes) than both performances with Szigeti.

Three short solo performances, taken from radio broadcasts, also deserve mention. Two small fragments from the Liszt Variations on a Theme by Bach are marked by Bartók's willful, quasi-improvisational indulgence, with rhythmic distortions and sentimental moonings present everywhere. It was the fragment of Bartók's playing of the Chopin Nocturne in C-sharp Minor, Op. 27, No. 1, which provided the specific occasion for much of Peter Davis's praise I quoted earlier; to my ears, however, this performance is marked by interruptions of rhythmic flow and incessant backings away that make the music sound at best like early and only partially formed Debussy.

Bartók's performance of the Brahms Capriccio in B Minor, Op. 76, No. 2, present here in complete form, seems flighty and even hasty, without achieving the composer's express indication of *Allegretto*; Bartók's hesitation on the second beats of both the second and fourth bars, in violation of the composer's clearly marked phrasing, adds a frivolous element to the entire enterprise.

It is clear, I think, that Bartók's accomplishments as a pianist were not all that considerable, either in his playing of the music of others or even in the playing of his own music. Other pianists, among them his student György Sándor,[6] have been more successful in communicating the essence of his work than Bartók himself. This is not to say that we have been in a great era of Bartók performance; the leading pianists of Bartók's day, including Horowitz and Rubinstein, were sadly unconcerned with his music, and today's young virtuosos, as is evidenced by the current spate of dutiful Hungarian records, come through the loudspeakers as little more than pallid curators of a boring heritage. What good playing of Bartók there is today comes only in his First and Second concertos, works that lend themselves to the steamroller and boiler-factory approach so congenial to pianists when they are young. Absorbing, vital, songful playing of Bartók's smaller solo masterpieces seems an art either lost or possibly never invented.

Perhaps the thing to say about Bartók's own pianism is that he played like a composer rather than a performer. To understand what this means it is necessary to realize that a composer does many things but a performer does only one. The composer writes all the notes of a piece as a more or less perfect replication of an immensely detailed, complicated, and multifaceted mental scheme. In its written state this scheme, now called a musical composition, still requires decoding by a performer. When a performer accomplishes this decoding well, when he is able to select identifiable elements—melody, phrasing, rhythm, harmony, architecture, timbre, and so on—and communicate them, he is said to have a *conception*, and to be an artist; if a performer takes these elements from his own gifts rather than from the work of art he is interpreting, he is said to have a *style*, and to be a star.

Yet no matter how well he does, the performer can only have utilized a few elements of a work's content or, in the case of the star, managed to substitute himself for the work altogether. The upshot is that there are innumerable ways, most of them seemingly of equal validity, to perform a composition. Which one the listener gets depends upon the exact nature of the selection the individual performer makes as he goes about his task of decoding.

For a composer, by contrast, every note he writes is of equal importance, because every note is an equal component of his aural vision; every part is the whole, and the whole is composed of every part. Thus when Bartók plays his own work, he is presenting all the musical elements he saw fit to put down in the music, not just those he has decided that we as listeners will be able to perceive and respond to. Because he does not pick and choose, we are not able to either, and Bartók's approach seems to go from disinterest to uninterest. This may well account for the impression of waywardness conveyed by Bartók's performances. To see in such performances the virtues which critics have attached to this piano compilation is not to listen but to succumb to that sentimentality which finds profundity in technological dimness, the passage of time, and the tragedy of physical martyrdom.

But to leave the whole matter on this negative note would be a mistake. Bartók was a great composer, and in particular a great composer for the piano. He wrote supremely well for the piano because it was an instrument he understood supremely well. As a result, his pieces, all the way from the touching sentiments of the *Mikrokosmos* to the pile-driving sonorities of the Sonata, from the dry and mysterious Sonata for Two Pianos and Percussion to the folk-evocative Third Concerto, are (to paraphrase a famous remark of Artur Schnabel about performance in general) masterworks greater than any single performance of them—his own or anyone else's—can ever be.

(*Commentary*, 1984)

9

KEITH JARRETT

JOINS THE BACH PARADE

Lo, poor Bach! Lo, for that matter, poor Domenico Scarlatti and poor Handel. For their ill luck in being born in the same year of 1685, they are being celebrated together this year, three not so glorious centuries later. This celebration will doubtless be perceived by the lovers of classical music as the tribute vice pays to virtue. The real danger, of course, is that the tribute will end up being the one virtue pays to vice.

An example of the dangers inherent in the possibility of winning converts from what might be called other musics was provided by the recital, in the middle of March at New York's Avery Fisher Hall, of the eminent, or at least eminently successful, jazz pianist Keith Jarrett. According to the biography contained in the concert program, Jarrett has recently forsaken the worldwide performance of the "spontaneously composed and improvised solo-piano concerts" which have occupied him for a decade. The recordings of these concerts, along with studio tapings, have sold "over five million copies worldwide." One live concert recording, from a performance in Cologne, has sold "over one million copies, making it the most popular piano recording ever released."

Having given up this artistic goldmine, Jarrett is now devoting himself to playing a demanding portion of the traditional keyboard repertory. Since 1982 he has performed the Second and Third Concertos of Bartók, the immensely difficult Concerto of Samuel Barber, two solo concertos of

Mozart, and a Mozart two-piano concerto—with the collaboration of another jazz star, Chick Corea. Jarrett has performed these important works with some of today's best-known ensembles, including the Philadelphia Orchestra, the San Francisco Symphony, the Saint Paul Chamber Orchestra, and the English Chamber Orchestra.

As part of his desire to "explore more fully the classical repertoire," Jarrett chose the Great Performers series at Lincoln Center to pay tribute to the three towering musical geniuses of the class of 1685. Bach, Scarlatti, and Handel are in no way unknown quantities in today's concert world. More than a century of "traditional" performances of their music is now giving way to "authentic" performances, which replace modern instruments with original ones, or their reproductions. The different sounds coming from these earlier instruments have impressed many sophisticates as providing a fresh look at a music they had come to treat as routine. Jarrett's playing of this music, coming as it does from an aesthetic world putatively foreign to that of early European art music, must have seemed yet another chance to hear old music in a new way. And at the same time, his legion of fans cannot but appear to the backers of classical music as new recruits to a flagging cause.

Jarrett's fans did indeed show up at Fisher Hall, along with some more conventional musical types who were there, presumably, to test the water. It was hard to tell what the pianist's fans thought. These predominantly well-groomed and well-dressed young people seemed on their best behavior. Only their tendency to whistle and laugh approvingly at Jarrett's stage behavior betrayed their discontinuity with the usual staid concert audience. One sophisticated music lover of my acquaintance—a critic, as a matter of fact—summed up the reaction of his own kind at intermission: "I thought Jarrett'd be off the wall in this music," he complained, "But he's really so *conservative.*"

It must be said that the stage setting was anything but typical of a solo-piano recital. Though the piano lid was fully raised (as is usual in solo playing), the music desk too was up, plainly signifying that the pianist would use music rather than play by memory. That the printed score was to be something more than an occasional aid was demonstrated by the provision of a page turner's chair to the left of the pianist's concert stool. Jarrett's first appearance onstage (followed by his page turner) was hardly conventional either. Dressed in a sloppy gray shirt and baggy black pants, he shambled out in a manner both tentative and cocky; it was as if he didn't know quite what he was doing there, but whatever he was doing, he was the best. There were some latecomers in the sold-out hall, and their coming down the aisle after Jarrett had seated himself at the piano seemed to discomfit him. Finally he shambled backstage and then immediately returned, to the slightly nervous amusement of the audience.

From the first notes of the first work on the program, the Handel Suite No. 15 in D Minor, it was abundantly clear why my critic friend's intermission judgment would be dead on. The sound coming from the piano, accompanied by soulful body movements and vocal murmurings, was round, fat, and thoroughly romantic. But it was monotonous, and quickly began to seem poorly focused, possibly because of some deficiency in Jarrett's technical training. Such rapid passage work as there was in this relatively simple Handel music was played with the kind of rhythmic unsteadiness that often marks amateur pianism and separates it from its professional counterpart. Though the frequent short trills and other ornaments the pianist employed were of an up-to-date scholarly character, the total effect was spoiled by his unfortunate tendency to delay the accompaniment to these ornaments in order to allow his fingers enough time to fit in all the notes. The total effect was far from the kind of motoric energy aimed at in the performances of Christopher Hogwood and the Academy of Ancient Music, today's exemplars of authentic baroque performance practice.

Another Handel suite, this one No. 13 in B-flat, followed. Again Jarrett seemed to have trouble ending his trills clearly, and his left hand often seemed clumsy and even slightly irregular. Next came two short Scarlatti sonatas, identified in the program by their keys—F minor and F major—rather than by the widely used (and more specific) Longo numbers or by the more recent chronologies of Ralph Kirkpatrick and Giorgio Pestelli. Perhaps in formulating his interpretive strategy, Jarrett put too much weight on the composers' birth-years, for under his fingers Handel and Scarlatti sounded very much the same. Completely absent was the rhythmic vitality with which Scarlatti must be played to avoid a false impression of tedium and wallpaper-like repetition. In its place was a kind of expressive mooning which, after generations of vapid playing, has come to be associated with weak-kneed performances of Chopin. Jarrett distorted Scarlatti's beautiful melodies and touching harmonic progressions by applying unvaried agogic accents—created by pausing before the arrival at important melodic notes and harmonies—and by suppressing normal dynamic stresses at climactic points. More than any of Jarrett's specific technical weaknesses, this backward approach helped to color his performances of this exciting music just about the same gray as his shirt.

The pianist's attentions now turned to the immortal Bach. First came the great French Suite No. 3 in B Minor, BWV 814. Once again there was no stylistic differentiation between composers; again, everything sounded the same. There was no progress, no momentum, no feeling of departure, and certainly none of arrival. Fast movement, slow movement, it didn't matter: all one could hear was a kind of pleasant, low-key, good-willed music-making. Though the concert was less than thirty minutes old, it already was painfully clear that Jarrett had only one way of playing a melodic line: start loud and get soft. Everywhere—and this included his performance of the Prelude and Fugue No. 11 in F Major from the second book of the *Well-Tempered Clavier* that followed—he showed a failed sense of rhythm, pulse, and bar structure.

After the intermission, Jarrett performed the *Italian Concerto*, perhaps Bach's most frequently played (and certainly most frequently studied) work for solo keyboard. In essaying this masterpiece, Jarrett was not just putting himself in competition with the "great performers" of the past, among them harpsichordist Wanda Landowska and pianists Edwin Fischer and Artur Schnabel, who have recorded the work. He was also placing himself among the throngs of players of baroque keyboard music now appearing before the public.

Unfortunately, Jarrett missed the mark in every way. His tempo for the opening movement, though blindingly fast, produced no feeling of excitement and tension, but instead only a sludgelike texture achieved by an almost invariable *forte* and an insufficient differentiation of touch and finger articulation. At the beginning of the sublime slow middle movement, Jarrett ignored Bach's plain notation, which requires the player's left hand to convey to the listener the existence of two separate voices. When the soprano melody entered, Jarrett resumed his old habit of starting loud and then backing away from every climax. Bach's noble cantilena ended up sounding like some kind of wayward salon kitsch. For those of Jarrett's listeners who knew the *Italian Concerto* in particular and the music of Bach in general, the result must have seemed peculiar and empty. For those coming to this great art for the first time, the insipidity of the performance did nothing to reveal the strength of the music. Nor were matters better in the work's last movement: a *fortissimo* beginning, an ignoring of Bach's directions for dynamic contrast, and a muddling of the distinctions between separate polyphonic strands—all of this served up a stew rather than presenting a precise and leanly conceived work of art.

The musical value of Jarrett's performances of Handel, Scarlatti, and Bach was, I think, just about nil. This music is vastly better performed by players known and unknown, young and old, live or on records. To hear Bach, one needn't go to Keith Jarrett.

But, it will no doubt be said, Jarrett was performing a valuable missionary function. Some will see him as a kind of Stokowski of our time, a propagandist for great music who puts not just his artistic talents but the very success of his performing career at the service of a music his audience will only be able to appreciate when it is presented through the medium of his charismatic personality. On this reading Jarrett's very shortcomings to "traditional" music lovers are artistic strengths making him fit for his holy mission. Preaching to the musical heathen, so the argument will go, is after all a very different matter from satisfying the needs of the already sophisticated.

Leaving the comparison with Stokowski aside—that complicated personality, whatever his sweet tooth for a mass success, did have his origins in the world of classical music—the problem of Keith Jarrett for the supporters of high musical art becomes one of trade-offs. Is what Jarrett is selling close enough to the real thing to justify his shortcomings in performance? Is the musical premise upon which his audience is being beguiled close enough to what animates the music of Bach (or Scarlatti or Handel) to make classical-music lovers out of the aficionados of jazz and other, more popular, musics?

There is no clear answer to these questions. On the Damascus road one does not choose one's epiphanies; it is possible to approach the goal of artistic insight in many ways. In fact what Jarrett does may well be close enough to instill in his listeners a hunger for real musical nourishment. Some of his listeners will doubtless like the music he is playing rather than the way he plays it; these souls will be ready to move on to something artistically better.

But to put matters in this way is to take refuge in a kind of relativism and self-doubt. There can be little question that Jarrett's audience is better served by his playing Bach, Scarlatti, and Handel than the kind of pap and worse which is so regularly served up by the superstars of commercial music. The real danger is that Jarrett's popular success, with all that it promises to artists and audience alike of money and glory, will become something to be emulated. Instead of his success being the means and high art being the goal, the order will be reversed. The result would mean the destruction of the very idea of an unsullied art, a world beyond—at least in our aspirations—the necessary contingencies of worldly prosperity. The worry that ought to be bothering the devotees of Bach, Handel, and Scarlatti as they contemplate Keith Jarrett's movement to their side ought not to be that his own audience will like what he does; it ought to be that they themselves, in their desire to become part of a cultural mainstream, will approve Jarrett's failed art merely because he is so successful doing it. Were this to happen, the current birthday celebrations of the wise men of 1685, rather than being sweet, would be sour indeed.

(*The New Criterion*, 1985)

10

THE PUPILS OF
CLARA SCHUMANN AND
THE USES OF TRADITION

The recent publication in England and simultaneous importation into this country of a nine-LP set on the Pearl label of recordings made by three pupils of Clara Schumann (1819–96) will doubtless excite interest among students and admirers of piano-playing.[1] It is not difficult to see why this should be so: Clara Schumann, of course, was the widow of the great Robert (1810–56) and a close friend over many years of Johannes Brahms; furthermore, she was by all accounts one of the great musicianly pianists of the second half of the nineteenth century. Because she was a renowned teacher, and because she gave lessons until her death in the mid-1890s, she taught several pianists who played professionally during the subsequent era of sound recording, and two of her pupils lived long enough to make private recordings at a time when tape recording made the capture of extended performances in lifelike sound possible.

It cannot be said that Clara Schumann's pupils included any names likely to be familiar today, either through the memory of live performances or through phonograph records. According to the most extensive list of her pupils I have seen—that contained in Wilson Lyle's recent and only partially satisfactory *A Dictionary of Pianists* (Schirmer Books,

1985)—the best-known ones included Richard Andersson, Leonard Borwick, Fanny Davies, Henry Eames, Ilona Eibenschütz, Adolf Frey, Carl Friedberg, Amina Goodwin, Clement Harris, Natalia Janotha, Louise Japha, Walter Lampe, Carolus Oberstadt, Edward Perry, Oscar da Silva, Anton Strelezky, Franklin Taylor, Lazzaro Uzielli, Mathilde Verne, and Marie Wurm. Of these, only Borwick, Davies, Eibenschütz, Friedberg, and Janotha are now remembered at all. But Borwick seems not to have recorded, and no evidence exists that Friedberg (well known to have associated with Brahms) actually studied with Clara Schumann. Janotha made four recordings in 1905 for the Gramophone & Typewriter Co., Ltd. (the precursor of His Master's Voice, which in 1931 was absorbed into EMI, the great English recording conglomerate). The most Harold C. Schonberg, perhaps our leading connoisseur of old pianists, can say of Natalia Janotha in his standard *The Great Pianists* (1963) is: "On the basis of her records, she was anything but a sensitive pianist, and certainly not a good musician, but at least she could get around the keyboard." That leaves Davies and Eibenschütz, though to this pair must be added, as we shall see, the name (unaccountably omitted by Lyle in his list of Schumann pupils) of yet another woman, Adelina de Lara.

It is these three pianists—Fanny Davies (1861–1934), Ilona Eibenschütz (1873–1967), and Adelina de Lara (1872–1961)—who make up the massive new Pearl set. The earliest recordings here, of short pieces by Brahms and Scarlatti, were made by Eibenschütz for G&T in 1903, though (according to Lyle) they were never issued in her lifetime; they are supplemented by noncommercial recordings of short pieces by Schumann and Brahms and excerpts from longer works by Beethoven and Schumann, along with a broadcast interview containing her reminiscences of Brahms, all dating from the early 1950s.

The representation of Fanny Davies on these new discs is rather more substantial. It consists of commercially released recordings, made for English Columbia in 1928, 1929, and 1930, of three major Robert Schumann works: the Concerto, the *Kinderszenen,* and the *Davidsbündlertänze.*

By far the largest part of the Pearl set is devoted to the playing of Adelina de Lara, in performances taped in 1951 and 1952. Indeed, so copious is the de Lara representation that it amounts to a conspectus of

Robert Schumann's major works for the piano. Included here are the *Davidsbündlertänze*, the *Carnaval*, the *Fantasiestücke* Op. 12, the *Etudes symphoniques*, the *Fantasie*, the *Kreisleriana*, the *Kinderszenen*, the *Faschingsschwank aus Wien*, the sonatas in F-sharp minor and G minor, and even (with the pianist Albert Ferber) the *Andante and Variations* for two pianos. There are also many smaller Schumann pieces here, including *Der Vogel als Prophet* and the famous *Arabeske*. As if all this weren't enough, these LPs also contain de Lara performances of the Beethoven Thirty-two Variations in C Minor, several short Brahms pieces, and (again with Albert Ferber) Brahms's *Variations on a Theme of Haydn*, Op. 56B, in the composer's own scoring for two pianos.

A mere description of the historical world out of which these nine LPs come goes far to suggest why they are being received as a privileged glimpse into a fantasy storehouse of nineteenth-century musical riches. As every music lover knows, despite the growth over the past decades of interest in preromantic music, the hearts of the audience—and especially the hearts of any large audience—remain in happy thrall to the masterworks written from Beethoven to Brahms and Tchaikovsky.

Nowhere is this more true than in the case of the piano, which was born in something like its present form during Beethoven's lifetime, and which achieved its mature form by the 1890s, or perhaps a decade earlier. The great works for the piano qua piano are not those of Bach, who wrote for the radically different harpsichord, or even those of Mozart, who clearly did not write for an instrument of the brilliance, volume, and tonal character of the modern piano. The great works begin, rather, with the Beethoven Sonata in C Minor, Op. 13 (1798–99), known best not by its key or by its opus number but by the very romantic name (assigned by Beethoven) of "pathétique." They go on perhaps as far as the famous Tchaikovsky Piano Concerto No. 1 in B-flat Minor (1874–75) and the last works of Brahms, which date from the early and mid-1890s. What was written later for the piano—including the works of Rachmaninoff, Debussy, and Ravel, to mention the three most consequential twentieth-century writers of idiomatic piano music—seems supplementary to the great tradition rather than central to it, no matter how popular such music is with performers and audiences.

This great tradition, then, spans the nineteenth century. It includes the piano solo music of Beethoven, Schubert, Chopin, Liszt, Mendels-sohn, Brahms—and, not least, Robert Schumann. Not so triumphantly profound as Beethoven, not so melodically charming as Schubert, not so elegantly yearning as Chopin, not so diabolically brilliant as Liszt, and not so solidly complex as Brahms, Schumann nonetheless found his own voice. It was his gift to combine the fantastic imagery associated with such romantic literary figures as E. T. A. Hoffmann with a melodic and harmonic instinct solidly rooted in German folk music; he brought this combination to bear upon the piano at a time when that instrument was increasingly to be found in middle-class homes.

Schumann does not seem to have been a first-class pianist himself. In an age of virtuoso pianists like Chopin and Liszt, this might well have been an obstacle to the acceptance of his music. But whatever failings he may have had as an executant were more than made up for by his wife's prowess. Her great reputation as a pianist went back to her earliest years as a child prodigy; by the time she reached adulthood, she was one of the leading pianists of Europe, admired above all for her musicality and for the quality of thought she brought to the music she essayed. During Schumann's lifetime she was the leading exponent of his music; after his death, with the help of her great friend Brahms, she became the keeper of the flame, not just as a performer but also as the editor of the collected edition of Schumann's piano works and as an immensely respected teacher.

Given all this prehistory, it is hardly surprising that the new Pearl set has been rapturously received, at least in some quarters. Alan Sanders, writing in the July 1986 issue of the English record magazine *Gramophone*, can scarcely contain his enthusiasm:

[N]ot only have some of these performances been retrieved from storage, cleaned, and put back on view in new frames, they have been rescued from irretrievable deterioration with the same care and devotion which picture restorers will bring to a fine work of art. . . .

Eibenschütz's only commercial recordings, made in 1903, convey a vivid impression of a brilliant artist who enjoyed a formidable reputation on the concert platform before her marriage and consequent retirement. . . .

Schumann's Piano Concerto is given a wonderfully vital and expressive perfor-

mance by Fanny Davies of a kind which you will just not hear in modern performances, faithful to the spirit and letter of the score and full of revelatory detail. . . .
The second movement is played simply and directly; it is the conversation between
soloist and orchestra Clara Schumann said it should be. . . . [T]he third movement
is equally telling, played as directed by Clara Schumann. . . .

. . . we must be eternally thankful to Michael Thomas that he persuaded de Lara
to play for the microphone, for her performances provided a great insight into the
Clara Schumann tradition.

. . . the more I hear them the less the mistakes matter and the more I am aware of
de Lara's strength and poetry, her love for the music and her veneration of the
tradition through Clara. . . . Adelina de Lara preserved a nineteenth century style
of playing into the second half of the twentieth century; it is an astonishing fact that
most of the Schumann works she plays here had been taught her by the woman who
influenced their composition over a century earlier. Her remarkable Brahms performances are equally authentic: the *Scherzo*, Op. 4 she even learned from the composer himself when he visited Clara Schumann.

All this, it seems to me, raises two questions. The first is whether we
ought to play Robert Schumann the way Clara Schumann did, or at least
the way she said we ought to—a question to which I shall return. The
second seems (at least to me) rather easier to answer: it is, quite simply,
what grounds do we have for taking the evidence of these records as
indicative of what Clara Schumann thought about and wanted in the
interpretation of her dead husband's music. It is plain that we cannot
now hear Clara Schumann play, though we can hear her pupils; it is
equally clear that we have no way of knowing how either their shortcomings or virtues stem from her.

However important and even magical the background of these LPs
may be, any evaluation of them cannot depend on a sentimental view of
a conjectured past; it must be based, rather, upon a hardheaded analysis
of the piano-playing they contain. And when the records are carefully
and dispassionately listened to, it must be said that they contain, not
riches, but rather something humdrum and on occasion unrefined, insen-
sitive, and even grossly in error.

It would be wrong for me to give the impression that the playing of
these three pianists is the same. It is not, and the differences among them
as piano performers and musical minds are immediately apparent. Eibenschütz is in many ways the most beguiling of the trio. Reasonably fleet-
fingered, she plays the A-flat waltz from the Brahms set on the 1903

G&T recording in a lightly attractive way, not perfectly but still with flair. Her Scarlatti on a disc of the same year is fast and sloppy, performed with a devil-may-care approach that barely manages to stay this side of triviality. Her performance, circa 1950, of the theme and first variation from the final movement of the Beethoven Sonata in E Major, Op. 109, is astonishingly fast and borders on the hard-boiled. The same, too, must be said for her performance of the "Chopin" movement from the Schumann *Carnaval*, again circa 1950.

The three pieces recorded commercially by Fanny Davies around 1930 are altogether more competent; they date, after all, from a time when electrical recording had vastly improved upon the original acoustic process used for the Eibenschütz G&Ts. There aren't many wrong notes here. Unfortunately, on the evidence of these recordings Davies seems to have been a cautious and even plodding pianist. Her playing of the beautiful melodic statement at the opening of the first movement of the Concerto, for example, in its ubiquitous, unvaried rolling of chords, comes across as a caricature of an empty, old-fashioned style; similarly, Davies's labored execution of the *Passionato* section is a revelation of how fifty years ago and more it was sometimes possible to make a solo career on the piano without being able to negotiate technical passages of moderate difficulty. And beyond these specific problems, everything in these Davies performances, whether inspired by the immortal Clara Schumann or not, is just dull, dull, dull.

And so we come to the major part of this set: the de Lara performances. There is, I suppose, romance aplenty in this story of an aging woman pianist whose stage career had been capsized by personal vicissitudes stretching over the first half of the century. This saga of performing art belatedly recognized is not unparalleled in recent musical history; there is an echo of the de Lara story in the widely publicized mid-1970s case of Ervin Nyiregyházi, the erstwhile Hungarian child prodigy who briefly rocketed, at the age of seventy, to the attention of piano aficionados in performances of virtuoso music first taped by an amateur at a San Francisco church concert and then commercially recorded by CBS.

In the case of de Lara, at the beginning of the 1950s a young piano enthusiast named Michael Thomas heard a set of recently made 78-RPM recordings issued by her grandson. These records featured the Schumann *Carnaval,* and other pieces as well, and inspired Thomas with the desire to record, at his own expense if necessary, the playing of this last surviving Clara Schumann pupil still giving concerts. He managed to make these recordings on tape in a room at the London Musical Club in March of 1951, at London's Wigmore Hall in a public concert in the fall of 1951, and again at the London Musical Club in the summer of 1952. The tapes were subsequently issued on LPs in small editions marked by variable sound; in the present Pearl set they are offered to the public for the first time in what we are told is the best sound obtainable from the original tapes, or from copies of the originals.

There is little musically similar about the cases of Ervin Nyiregyházi and Adelina de Lara, except for their disappearance and then partial rediscovery through the medium of recordings made in old age. Nyiregyházi's playing, because of his concentration on the flashiest and most meretricious pieces of Liszt in vulgar and souped-up performances, represented a throwback to a now dead tradition of mindless pianistic display before mindless audiences. By contrast, de Lara's playing takes the high road of total dedication to what is universally acknowledged as great music.

Because there is so little understanding these days of what exactly it is that a great pianist does, I think it would be useful at this point to place the whole idea of keyboard performance in some kind of intellectual context, to explain briefly just what it seems to me is involved in the playing of the most important piano works for an audience. It can be briefly, though certainly unsatisfactorily, put: to be a great pianist is to be so in command of the means of performance that the foundation necessary for the communication of the character of the performer, no less than of the music, can be taken for granted.

It must not be thought that what I have called the "foundation" means absolute, constant, and replicable accuracy; the great piano recordings of the past include performances in which there are, as the old saw goes, enough wrong notes to write another piece. Nor does this "foundation" mean musicological scholarship, fidelity to the composer's presumed wishes, or knowledge of or a subservience to the regnant performance style of the day; the great pianists of the past have rarely been scholars, have always been supreme egotists, and have invariably made styles, not reflected them.

The issue here is command: pianistic, musical, and what for want of a better word I must call emotional. Pianistic command—it must be stated over and over again—in these days of perfect performances made by tape-splicing is by no means simply a matter of hitting all the right notes. It is also by no means simply a matter of the greatest facility in traversing the most difficult passages, for it is a sad fact that the most difficult passages from a purely digital standpoint are usually to be found in the musically thinnest and least interesting pieces.

In technical terms, the basis of pianistic command is firm tone and firm rhythm. Firm tone refers to the depth and articulation of the sound the pianist draws from the piano in individual notes, melodic and running passages, and chords; firm rhythm refers to the solidity of the basic metrical pulse with which the pianist communicates chosen tempos, the natural flow with which those tempos are varied, and the crispness with which rhythmic patterns are made clear and memorable to the listener.

Musical command involves, at the outset, the ability to make clear the differences between musical styles. Even more important, it requires the ability to keep in mind the structure of the work being played, to make clear to the listener how the different sections and features of the work fit into a coherent plan devised by the composer and also, to some extent, by the performer. Above all, musical command makes it possible for the performer to keep the listener aware that the work has a beginning, middle, and end, and to keep him aware of just where the composer, the performer, and by implication the listener are in the work.

Emotional command is perhaps more succinctly put by the word "personality." The most frequent use of emotional command, of course, is to impress the performance and the performer on the audience. In this use, it is emotional command which distinguishes one performer and performance from another; it is emotional command which enables each musical performance to become a distinct entity in the mind and the memory of each listener. It need hardly be added that it is this use of emotional command which is responsible for the making and keeping of performing careers.

There is another, and perhaps higher, use of what I have chosen to call emotional command. This use involves the putting of the performer's power at the service of the music being played, so that the impression of vibrant personality not only appears to stem from, but actually does stem from, the musical work rather than from the performer's superficial individuality. For listeners of one bent—and Harold Schonberg would seem to belong in this camp—it is the performer's personality in a relatively pure state which makes music come to life; for listeners of what some would call a more serious orientation, the submerging of the performer's personality in the composer's work of art is required for that work of art to come across in undefiled form. But either way, the existence of a powerful performing personality is a sine qua non for the communication of music.

There is now a vogue, made possible by the existence of sound recording, for the great musical performers of the past one hundred years; it is this vogue that underlies the rapturous reception which this Pearl set is receiving and undoubtedly will continue to receive. There are indeed, on hundreds of old 78-RPM records now being well transferred piecemeal to LP and compact discs, remarkable performances, many of them involving illustrious pianists. In this regard, I think immediately of the large recorded repertory of Artur Schnabel, Edwin Fischer, Alfred Cortot, and Walter Gieseking; of the early discs of Arthur Rubinstein and Vladimir Horowitz; of the few recordings of Josef Hofmann and the almost forgotten Ricardo Viñes; and of the extraordinary performances of Sergei Rachmaninoff. Some of these pianists—especially Hofmann— had great technical equipment; others—in particular Fischer—possessed much more limited resources. Some of them—Schnabel and Cortot in particular—at times tended to be sloppy; others—Gieseking and Rachmaninoff, for example—were usually immaculate executants. Some of them—Schnabel and Fischer among them—were "intellectual"; others—Cortot in particular—were often outrageously "romantic." But all of them demonstrated that triple *command* which seems so necessary to the existence of piano performance on the highest level.

Adelina de Lara, on the evidence of the seven LPs in this set devoted to her playing, did not possess this command. It will be argued that these performances come from her old age and not from her vigorous youth or solid middle age. The only possible answer to this rejoinder must be that one can only listen to what is before one; one cannot listen to that which, for whatever regrettable reasons, never existed. On these records at least, de Lara sounds not like a great pianist, but like a teacher doggedly demonstrating for students how the pieces go.

I would not want what I have just written to be taken as an indictment of piano teachers, or even as a reflection on the necessary practice of music teachers playing for their students. I am doing nothing more here than stating the obvious: there is a world of difference between knowing well enough how works go to be able to communicate them to students in the private atmosphere of a lesson and being a great performer. De Lara's playing satisfies the first requirement. But, despite all the understandable historical nostalgia that is being brought to these records, it does not satisfy the second.

There seems little point in attempting to describe de Lara's performances on these discs in any detail. There are so many wrong notes as to make the harmonies obscure; tempos are often physically out of control, not so much in speed as in their headlong, hurtling character; the difficult rhythms Schumann writes are often distorted out of recognition for technical reasons; the piano tone is heavy and unvaried. And there is in these performances no communication of the differences among these great works of Schumann—between the light and graceful fantasy of the *Carnaval*, the moody introspection of the *Fantasiestücke* Op. 12, the earthy, quasi-peasant humor of the *Faschingsschwank aus Wien*, the virtuoso display characteristic of the *Etudes symphoniques*, the massive architectural structure of the *Fantasie*, and the small, gentle scale of the *Kinderszenen*.

Matters do not improve, furthermore, when we come to de Lara's performances of music by composers other than Schumann. The Brahms-Haydn Variations for Two Pianos are so disfigured by caution, technical incompetence, and a certain weak-kneed sentimentality as to seem almost unrecognizable. The Beethoven Thirty-two Variations, a testing piece for any virtuoso pianist (and beautifully recorded as such in the early 1930s by Horowitz), becomes in de Lara's hands a mass of stops, lurches, and oozings. There is in fact a prevailing character to all these performances by de Lara. This character is one of undifferentiated dullness, of the dogged grinding out of music well beyond the pianist's capacities as a performer. It would be sad if the nostalgia buffs were to have their way and convince anyone young and talented that technical incompetence, nondescript emotional content, and the infirmities of age were qualities to be replicated.

Thus, far from making the case that there is a great line of descent from Clara Schumann in which the artists of today should humbly and gladly take their place, these records by Ilona Eibenschütz, Fanny Davies, and Adelina de Lara accomplish exactly the opposite. So massive is my disappointment in these records that I find it hard to avoid asking more basic questions. Even assuming the task could be accomplished, is there a supreme value in playing this music as Clara Schumann said it should be played? Can it really be the case that Robert Schumann's piano music exists best, or perhaps exists only, in performances that in some obscure way have been mediated through his widow? Is tradition to be the final guide to how great music should be interpreted?

If the art of piano-playing is to go on as a living artistic organism, the answer to these questions must be unequivocally no. The proper relation of a performer to a work of music is directly to that work, not to that work as it has been digested, domesticated, and merchandised by generations of other performers. The essence of great piano music, whether Robert Schumann's or any other composer's, is in our best contemporary perception of the text of the music, not in the way it has been performed in the near and distant past. Each generation must find its own way back to the hallowed works of the past, so that they may be possessed directly. It was this act of rediscovery that made performances great in the past, when they were indeed great. The same is true for today's artists. There is nothing for contemporary pianists in these sadly deficient recordings—even if they were made by pupils of Clara Schumann.

(*The New Criterion*, 1986)

DOES THE PIANO HAVE

A FUTURE?

I am now fifty-five years old. I have been playing the piano for the last fifty-two years, and I suppose that in some way I shall continue to play it for as long as—or perhaps even for a bit longer than—my fingers are able to move. *My* intention, at least, is clear; what is murky is how long the piano will be around.

The present-day piano is the successor to the aristocratic harpsichord, but unlike its elegant ancestor its strings are struck rather than plucked. It is a ponderous agglomeration of wood, metal, and cloth; its more than two hundred strings are hit with considerable force by compacted felt hammers, and its cunningly designed sounding board enables the struck strings, and their sympathetic neighbors, to project their rich vibrations into grand public spaces. In varying designs—long (a "grand"), high (an "upright"), or short and low (a "console" or "spinet")—the piano is played by applying the fingers to a keyboard containing, in its final, fully developed form, eighty-eight keys. At least ten of these keys may be struck by the pianist at any one time; with the help of a sustaining pedal, actuated by the right foot, all the notes may be made to go on sounding long after the initial impact of hammers upon strings.

Almost all the greatest composers of the past two centuries have written for the piano; in the case of several, notably Beethoven, Schubert, Schumann, Liszt, Brahms, and Debussy, they entrusted to it some of their most profound—not to say attractive—thoughts. Equally important, the piano throughout its history has arrogated to itself music written before its own modern development, including that of Bach, originally composed for the thin-sounding harpsichord, the whispering clavichord, and the majestic, albeit unwieldy, organ. Haydn and Mozart, too, both of whom wrote marvelous music for the fortepiano, a transitional instrument between the harpsichord and the modern piano, were quickly gathered up to feed the new instrument's imperial triumph.

Great and even mythic careers have been made playing the modern piano. Past celebrities, beginning on the highest level with the composer Liszt and the hardly less popular Rachmaninoff, have included Anton Rubinstein, Josef Hofmann, and Ignace Jan Paderewski. Closer to today we have witnessed the meteoric careers of Arthur Rubinstein, Artur Schnabel, and Vladimir Horowitz, and still more recently, the brief access of Van Cliburn, rocketed to fame in 1958 on the imprimatur of Nikita Khrushchev.

The piano could hardly have become so popular had the music written for it not occupied a position at the top of European culture, and had that music not been immediately recognized as among the highest achievements of world civilization. But at the same time the piano has always served as more than a medium of musical greatness. Throughout the nineteenth century, it was the indispensable item of middle-class home furniture, its possession a sure sign, on the one hand, that art was no longer the birthright of an increasingly redundant and superannuated aristocracy, and, on the other, that a household prosperous enough to own a piano had permanently escaped the coils of the peasantry and the working class.

Much more can be said, of course, about the piano's appeal. To take only one example: for several generations of upwardly mobile Jews in Western and Eastern Europe and later in America, the piano provided a wholesome vehicle for indulging the cultural aspirations kindled in them by the Enlightenment. Always concerned first with the education of their children, Jewish parents soon noticed that more was at stake in playing the piano than simple—in its working-out, hardly so simple— acculturation, social progress, or, on a higher level, what the Germans called *Bildung* (the formation of character and mind through the acquisition of civilized learning). In fact, given the rage everywhere for classical music, those Jewish children who showed remarkable talent were quickly able to become successful figures of European and even world importance.

To understand what the piano has been in the past and is today, and what its future might hold, we must examine four areas: the instrument, its public, its players, and its music. Between them, two books published in the past year go much of the way toward mapping this territory.

The first, *The Piano in America, 1890–1940,* by the business historian Craig H. Roell,[1] is an example of an emergent trend in the social sciences toward descriptions of the tangled relationship between culture and commerce. Despite the title, it is not Roell's purpose to describe the different pianos made in America; his interest is clearly not in manufacture but in marketing, and his book offers a detailed account of the way piano-makers, during the heyday of the American industry, attempted to sell their products in an environment of rapid and sweeping changes in consumer tastes and behavior. The second book, *The Art of the Piano,* by the music historian and broadcaster (and sometime pianist) David Dubal,[2] is a more traditional omnium-gatherum directed at present and prospective devotees; it consists of brief sketches of well-known pianists yesterday and today and the repertory they have played, together with lists of the most important recordings (in Dubal's opinion) of this repertory available since 1949 on LP, and now on compact disc.

First, then, the history. The tale Roell tells begins late in the nineteenth century, when the piano was already indispensable to serious music and well on the way to becoming a fixture in comfortable homes everywhere. It ends (in 1940) with the American piano industry engaged in a determined effort to sell an expensive object that no one really needed but that everyone, it was hoped, could be made to desire.

There is little doubt that, historically, the piano was uniquely suited to be such an object of desire. As Roell sees the matter, the piano, requiring study and practice to play, could easily be regarded as an exemplar of the Victorian work ethic. Because it could be learned and played in the home, it could become a means whereby women, trained in the gentle art of music, might civilize their always potentially barbarous men. And because music itself was elevating, it could lead everyone who came under its sway toward what has lately been called a "kinder, gentler" world.

Unfortunately, there was a serpent concealed in the conception of Eden harbored by piano-makers, and by their customers. That serpent, to mix metaphors, sailed under the old, familiar flag of "something for nothing." Though the piano did indeed require great effort to play decently—and Roell is nothing if not candid on this score, bestowing many derogatory comments, only some of them deserved, on old-time lady piano teachers—and thus amply justified its place in the Victorian hierarchy of values, all the suffering one might undergo did not guarantee a reward. Then, as now, great numbers studied the piano, many practiced it, but few actually learned to play it.

And so, in the early years of the present century, the player piano was born. By means of perforated paper rolls containing the punched-in records of great, or at least efficient, executants' performances, this devilish triumph of mechanization enabled a specially designed home piano to burst forth with a stunningly rapid clatter of sounds. Somewhat in the fashion of cake mixes that allow the person opening the package to exercise a creative function by adding an egg, the player pianos made provision for a person sitting at the keyboard to vary the monster machine's speed, dynamic level, and pedaling.

Not only did such an appeal to enlightened sloth prove commercially attractive, it was reformist as well: in the best democratic fashion, the player piano enabled everyone, not just the talented and the hard-working but also the untalented and the lazy, to share in the satisfactions of making music. Not that one should overrate the quality of the music rendered by player pianos: in fact, their vogue coincided with the ragtime craze in American popular music, and as Roell quite correctly points out, authentic ragtime is very difficult to play. I can remember my own attempts, undertaken in order to impress the fairer sex, to master the cross-rhythms, accuracy in jumping around the keyboard, and physical endurance necessary for a proper ragtime performance. For the player piano, with its ability to employ all the keys at once, ragtime was duck soup.

For a time player pianos were big business. By 1919, out of some

350,000 pianos sold in the United States, fully 53 percent were player pianos; by 1923, the figure had risen to 56 percent. Ironically, however, all this was soon to change: the market for passive music-making so prosperously excited by the player piano would come to be filled not by a musical instrument but by that child of electricity, the radio. Not only was performed music, of whatever kind, soon to be accessible without any effort on the part of the erstwhile amateur producer, now consumer; best of all, it was to be available without any cost save the initial, relatively low, price of the radio and the trifling amount of electricity required to operate it.

The radio arrived in the mid-1920s. By 1929—before the onset of the Great Depression—the piano business was irremediably marked by the hostile winds of change. Despite the widespread popularity of music, and even of serious music; despite the growth of music education in the schools; despite a more musically aware population than America had ever before known, the piano industry was now bankrupt.

At first the depression, with its drying-up of economic activity and massive unemployment, seemed only to complete the work of electrically assisted mass culture in destroying the viability of piano manufacturing. Many firms failed, and many were forced into combinations that overnight obliterated decades of hard-earned distinctions among competing trademarks and makers. Even the august firm of Steinway & Sons, so beloved by great artists that it could justifiably advertise its product as "The Instrument of the Immortals," was forced to cease building pianos from 1931 to 1933.

But what the depression took away the depression was also to give back, if in a different form. For amid the economic dislocations that followed the 1929 crash there now arose the possibility of a return to a view of music as uplifting, as a noble human activity that contributed to the maintenance of traditional values.

As Roell puts it, with only a hint of condescension:

[T]he hard times brought a revival of Victorian values and provoked a new interest in the importance of home and family life. Movies and much of the literature glorified traditional American values, seeking to establish a sense of security, an identity with a somewhat mythical age of cooperation, justice, and moral economics. Iron deer reappeared on lawns, old-style wallpaper became popular, the waltz replaced the Charleston, and the flapper was urged home again.

Led by Steinway and Baldwin, then as now the only domestic competitors for the quality piano market, manufacturers were quick to appeal to the new turn of the public mind. In doing so they were only behaving naturally, for the piano industry, and especially its leaders, had always been more comfortable representing their product as a facilitator of art and uplift than as a medium of easy entertainment. Roell is generous in recognizing their high interests:

[They] were patrons of culture as well as business. They cultivated sales, but concurrently sought to uplift society through their product and its characteristic bond with art. In so doing, they encouraged their society's appreciation of music. And as that society became more consumption-oriented, they fought to regenerate the importance of making music and of self-expression. In this, because the consumer culture can never be wholly absorbing, they were successful.

The Piano in America, 1890–1940 closes on an ambivalent note: the piano industry had survived, in a healthy but reduced state, by insisting at one and the same time on the piano as art and as a "symbol of a past age" (in Roell's inevitably dismissive phrase). During World War II—to go for a moment beyond Roell's terminal date—the industry was quickly converted to war production, and it was not until 1946 that a flood of new pianos again began reaching American consumers. As for the more recent story of the piano business, including an account of the takeover in the past two decades of the American market by pianos made in the Far East, this remains to be written; Roell seems a worthy and likely candidate for the task.

There is, however, one curious and significant lacuna in his excellent effort. Roell writes much about pianos, their makers, their buyers, and the terms on which the public and the manufacturers met. But though he discusses the way piano-makers appealed to art in marketing their wares, he has very little to say about the art that underlay the appeal and that must have been so important both to sellers and buyers. That art, of course, was the great music written expressly for the piano, and performable only on it, over a period extending approximately from the beginning of the nineteenth century to the time of World War I.

In Roell's index there is but a single page reference to Beethoven, and the text in that instance offers merely a glancing account of Beethoven's preference in piano-makers. There is no mention at all of Chopin, the quintessential composer of piano music playable in the home to the supreme gratification of amateur performers and casual listeners alike. Famous pianists are mentioned on occasion, but always as entertainers rather than as the communicators of high art. Roell displays a welcome willingness to treat *recherché* entities like Victorian values and cultural uplift as real and consequential determinants of human behavior; despite this, he seems sadly unable to come to terms with the piano not only as an instrument which, when well played, astounded and mesmerized with its brilliance—though it surely did that—but also as an instrument for which great composers were writing great music.

David Dubal's *The Art of the Piano* hardly suffers from a lack of talk about art. As the profiles of pianists pile up in this book, all in alphabetical order, and composers follow suit, one begins to appreciate just how massive an artistic effort has been devoted to the piano over its history. Inevitably, Dubal retraces much of the same ground covered by the former *New York Times* music critic Harold C. Schonberg in his *The Great Pianists* (1963, widely available in an updated version in paperback); but unlike his predeccessor, Dubal eschews the vulgar, albeit often telling, anecdote in favor of the sober recounting of biographical fact.

In listing pianists, Dubal is satisfactorily inclusive; the omissions I found were few, and, with the possible exception of the Spaniard Eduardo del Pueyo, none seems in any way central. As might be expected, more space is given to the famous than to the little-known. If we take the number of words as indicative of Dubal's musical esteem, the clear winner is Vladimir Horowitz, at eight-plus pages; by contrast, Arthur Rubinstein, Horowitz's only competitor for the post-1945 celebrity title, receives a scant three pages. Fittingly, the back jacket of *The Art of the Piano* is adorned with an extravagant blurb by Horowitz: "It must be read by everyone who loves the instrument."

On occasion, Dubal can be harsh in his comments. Thus, of the flamboyant Earl Wild, a specialist in virtuoso (and for many, including me, meretricious) salon transcriptions, he remarks: "He is lavish in his use of rubato. A witty man, he once told me that his performance of the Chopin Ballade in G minor one evening had had enough rubato to last for two years. (I remember thinking how ghastly the performance had been.)" Dubal is hard, too, on the hyperserious Czech specialist Alfred Brendel, whom he finds (despite commendable artistic seriousness) often dry, lacking in suggestiveness, and without real technical flexibility. He is even hard on Josef Hofmann, beyond reproach to many piano lovers, whom he accuses of frequently playing in order to shock the audience rather than to illuminate the music; he is also tough (in my opinion correctly so) on Hofmann's pupil Jorge Bolet, whose playing—especially on records—he describes in such terms as tired, earthbound, humdrum. By contrast, he seems very kind to the many young pianists about whom he writes briefly, stressing their achievements and minimizing their flaws.

Yet even taking into account his reservations, it is difficult to avoid the impression that Dubal is a fan writing for other fans. He concentrates on saying good and frequently extravagant things about the scores of pianists he has heard in concert and on record, and he has equally good things to say about the scores of earlier artists about whom he has only read. In addition to being a great fan of pianists, Dubal is a great fan of piano music. The almost two hundred pages he devotes to a discussion of the important works of the repertory are universally enthusiastic; furthermore, in listing recommended recordings—often as many as ten—of each work or group of works, Dubal declines to rank competing versions but is content to list them alphabetically.[3]

What seems finally so curious about Dubal's approach is just this unwillingness to take sides. Reading his book, one is fully aware that he likes the good pianists and dislikes the bad; more than that, one is aware that he is mightily impressed by individualistic playing, whether oriented toward technical display or toward musical expression. It is also plain that Dubal wants to avoid comparing the work of today's pianists with the work of past masters. But what is so difficult to tell is just what *kind* of playing he really prefers.

There are, after all, great differences among pianists, expressed both in the individual and characteristic features of their art and in the nature of their appeal to sophisticated and unsophisticated listeners alike. Pianists are young, middle-aged, or old, tense or relaxed, brilliant or refined, direct or subtle, and (dare it be said?) male or female. Even excellent pianists possess widely varying amounts of technical equipment and musical knowledge; even successful and famous pianists exhibit widely varying levels of mastery. And beyond all these relatively easily identifiable characteristics, each artist displays, and displays the more on closer acquaintance, a world of subtle differences—expressed through dynamics, tone, phrasing, rhythm, and pulse—of individual style, personality, and communicated emotion. Put another way, the differences in the F Minor Sonata Op. 57 (the "Appassionata") of Beethoven as played by Rubinstein, Schnabel, or Horowitz (to choose three incontestably great artists, each of whom recorded the work in the past) are so great that, excellent though each may be, a sophisticated listener is all but compelled to choose among them.

Then, too, there are the various nationalities of pianists—German, Russian, French, Spanish, English, American. Despite the endless variations within each nationality, it can be said that each country as a whole has produced a school of playing. Moreover, each national school has a national specialty, invariably made up of national composers, and these groups of composers also make up schools of composition, each widely different from the next and instantly recognizable. In the close relationship between national composition styles and national playing styles—between, for example, Germanic pianists and Beethoven and Schubert, or between Polish pianists and Chopin, or between Russian pianists and Rachmaninoff, or between French pianists and Debussy and Ravel, or between American pianists and Gershwin and Samuel Barber—lies perhaps the best chance that a given composer's intentions will be realized (though even the best such rendering is unlikely to be equally beloved by all).

It is a remarkable characteristic of musical life today that we no longer feel comfortable making clear statements of our own preferences in individual artists or in conflicting national schools. This attitude is new. It used to be that every lover of the piano had his favorites. When I was growing up in the 1940s the fur always flew when the merits of competing artists were being discussed by knowledgeable and experienced concertgoers. Today, discussing his selection of repertory, David Dubal can write: "After each composition, I have listed various recordings which represent the widest diversity of interpretation. If, for example, listeners were to hear each of my selections for the Brahms Second Piano Concerto, they would form through such 'comparative listening' a great knowledge of the work's potential and interpretive possibilities. From such listening one becomes open-minded, and always curious as to the next performance."

The end result is that Dubal has succeeded in writing a book not of criticism but of appreciation. It can be argued that these days, appreciation is just what we need. Even if this were so, however, it is impossible to ignore the loss to living art implicit in the sacrifice of hard judgment to the cause of an unbounded admiration.

Dubal's good feelings are especially evident in a passage summarizing his attitude toward the present and the future:

One thing is certain: the piano and piano playing are here to stay. More countries produce pianos that ever before—Korea, Brazil, Switzerland, Czechoslovakia, China, Thailand, Australia, and many others—while Japan has become the world's largest piano producer. The Orient, in its obsession with things Western, has been captivated by the instrument. Asian pianists are filling conservatories and winning competitions. The future of the instrument and its literature are becoming international. Had Beethoven or Liszt ever thought of a Japanese or a Korean pianist?

This forthright statement hardly specifies just what music all the new pianists are to play. David Dubal's book is full of the names of great pianists who wrote great music and themselves played it supremely well: the line connecting Beethoven, Chopin, Liszt, and Brahms to Debussy and Rachmaninoff is central to the development of playing no less than to that of composition. But this happy condition no longer obtains, for quite without exception today's best pianists do not compose. Are there, then, nonpianists who are writing great piano music today?

Dubal's answer to this vexing question is, once again, forthright:

"[A]lthough many think that composers no longer love the piano as they once did, the piano literature of the twentieth century gives abundant proof to the contrary. Indeed, one of the great challenges for the contemporary pianist will be to reveal the wealth of the twentieth century's piano literature to audiences worldwide."

It should hardly be necessary to remind ourselves that the twentieth century is now nine-tenths over; very few people, musicians or otherwise, who were born in its early years are still with us today. Though Debussy wrote his great piano music in this century, and though in his day he must have seemed modern indeed, he surely belongs not to our time but to the increasingly far-distant world of pre-1914 Europe. Ravel wrote marvelous music for the piano into the 1930s—but his compositional style was largely formed already by the turn of the century. The still very modern-sounding Béla Bartók was dead by 1945, almost a half-century ago; in fact Bartók's Third Concerto, almost finished at his death, is the last work for piano and orchestra to enter the international repertory. Significantly, Prokofiev's last piano sonatas, though they are still used to fill the "contemporary" niche on recital programs, were all in place by 1947, just two years after the Bartók Third Concerto.

Thus, most of what we today call modern music is in fact old music. If we are to be honest in using the category of contemporary music, it seems clear that it should apply to *new* music, music that is being written now rather than that which comes out of a (properly) hallowed past. And just where, one must ask, is this marvelous new music? Wherever it is to be found, one thing is certain: there is precious little of it mentioned in David Dubal's book.

Scattered among his profiles of the famous there are indeed several composers whose works are still unassimilated into the musical vocabulary either of pianists or of audiences. Yet all of them, living or dead, were born more than six decades ago. Among them are Arnold Schoenberg (1874–1951), Anton Webern (1883–1945), Roger Sessions (1896–1985), Luigi Dallapiccola (1904–75), Olivier Messiaen (b. 1908), Elliott Carter (b. 1908), Luciano Berio (b. 1925), Pierre Boulez (b. 1925), Karlheinz Stockhausen (b. 1928), and George Crumb (b. 1929). Several of these composers have written highly interesting works for the piano, yet not one of them shows the slightest sign of entering the standard piano repertory—the music through which a great piano career is made.

Dubal does add a few pages describing briefly a category of music he deems "worth examination and study . . . [by] composers of special quality who have explored the piano with high ideals and particularly understand the instrument's resources." In this category he lists 106 composers, fully 54 of whom were born before 1900 and another 33 between 1900 and 1920. The remaining 19, the "now generation," there is no point in enumerating. They write in styles ranging from the academic to the avant-garde. I am sorry Dubal left out, in his discussion of the works of older composers, the massive Sonata (1983) by the American composer Hugo Weisgall (b. 1912), a work I have played several times and have always found moving and rewarding.

As for the younger composers Dubal mentions, my own experience of many of them gives me little hope that their music will ever be more than objects of curiosity, programmed by few pianists and heard only by that exiguous public of colleagues who make up the serious contemporary-music audience today. Sadly, but also tellingly, it is necessary to note that though Dubal places great weight on the present and future of the piano in the Orient, he does not discuss the music of a single Asian composer.

It is now time to return to the question with which I began: whither the piano?

There are three parts to any answer to this question. The first part must address itself to the current level of piano-playing. Is it sufficiently high to communicate the great works of the past to new, and lamentably untrained, audiences? The second part must consider whether a living tradition of performance can exist without new compositions on which to build. And the last part must look to the nature of a cultural enterprise tied as this one is to the artistic, intellectual, and social values of the past. Can such an enterprise survive in a world increasingly given to defining itself not by its continuity with the past, but by its breaking with, and destruction of, that past?

As to the first part, the present level of performance, I myself have grave doubts. Today's pianists, whether from the Orient or from the Occident, play accurately but no more than accurately; as compared with artists of even the fairly recent past, they lack a wide knowledge of the literature, technical flair, unforced projection of tone, the ability to communicate the differences among composers' styles, and, above all, emotional power. The result of these shortcomings is a gap between the content of the music being played and the audiences' perception of that content. In the piano literature perhaps more than in any other area of serious music (save opera), what is being heard by the musical public today is only a simulacrum, not the reality, of incontestable masterworks.

As to the second part: because of the absence of new piano compositions that go via the ears and minds of listeners to their hearts, performers have been robbed of their best approach to an audience: the communication of an art arising directly out of the performers' immediate life experience rather than out of imitation, no matter how accomplished, of predeccessors. Such imitation is inevitably an act of re-creation rather than of creation, and it makes of today's pianists merely ingenious antiquarians and painstaking curators; the current stampede to original performance styles provides ample evidence both of the desperation of today's most intellectually active performers and the narrowing and debilitating effect produced by such concentration on the past even in the performance of the music of the past itself.

Finally, it has become the fashion today, as we approach the millennium, to speculate about a possible end to various fundamental processes—an end to war, or to history, or perhaps even, for the gloomy among us, to culture. Yet fashion or no, little in the condition of serious music today and little especially in the condition of the piano as an instrument for the continuing performance of great music can inspire optimism about the future.

It is difficult to believe there is a shortage of talent in the world; it is equally difficult to believe that we now know less about music than did our forebears. What does seem clear, however, is that the human basis for the creation of great music, whether that basis is understood in terms of the individual, the family, the home, the folk, or the nation, is now somehow eroded. What we have is prosperity, freedom, perhaps even satiation. What we do not seem to be able to manage is the creation of permanent culture. For hundreds of years now, such creation has often manifested itself in the writing of great music. This time of glory does seem to have come to an end.

Still, as for me, and others like me, it will be hard to stop playing, or at least practicing, the beloved piano.

(*Commentary*, 1989)

PART THREE

CONDUCTORS

12

WILLEM MENGELBERG

AT THE PHILHARMONIC

The flood of fascinating CD reissues of marvelous old 78-RPM discs continues without interruption. The enterprising Pearl label in England has just released some, though unfortunately not all, of the electrical recordings made by the great Dutch conductor Willem Mengelberg with the New York Philharmonic (then called the Philharmonic-Symphony Orchestra of New York) between 1925 and 1930.[1]

There is little doubt that Mengelberg was one of the great conductors of the century. Born in 1871 in Utrecht to German parents, he studied in Germany at the Cologne Conservatory, and in 1891 became conductor of the municipal orchestra in Lucerne. In 1895, he became conductor of the Concertgebouw in Amsterdam, a post he held until 1945. Mengelberg was also the leading conductor of the New York Philharmonic from 1923 to 1929, when he was replaced by Toscanini, though he continued to conduct the orchestra into the 1929–30 season. Throughout Mengelberg's career, he was a champion of the works of Gustav Mahler; in 1920, he celebrated his twenty-fifth anniversary at the Concertgebouw with a complete Mahler cycle. He was also devoted to the works of Richard Strauss. *Ein Heldenleben* was dedicated to Mengelberg; he gave its first performance and remained its most persuasive performer.

Mengelberg spent the last years of his life under the cloud of a deserved reputation for pro-German sympathies (and for conducting in Germany) during the World War II occupation of Holland. Earlier, he had championed the music of the Jewish Ernest Bloch and Darius Milhaud, and during the time of Hitler he helped Jewish orchestra musicians escape. Because of his eminence in national life, he was barred from musical activity, and until his death in 1951 lived in forced retirement in Switzerland. His death seemed to efface some of the bitterness toward him in Holland. A memorial concert was given in Amsterdam just nine days after he died; it was played by his beloved Concertgebouw Orchestra and conducted by Otto Klemperer, himself a Jewish refugee from Hitler. Nonetheless, his complaisant behavior toward the hated Nazis had destroyed his career, and his sad end provides many cautionary lessons for those artists who would cooperate with tyranny.

But when Mengelberg was working with the Philharmonic, this denouement was still some years in the future. His first recordings with the orchestra, made by the old acoustic process, included *Les Préludes* of Liszt, the Beethoven *Coriolan* and the Weber *Oberon* overtures, a movement of the Beethoven Fifth Symphony, and the second and fourth movements of the Tchaikovsky "Pathétique" Symphony. But acoustic recordings, for all their value in documenting the voices of the golden age of Italian operatic singing, are usually but travesties of the real sound of an orchestra. And so it is to Mengelberg's electrical recordings with the Philharmonic, made at the very dawn of this vastly superior process, that we must look for information on just what he achieved as a conductor in New York.

The Mengelberg electrical Philharmonic recordings, all done for the Victor Red Seal label, begin with a 1925 performance of Wagner's Overture to *Der fliegende Holländer;* the next Mengelberg recording with the Philharmonic, made in January of 1928, is again of Wagner, this time the *Waldweben* from *Siegfried.* At the end of the same year, Mengelberg and the Philharmonic recorded the Strauss *Ein Heldenleben.* They recorded several shorter pieces in January of the next year, including the Coronation March from Meyerbeer's *Le Prophète,* Saint-Saëns *Le Rouet d'Omphale,* the "War March of the Priests" from Mendelssohn's *Athalie,* a suite from Handel's *Alcina,* the famous Air from J. S. Bach's Suite in D

Major, and J. C. Bach's Sinfonia, Op. 18, No. 2, in B-flat Major. At the end of 1929, Mengelberg and the Philharmonic recorded the Beethoven Third Symphony, the *Eroica*; in January of 1930, they recorded the Beethoven First Symphony. In the same month, they also recorded the overtures to Mozart's *Die Zauberflöte,* Beethoven's *Egmont,* and Humperdinck's *Hänsel und Gretel.* The Pearl CD includes all the performances listed above, with four exceptions, the last three of them major: the Wagner overture, the Strauss *Ein Heldenleben,* and the two Beethoven symphonies.[2] While one might lament the relatively small number of Mengelberg recordings with the Philharmonic, there is still enough here, not just to afford high musical pleasure, but to pass judgments both on Mengelberg in his prime as a musician and on the New York Philharmonic as it entered the Toscanini era. These judgments are overwhelmingly favorable, and in making them we will learn much that is surprising about the standards and goals of musical performance sixty and more years ago.

The great distinction of these recordings leaps out from the pre-romantic works with which the Pearl CD opens. It is now the fashion for musicians and critics to assume unthinkingly that the 1920s and before were a musical dark age, a time when Handel and Bach, not to mention Bach's sons, were either not played at all or, if played, were so mangled that their music was not recognizable.

The Pearl CD gives the lie to this fatuous (and often self-serving) assumption. In Mengelberg's performance, the *Alcina* Suite is Handel before the age of Handel specialists. Here is Handel performed without the attempt to be anything more than *musically* authentic: here is vital rhythm, a half-century before the authentic-performance specialists discovered—and exaggerated—short upbeats; what makes the rhythm so gripping is its foundation in the conductor's strong feeling for pulse and tempo, a feeling that extends throughout whole movements rather than peters out, as so often happens today, in heedless forward motion. Mengelberg manages another miracle in the Handel: he makes the varied tempos of the separate movements cohere, so that each successive speed is both different and related to what has gone before.

Mengelberg's miracle in the slow movement—the famous "Air on the G String"—from the Bach Suite is nothing less than the glorious playing of a glorious melody. He uses Mahler's arrangement, and thereby gives us some insight into Mahler's own dedication to this music. Doubtless the incredibly moving string tone owes much to the use of gut, rather than the later steel-wound, strings; the quality of consolation—for life and in life—must equally come from Mengelberg's own passionate attachment to the melody and his ability to transmit that attachment to his musicians.

Mengelberg and the Philharmonic's playing of the J. C. Bach Sinfonia possesses all the virtues of their Handel, with perhaps an even greater depth of string tone and a marvelously elegant oboe solo by the great Bruno Labate. J. C. Bach, like all his contemporaries, is now played, as it were, by the yard: conductorial reputations on record—one thinks immediately of that of Neville Marriner—are currently made not by how specially each piece is played in itself but by how many pieces the conductor manages to tape. Here Mengelberg conveys the impression that this piece is not just the most beautiful and absorbing piece of J. C. Bach but is the most beautiful and absorbing piece in the world.

The Mozart and Beethoven overtures are among the incontestably great works of our tradition. Mozart's *Die Zauberflöte*, including its overture, has now achieved cultic significance, while Beethoven's music to Goethe's prose tragedy *Egmont* is now ignored, save for its oft-played overture. But familiar as these two overtures are, Mengelberg treats them as special, and as conceptually free-standing. In the Mozart, the opening chords are models of precise ensemble, played without the tonal tightness that the drive for orchestral accuracy so often engenders; the fugal passages with which the work abounds are played not just correctly, but with the greatest delicacy. In the *Egmont*, Mengelberg's canvas is properly much larger. Here is not only wonderful orchestral playing, including once again Labate's oboe and also the horns, led by the famous Bruno Jaenicke; Mengelberg also provides an amalgam of strength and warmth, each quality making up one-half of Beethoven's genius. The effect of Mengelberg's performance is so natural, as if he and the orchestra had played the piece together every day of their lives. In this regard, it is instructive to compare the comfort of this Mengelberg performance with the knifelike edge of Toscanini's 1939 NBC Symphony broadcast performance of the work;[3] the impression conveyed by Toscanini is not one of comfort with the music's splendor, but of an almost angry discovery of the music for the first time.

The rest of the Pearl CD, including music of Mendelssohn, Meyerbeer, Wagner, Humperdinck, and Saint Saëns, seems of less interest, not because of any less value in its performance, but because the works themselves seem to ask for less from us as listeners. For what is more significant of Mengelberg and the Philharmonic, we must go to their major recordings that are as yet unreleased on CD.

The best-known of these recordings, both because it was very successful on its release and because it has been available on an LP transfer, is the Strauss *Ein Heldenleben*. Opinions vary about this enormous work: for some, including me, the work's many beautiful passages are overwhelmed by Strauss's tendency (at least in this period of his development) to a self-regarding vulgarity. But though rather less-played than such earlier Strauss tone poems as *Don Juan, Tod und Verklärung, Till Eulenspiegel,* and *Don Quixote* (and perhaps even *Also Sprach Zarathustra*), *Ein Heldenleben* retains its place in the repertory as an orchestral, and therefore as a conductor's, showpiece. And that is how Mengelberg treats the work. Considering the fact that the performance was recorded in 1928, using the still primitive technology then available, the orchestral writing is amazingly clear. Compare, for example, the precise execution of the mammoth opening arpeggio in the horns, cellos, and basses in the Mengelberg recording with the slippery and diffuse playing of the Vienna Philharmonic in the composer's own 1944 recording; the reason for the superiority of Mengelberg lies in his willingness to alter Strauss's phrasing so that what the composer wrote might be heard.[4] The comparison of the two performances is instructive in another regard as well: given all the yards of writing these days about how much more composers know than mere performers about how their music should be played, it is remarkable just how much more persuasive Mengelberg's performance in this inescapably rhetorical work is than that of Strauss. And no consideration of the Mengelberg recording can possibly omit a tribute to the splendid solo-violin playing of the Philharmonic's concertmaster, the now-forgotten Scipione Guidi.

Finally, we come to the Beethoven symphonies. As was the case with the *Egmont* Overture, the required comparisons are with Toscanini. There can be no doubt that Toscanini's Beethoven symphonies are on the highest level of any of the performances of these works of which we have recorded (or concert-hall) evidence. I have earlier referred to Toscanini's performance of the *Egmont* as sounding like an almost angry discovery; for Toscanini, it is difficult to escape the conclusion that Beethoven—and despite Toscanini's much-demanded fidelity to the notes and nothing but the notes, he must indeed have had a mental image of the composer—was not so much human as mythic; the operative myth must have been something like Prometheus defying Zeus. The result was that Toscanini's Beethoven belonged not to heaven, if by heaven we mean a place of divine mercy to man and human love for God; his Beethoven belonged to the pagan heavens of the gods and their terrors.[5] What marks Toscanini's Beethoven is not love for man but always a strict love, and often a painful love, for music.

By contrast, Mengelberg's Beethoven belongs to this world. The tone is always rich, always vibrant; the notes, no matter how short, are always rounded; the rhythms, no matter how pert, are always fully sounded, never snapped off; even the most powerfully made gestures are always shapely, never angular. Every melody is not just sung but shaped. Strange as it is to say so, in Mengelberg's *Eroica* the opening melody in the cellos is played almost tenderly, as if heroes too can be gentle. And the orchestral playing is superb; merely to listen to the opening of the last movement of the First Symphony, with its treacherously exposed passage for the first violins, and to the equally treacherously exposed passage for the horns in the scherzo of the *Eroica,* is to know that the Philharmonic in 1930 (due to Toscanini as well as to Mengelberg) was a supremely great orchestra.

How did Mengelberg achieve his results? He must have had a marvelous ear, and he was willing to take infinite pains over details, taking excruciatingly many minutes at the beginning of each rehearsal to tune the orchestra.[6] In at least one rather obvious respect, he was a very old-fashioned conductor: unlike today's businesslike and efficient leaders, Mengelberg liked to lecture the orchestra, it often seemed by the hour, about the composers and the music to be played. Such an indirect approach was sometimes resented by the musicians. An old and perhaps unreliable Philharmonic story has the oboist Labate interrupting one of Mengelberg's extended talks with the trenchant words, "Hey Mist'! You talka too much." But conducting is at bottom a form of alchemy and perhaps even of necromancy; what counts is not the process but the outcome.

To sum up, then: as I listen to these recordings, three words come immediately to mind: brilliance, freedom, and warmth. I am tempted to add that the greatest of these is warmth. As much as Mengelberg may have demanded it, the brilliance belongs to the orchestra: virtuoso playing in the strings, the winds, and the brass; razor-sharp ensemble, and, above all, a feeling for ensemble playing always attentive to the playing of other instruments and other sections. The freedom was Mengelberg's: more accelerandos and ritardandos than are fashionable today in our musically prim age; violent dynamic contrasts, often combined with major changes in basic tempos; and, perhaps most significant, a willingness to vary the explicit demands of the printed notation, either to make the performance more faithful to what he divined were the composer's intentions or to make the music more communicable to the audience. But it is the warmth in these performances that takes pride of place: an intensely human quality in melodic playing, especially in the strings, that always seems to speak personally and directly. It is hardly too much to apply to these performances the words that Cardinal Newman, a passionate lover of the violin and of the Beethoven quartets, chose for his motto: *cor ad cor loquitur*—the heart speaks to the heart. Can there be greater praise for a conductor—or for an orchestra?

(*The New Criterion*, 1991)

13

PIERRE MONTEUX'S SUCCESS

It may safely be said that personal striving—vulgarly called ambition—
is the hallmark of modernity. To be satisfied with one's lot, we are told,
is to default on our duty to self and world alike; to be all that one can be,
and perhaps even a bit more, seems the only success we can have fully
within our grasp.

Pierre Monteux does not fit well into our contemporary world of push
and shove, get-up-and-go. Those who were privileged to know him as a
teacher remember a musician *pur sang*, a man of simple pleasures and
worldly interests but always a man of the most total devotion to a Pla-
tonic ideal of music and its performance. For example, his students inevitably have graven on their minds his conception of the *tempo juste*: the
speed neither too fast nor too slow at which a piece of music is not just
plausible but *right*. Indeed, the truth is that for this sometimes jolly,
sometimes irascible giant of musicality, there were no two ways about
anything musical, as there were no two ways about his own relationship
to his art: by the very rules of his being, music was life, and life was
music.

It cannot be said that Pierre Monteux was unrewarded by the fates for
his dedication. He has an assured place in the musical history of our
century as the courageously persistent conductor of the 1913 premiere
in Paris of Stravinsky's (and Diaghilev and Nijinsky's) *Rite of Spring;* in
addition, he conducted the premieres of Stravinsky's *Petrushka* and *The
Nightingale,* Ravel's *Daphnis et Chloé,* and Debussy's *Jeux.* A winner (with

Jacques Thibaud) of a *premier prix* at the Paris Conservatoire, he was already a conductor by 1887, when at the age of twelve he led an orchestra "in Paris and elsewhere"—as the *New Grove* tells us—with the pianist Alfred Cortot as soloist. In a conducting career that spanned almost eight full decades, Monteux led the Boston Symphony Orchestra from 1919 to 1924, served as the second conductor (after Mengelberg) of the Concertgebouw in Amsterdam from 1924 to 1934, founded the Orchestre Symphonique de Paris in 1929, serving as its conductor till 1938, and became the music director of the San Francisco Symphony Orchestra in 1936, where he remained until 1953. In a brilliant Indian summer, the seventy-seven-year-old Monteux began an international career as a guest conductor, returning repeatedly to Boston and even for a short time gracing the Metropolitan Opera with his sure grip of Offenbach's *Tales of Hoffmann*. Above all, he was successful in England, where in 1961 (at the age of eighty-six, and just three years before his death) he accepted an appointment as chief conductor of the London Symphony Orchestra.

Monteux began to make records in Paris in the early days of the electrical process.[1] These first efforts included a ragged 1929 *Rite of Spring*[2] and a volcanic 1931 Ravel *La Valse*.[3] A bit later, he collaborated on several recordings with the adolescent Yehudi Menuhin. Among their work together is the classic 1932 performance of the Bach Concerto for Two Violins, in which Menuhin is joined by his teacher, Georges Enescu.[4] Profiting by the dearth of new material coming out of Europe during World War II, Monteux made many remarkable discs in San Francisco, ranging from Beethoven and Brahms through Chausson and D'Indy to Rimsky-Korsakov and Stravinsky.[5] In the mid- and late 1950s he made the now standard Boston recordings of the Fourth, Fifth, and Sixth symphonies of Tchaikovsky[6] and of Stravinsky's *Petrushka* and *The Rite of Spring*.[7] Finally, there were numerous recordings for Philips and Decca in Europe, including all the Beethoven symphonies and some of the masterpieces of the French literature. In a sadly belated tribute to Monteux's genius in opera, EMI brought out a marvelous complete *La Traviata* under his direction.

No assessment of Monteux's career could possibly fail to mention his dedicated work as a teacher. He founded the Ecole Monteux in France in 1932, and with the coming of World War II moved it to the simple village of Hancock on the coast of Maine. For Monteux, a school was about teaching and learning, not administrative redundancies; about music-making, not career empire-building. The hundreds of aspirants who came to him over the years were taught not just how to *conduct* music but how to *construe* it. For Monteux, music was not a matter of feelings. It had its own ontology, an independent existence: now serene, now lively, now sensuous, now stormy. If his students were talented— very talented, I should add—they might divine what music was and how it went; if they were not, it was a good idea for them to get out of the way instanter. Direct and tough, witty and sometimes barbed, Monteux's performing injunctions were based on his own complete musical knowledge and perfect ear; as his final approving audience, he had in mind no one but Euterpe and her sister Muses.

How far away is the musical world of today from the world of Pierre Monteux! A new year has just dawned in our calendar, but I think none of us is so foolhardy as to think that with the change in calendar will come a better era in music. Those of us who owe so much to Monteux— those of us, that is, for whom the expression *Harmonielehre* suggests Arnold Schoenberg, not John Adams—cannot but look with dismay at today's paucity of significant new works, so unlike the constant replenishment of the repertory that took place before Monteux reached the biblical promise of threescore and ten years. Similarly, it is dismaying to find so many of the new "superstar" conductors—I will forbear listing their names so as not to assist the mills of public relations—conducting fewer and fewer pieces in less and less interesting ways. As the CD has replaced the LP, we realize that we have no interest in Herr X's *Eroica*, in Sir Y's *Messiah*, or in Maestro Z's *Rigoletto*. And yet the CDs keep coming, and the music directorships of American orchestras continue to go to an epigonic generation of European conductors who are paid astronomic salaries for part-year work. Many of us, indeed, think of Maître Monteux—for so he was ineluctably called—and we weep.

We weep for ourselves because we have not his like today. But we weep also for him, because we realize that by today's standards Monteux wasn't really all that successful. His reputation, like whatever monetary compensation he earned, pales into insignificance beside what was accorded to such estimable figures as Arturo Toscanini, Leopold Stokowski, Wilhelm Furtwängler, Serge Koussevitzky, and Bruno Walter, to say nothing of today's star conducting personalities.

To begin with, Monteux always received, and receives to this day, surprisingly little discussion in the critical press. To cite more or less at random from two books I happen to have on my shelves: in Harold C. Schonberg's *Great Conductors* (1967) Monteux receives a scant three pages—as part of a chapter on "The Modern French School"—rather than one of the separate and extended chapters devoted to the truly famous; worse, he is not discussed at all in Kurt Blaukopf's *Great Conductors* (1955), a survey that manages to find room for the likes of Adrian Boult, Paul Kletzki, Josef Krips, and Hermann Scherchen. Monteux was never the subject of the Great Human Being worship that is traditionally reserved for those perceived to be the major performing musicians of the moment; even in the London musical world, where he was so successful at the end of his life, he never received the canonization so fulsomely awarded to Otto Klemperer for the Divine Services of Beethoven symphonies he presented at the Royal Festival Hall.

The fact is inescapable that, when it mattered most, Monteux was not the music director of a great world orchestra rooted in a great world city. While conductors of approximately his age conducted in New York, Boston, and Berlin (in Philadelphia, Stokowski had already created a great orchestra and left), Monteux only emerged from San Francisco for infrequent guest-conducting appearances. Even when he began a life of international guest conducting, he still lacked—and was to lack for the remainder of his life—the secure power base provided by the music directorship of a great orchestra.

Then, too, Monteux made fewer recordings in San Francisco than Toscanini made with the NBC Symphony Orchestra and Koussevitzky with the Boston Symphony; and he made many fewer than Ormandy in Philadelphia. Unlike Toscanini, whose weekly NBC radio broadcasts during the winter season were nationwide events; unlike Stokowski, whose every musical sigh was available on screen and radio; and unlike whoever was conducting the weekly broadcasts of the New York Philharmonic, Monteux was restricted to a few hour-long broadcasts each year on a Pacific Coast radio hookup.

As we look for the reasons why Monteux did not have a greater career, we must begin with the fact that his incarceration was on a West Coast not as yet tied to the East by jet air travel. There can be no argument: the San Francisco Symphony Orchestra in the Monteux years, for all the yeoman work he did there, was not a great orchestra. Despite the city's unsurpassable physical beauty, San Francisco has never been able to compete for intellectual excitement or serious cultural activity with Chicago and the great cities of the East. A cultivated core audience and a vastly sophisticated group of patrons supported Monteux loyally for sixteen years, but the total audience remained limited, and as a result the season was relatively short. As important, the musicians' union, always distrusting of outlanders, made it difficult and often impossible for Monteux to improve the orchestra's personnel; as a result, the kind of finely textured ensemble he did succeed in building in San Francisco lacked its proper complement and permanent foundation in individual instrumental excellence.

Just how great the distance was separating the San Francisco orchestra from the majors is poignantly demonstrated by two reviews Monteux received in the mid-1940s from the subtly discerning Virgil Thomson, then at the height of his power.as the chief critic of the *New York Herald Tribune*. In 1944, Monteux conducted the New York Philharmonic[8] and elicited the following observation from Thomson, one that, in its implicit judgments of the orchestra's usual performance standards, applies equally to the Philharmonic of today:

Pierre Monteux's two-week visit as guest conductor of the Philharmonic-Symphony Orchestra, which ends today, has led music lovers of all schools (the critical press included) to two conclusions: namely, that this conductor has drawn from our orchestra more beautiful sounds and more beautiful mixtures of sound than any other conductor has done in many years, and that his readings of Brahms are highly refreshing. . . . It has remained for Pierre Monteux to achieve what many of us thought was hopeless. He has made the Philharmonic play with real beauty of tone, many kinds of it, and with perfect balance and blending—to sound, in short, like an orchestra, a real, first-class orchestra requiring no apology.

But lest one think that all that counts is the conductor, here is Thomson on a Monteux concert with the San Francisco orchestra less than three years later:

Pierre Monteux, who conducted his own orchestra, the San Francisco Symphony, last night in Carnegie Hall, is one of the greatest among living conductors. His orchestra, unfortunately, on account of budgetary limitations, is not so perfect an orchestra as he is a musician. . . . Both the brasses and the woodwinds of this orchestra are of good quality. It is the strings that are weak. . . . All the animated passages sounded last night, in consequence, in spite of Mr. Monteux's admirable tempos and careful phrasing, a little rowdy.

Others, less discerning in taste and less acute in hearing than Thomson, have identified Monteux's problem as a lack of "personality." Thus, in David Wooldridge's *Conductor's World* (1970) Monteux is patronizingly compared to Koussevitzky and found wanting in certain crucial respects:

Whatever may have been the merits of the late Pierre Monteux—*and as a conductor he possibly possessed greater musicianship than did Koussevitzky* [emphasis added]—he could not by any stretch of the imagination have been called a personality in the sense that that term is usually intended to convey. His extreme vanity and exaggerated sense of *amour propre* were never of an order to sustain the burden of the great tradition of musical personalities who—though their nature be extrovert or introvert—must always be *seen* to be musical personalities, and larger than life. In the language of our American friends, Monteux was, in short, something of a "cold fish."

Whatever the merits of Wooldridge's characterization, he has identified an aspect of Monteux's art that might strike the ignorant (a category that perhaps includes Wooldridge) as indeed responsible for a "personality" deficit. I refer here to Monteux's insistence on improving the taste of everyone involved, players and listeners alike. Monteux was, I suspect by design, a teacher in everything musical he did, not just when he instructed the young but also, and above all, when he performed. To his students, he taught the technical material of conducting; to his players and his listeners he taught the repertory and the proper fashion of its performance.

In the area of repertory, Monteux programmed unfamiliar, difficult, and often new (and American!) twentieth-century music. (It should be remembered that during Monteux's years in San Francisco, this century was but a few decades old, and its radical break with the music of the past was relatively recent.) Because Monteux was a deeply proud

Frenchman, he shifted the balance of the repertory away from the Austro-German classics—so beloved, for instance, of New York Philharmonic audiences of the 1920s and 1930s—and toward French music, from Berlioz to Milhaud and even Messiaen.

In performance, Monteux lessened the interest in superstar soloists playing superstar concertos, those fabulous star turns perceived to be so vital to the commercial success of most second-tier orchestras. He also brought to the music he conducted a performance style concerned with realizing the structure of the music and the details by which that structure might be articulated. He was, too, faithful to the text, not in today's quixotic sense of historical re-creation, but in the rather more straightforward, if arduous, sense of clearly playing the right notes in tune, at the right tempo, in the right rhythm, and in the notated phrasing.[9]

I must assume that many people saw all this as stuffy didacticism, and perhaps even as pedantic moralism. It will rightly be objected that every major conductor, and every great musical performer, sees what he does in terms of black and white, of right and wrong; it will further be maintained, quite properly, that it is in communicating how artistic matters should be, rather than merely how they are, that great artists distinguish themselves from routine executants. But the conductors with the very greatest careers—here I particularly have in mind Toscanini, Furtwängler, and Stokowski—communicated their private visions of musical truth by directly powerful emotional means. At their best, these means, involving the use of what Thomson called the "wowing technique," were grandly eloquent, and the results profound;[10] at their worst, they were openly crass, and the results overwrought or sentimental. Even the musically refined Herbert von Karajan, in my opinion the greatest conductor to emerge since World War II, is not entirely free of the charge of vamping a gullible public through the projection of a spuriously prophetic and trancelike image on the podium.

Needless to say, Monteux did not see his task this way. He did not cultivate the body beautiful but rather looked like a pear; he did not walk sinuously onto the stage but rather waddled; he didn't jump around while he conducted but often seemed to disappear once the music had begun. His aural persona didn't call attention to itself either. Monteux's musical model, not surprisingly, was French, and furthermore, I suspect,

Ravel-French and not Debussy-French. I remember him reacting with noticeable irritation when anyone sloppily called the new French music written around the turn of this century "impressionist." No matter how fast the tempo Monteux demanded—and his tempos were often blindingly fast—everything had to be audible. The dynamics, too, had to be containable within a classical framework. To sum up, Monteux's goal for the performance of his beloved music was total clarity, not overwhelming impact. His message to all was the same: if we do our job properly, the music will make its way, not ours.

Monteux's rustication with a regional orchestra in sunny California, his lack of identification with the standard works of the Austro-German repertory, his unphotogenic platform behavior, and, above all, his omnipresent pedagogic and self-effacing musical impulse—these factors plausibly explain why he never became one of the ballyhooed conductors of the age. To stop there, however, would be to settle for the kind of self-gratification we so comfortably indulge when we say, in thundering imitation of Dr. Johnson, "The public, Sir, is a great fool!" To stop there, it seems to me, would be to do less than full justice both to the musical public and to the surrounding world in which music must make its way.

It goes without saying that our century has been a time of unprecedented cataclysms, of wars and liberations, of revolutions and tyrannies, of weapons of destruction and potions of healing, of supreme hopes and terrifying disappointments. It has also been a time of involuntary movements of peoples perhaps unprecedented in history. Viewed against this tumultuous background, music—and the other arts as well—can hardly fail to be buffeted by forces beyond its control. The same impotence which thus affects a mere art must also mark the lives of its practitioners.

So we must not be surprised that musical careers will reflect their times, and that great careers will greatly reflect the world that makes them possible. To make this point concretely, we might consider two powerful images, each rightly bound up with the career of a great conductor. The first image, from the career of Toscanini, is heroic and indeed triumphant; the second, from the career of Furtwängler, is horrifying.

To begin with Toscanini: imagine, if you will, a summer day in the spacious gardens surrounding Triebschen, the beautiful lakeside villa just outside Lucerne in Switzerland. It was here that Richard Wagner, between 1866 and 1872, completed *Die Meistersinger,* practically completed *Siegfried,* and wrote and first performed (as a gift for his wife on the birth of their son) the *Siegfried Idyll.* The time now is that of the August 1938 Anschluss, Hitler's unresisted rape of Austria. There is again music at Triebschen, very much including Wagner, but it is not performed by the composer; in the audience one will not find, as had been possible in happier days, Franz Liszt and Friedrich Nietzsche. Instead, the conductor is Toscanini, no longer willing to be a guest at Salzburg and eager to demonstrate his opposition to Mussolini and Hitler as the inevitable European war draws near. In the audience are, in the words of Harvey Sachs, "Italian music lovers and the cream of Italian society"; for these listeners' pains, their automobile license-plate numbers are taken down by fascist informers, and the names of the owners are published in the Italian press.

We will hardly extract such an edifying picture from the life of Furtwängler. Here I have in mind the splendid photograph of the conductor in action which adorns the jacket of an epochal concert recording by him of the Beethoven Seventh Symphony.[11] Both photograph and recording were made in the old Philharmonic Hall in Berlin before its destruction; the performance took place at the end of October or perhaps the beginning of November 1943. Think back to the days when the concert was given: the bloody German retreat from Russia in progress, the Allied bombing offensive taking out German cities by day and by night, Italy already driven out of the war, the Holocaust more horrible with each passing day—and Beethoven goes on. To tell us how it felt to be in the Philharmonic Hall itself, we have the jacket photograph, showing an absorbed audience massed behind Furtwängler and the orchestra. Verily, the dream within and the nightmare without, but amid the horror: music and musicians, the dead Beethoven and the living Furtwängler, on the edge—not of art but of life.

I have chosen these two images, the one sublime and the other grotesque, not to make an argument for the amorality of art, for I am not at all clear that the Furtwängler image tells us anything more than that man, as part of his nature, bears the capacity to befoul even his own most wonderful achievements. Instead, I have attempted to show how the great, and today unparalleled, careers of Toscanini and Furtwängler drew their resonance from the world outside music. When we think of them, we know they fully lived, one for glory and the other for shame—but we know they fully lived. Viewed against the touchstones of these careers, the dear, beaming, decent Pierre Monteux seems to have been forced by destiny to be merely a great musician making beautiful music under conditions of peace.

Perhaps there is a lesson in Monteux's career for us in America, as we continue to wonder why our own composers and performers seem to lack the kind of universal status we expect musicians to be accorded. We in America have been fortunate: we have had no foreign wars on our soil in almost two centuries, and no major civil strife since the Civil War. Two world wars brought us victory and world power with little suffering; even Vietnam, as painful as it was, took place in a faraway country of which we knew nothing. Like the children from some happy fairy tale, we remain forever children, taking our heroes from the ranks of the real adults. Is is any wonder we are still waiting for our Toscanini or our Furtwängler?

The last word, however, belongs to Pierre Monteux. Fittingly, he now lies in the earth of the Maine he grew so much to love. One intuitively knows his fate to be something of what Goethe envisioned, for a poet-musician, in his immortal *Anakreons Grab*:

> Wo die Rose hier blüht, wo Reben um Lorbeer sich schlingen,
> Wo das Turtelchen lockt, wo sich das Grillchen ergötzt,
> Welch ein Grab ist hier, das alle Götter mit Leben
> Schön beplanfzt und geziert? Es ist Anakreons Ruh.
> Frühling, Sommer und Herbst genoss der glückliche Dichter,
> Vor dem Winter hat ihn endlich der Hügel geschützt.

> [Where the rose blooms, where vines and laurel are entwined,
> Where the turtle-dove calls, where the grasshopper takes his delight,
> What is this grave, that all the gods with life
> Have so beautifully planted and enlivened? It is Anacreon's repose.
> Spring, summer, and fall supported the happy poet;
> From the winter he has been protected, at last, by the hill.]

Is this success not success enough?

(*The New Criterion*, 1989)

TOSCANINI AND THE
LOVE OF GREAT MUSIC

Once upon a time, the work of great musical performers died with them. It is true that, for a few years after the death of these titans, the memories of admirers served to grant them a spectral presence. But soon even the most tireless fans also went on to their reward, and nothing remained of their heroes but more or less passing mentions in ephemeral periodicals and dusty histories. It has been argued, not altogether convincingly, that this rule of forgetfulness meant a better time for music, for the presence of the illustrious dead had no power to overshadow the struggling work of living performers. Perhaps more important, it is often suggested that when the work of performers died with them the way was clear for a proper and continuing attention to be given to the music of living composers.

It is hardly a secret that this obligatory sentence of oblivion no longer obtains. Through the miracle of sound recording, the reality of the best work of the most distinguished performers is available, on the whole in ever-improved technological form. Indeed, through the preservation of radio broadcasts from a time unlike ours, when the commercial media felt some responsibility for the diffusion of high culture, a wealth of hitherto forgotten musical treasures has been rediscovered and brought to market.

If tenor Enrico Caruso, now helped by computer-aided sonic reconstruction, remains the prime beneficiary of the very primitive acoustic recording process that flowered in the first quarter of the century, it is clear that Arturo Toscanini, aided mightily by the collateral phenomenon of radio, remains perhaps the prime beneficiary of electrical recording. I have seen it stated that Toscanini sold some twenty million records before his death in 1957, most of them doubtless LPs. Since then, his records have never ceased to be popular. The latest Schwann artist catalogue, very much an incomplete source, contains more than forty Toscanini entries, many of them on the now triumphant compact disc. Indeed, the parallel with the Italian super-tenor holds for the Italian super-conductor; for a new generation of music lovers, Caruso remains the archetypal tenor, and Toscanini remains the archetypal conductor.

It is curious that an age so given to the whorish adoration of fame and glamour as ours should also specialize in what can only be called the shattering of idols. The same approach that has raked up so much muck about our political leaders is now being applied to a once sacrosanct class of artists. Even the sainted Mozart was fair game in Peter Shaffer's hit play (and movie) *Amadeus*, emerging as the very model of the child-in-the-artist. Worse yet, from the musico-Freudian netherworld can currently be heard rumblings connecting Schubert with a life of sexual inversion.

All this has recently come home to the admirers of Toscanini with the publication of Joseph Horowitz's much discussed *Understanding Toscanini: How He Became an American Culture-God and Helped Create a New Audience for Old Music* (1987). This lengthy book, a sociological tract in the guise of a musical, biographical, and historical study, made three major attacks on the conductor, only two of them contained in the ponderous subtitle. The attack that went unmentioned on the title page was the purely musical element in a book which ended up having rather little to do with music qua music: I refer to Horowitz's pervasive unhappiness with the presenting face of Toscanini's music-making, a face that only grew clearer as the conductor grew older. Even on the evidence Horowitz presents, this critical unhappiness with Toscanini the musician had always existed; it is also only fair to add that the reaction to Horowitz's book has only shown that there are new recruits to the pro- and anti-Toscanini parties, not that musical opinions about the conductor have themselves changed over the better part of a century.

There are many ways of describing Toscanini's way of performing music: it has been called "objective" because of its seeming literalness, "exciting" because of its ability to communicate a quality of total integration and concentration, "Italianate" because of its emphasis on melodic clarity rather than harmonic richness, "motoric" because of its tendency to find and keep one tempo, and "willful" because of its tendency to concentrate attention on the orders of the conductor rather than on the instincts of the individual orchestral musicians. There is no reason here to point out the manifest contradictions among these various appellations; suffice it to say that all of them, taken together and shorn of their pejorative implications, serve to sum up how we identify a Toscanini performance. That Horowitz has in general a low opinion of most of these performances, that on the whole he would prefer the very different sound (for example) of Wilhelm Furtwängler, serves as a characterization of his musical taste as much as it does of Toscanini's work. This is as it should be, and it would be supererogatory for me to behave as if Arturo Toscanini needed *musical* defense from Horowitz's charges. In this matter, with such recordings as Toscanini made, even the best musical lawyers are surely unnecessary.

In any case, it is my impression that most of the reviewers of *Understanding Toscanini* concentrated the major part of their attention on the conductor's status as a performer and on the author's accuracy in assessing that status. Unfortunately, this narrow concentration tended to overshadow the two rather less easily demonstrated charges that Horowitz placed in his subtitle. It will therefore be my concern here to deal with the wider accusations, at once musical and cultural, that Horowitz levels against Toscanini.

The first of these two charges, and for me the less interesting, is that Toscanini collaborated with, and even cunningly manipulated, the glorification of his personal image that was such a significant factor in his career at least from his arrival at the Metropolitan Opera in 1908 to his death almost fifty years later. I suppose there can be little doubt that had Toscanini been a *gemütlich* conductor, his publicity would have reflected that fact; had he felt the musical tastes of his colleagues to have been more valuable than his own, he would have followed their tastes, not his own; had he not wished to perform before a large public, he would have refused to do so; had he not wished to earn high fees, he would not have charged them; had he not wished to make recordings, he would not have made them, and would certainly not have made so many of them. In other words, had Toscanini been different, he would have been someone else. It seems to me that there is in life a rough equivalence between professional bent, private personality, and public image, and it further seems to me that, when we are considering a career extending over decades, that equivalence becomes a virtual congruence. I would further say that even the most powerful—and often, from my standpoint, the most malign—engines of publicity manifest a deeper, though often unpalatable, truth about their beneficiaries.

The point of all this is that it seems futile to ask that Toscanini, given that he was the musician and the person that he was, should have chosen a different way to make the public career that clearly was his raison d'être. It is thus my sense that the Toscanini who can be seen in the remarkable Hupka photographs on RCA-record jackets, and the Toscanini who was ballyhooed by NBC as the world's greatest conductor conducting the world's greatest orchestra and who was, in Horowitz's ambivalent coinage, perceived as a "Culture-God," was the very same Toscanini we still hear today on records. And so it all does seem to come down to a musical judgment: what do you think of Toscanini, not as a "Culture-God," but as a conductor?

Horowitz's second charge against Toscanini, presented in his subtitle as "How He . . . Helped Create a New Audience for Old Music," strikes me as rather more significant. This charge takes many forms, even on occasion becoming vastly patronizing, as when Horowitz remarks early on that Toscanini became "the dominant figurehead for Great Music." But perhaps the most complete formulation occurs in an attack on several music critics of the day, all supporters of Toscanini and therefore among the book's chief villains. I will quote from this attack at length not just because it is an excellent summary of the position but because it well conveys the rhetorically supercharged atmosphere of *Understanding Toscanini*:

The argument now emerging was that only great music was good enough for a great conductor. The Toscanini disciples would become guardians of a canon of master-pieces—in [*Brooklyn Daily Eagle* and later *Nation* critic B.H.] Haggin's phrase, "the finest, the greatest music"—of which Toscanini was the one great purveyor. This holy of holies—even Beethoven's Violin Concerto and the "Pastoral" Symphony could not gain admittance—would comprise the best of Haydn, Mozart, Beetho-ven, Schubert, Brahms, and Wagner, with gilding by Mendelssohn, Berlioz, De-bussy, and Richard Strauss. No premiere, no enterprising revival could give greater pleasure than a certified major work. As [*New York Times* critic Olin] Downes put it upon hearing Toscanini conduct *Ein Heldenleben* following seventeen Philharmonic performances under three conductors the preceding eight seasons: "Mr. Toscanini interpreted the score for the first time in New York, and a first time by Toscanini can well be more important than a novel composition."

Horowitz's next words draw the net, or perhaps the noose, tightly around the conductor: "To give Toscanini his due, notwithstanding his admitted weakness for Italian cameos, he stuck as close to the canon of acknowledged masterpieces as any disciple could have reasonably de-sired."

There are other targets than mere music critics in Horowitz's cast of villains. He has a particularly angry pen for "music appreciation," which he seems to see as no more than the teaching of pap to pups. He takes particular pleasure in attacking the conductor Walter Damrosch, who became what we would today call a media personality by being the avuncular host of the long-running weekly daytime radio program "The NBC Music Appreciation Hour." For Horowitz, Damrosch

was in some respects all too plausible. His paternal manner (he began each lesson by intoning "Good morning, my dear children!") made him seem even older than he was. His German pedigree (born in Breslau, trained in Dresden) made him seem the more distant. . . . For his young listeners Damrosch's distant yet soothing aura per-vaded the music he appreciated. He taught music listening, not music making. Moreover, he prescribed a pantheon of dead Germans and Austrians. . . . When in 1932 Leopold Stokowski proposed broadcasting "modernistic" music to children so they could "develop a liking for it," Damrosch issued a press release "deeply deploring" Stokowski's plan. "Children should not be confused by experiments," he wrote. For Damrosch's schoolchildren, music as a contemporary art form ceased to exist except as a dilute residue of the nineteenth century.

I might add that Horowitz not only castigates the broadcasting of Damrosch's educational programs but also goes on to attack RCA for its nineteenth-century-based music-appreciation efforts and Hollywood movies for their use of classical sound track material. I must say that these strictures, when written and read in today's debased cultural atmosphere, seem nothing if not bizarre. Perhaps Dante's immortal words in the *Inferno* apply here as so often elsewhere in life: *Nessun maggior dolore,/che ricordarsi del tempo felice/nella miseria* ("There is no greater sorrow than to recall a time of happiness when in misery").

Horowitz, having tied together Toscanini, his critical supporters, the network that made his concerts possible, the label that sold his records—and even the film industry that capitalized on the resulting popularity of classical music—is ready for his culminating charge against what he sees as the Toscanini cult, disciples and all:

At least five worlds of American music were omitted from the curricula of music appreciation and of the Toscanini cult. . . . The first was . . . the come-of-age American composers of the twenties and thirties. . . . The second was a maverick sidebar to the first: rangy American originals in the tradition of Whitman and Melville, beginning with Charles Ives and including Edgard Varèse, Harry Partch, and John Cage. The third . . . was of American musical theater: Gershwin, Cole Porter, Irving Berlin, Richard Rodgers. The fourth—endorsed by [the quarterly review] *Modern Music,* Ives, and Gershwin, denigrated by highbrow music appreciators— was jazz, its precursors and forms: gospel, blues, ragtime, swing. The fifth . . . [was] the most thorough attack on the "masterwork" idea, with its elaborate distinctions between "serious" and "popular," "art" and "recreation." . . . [I]t prophetically embraced the music of Asia, Africa, and South America, accommodating listening modes more meditative or ceremonial than those of the modern West.

Here, finally, is the material to support Horowitz's earlier explanation for the course American serious music took after World War II: "Ultimately repulsed by music appreciation's new audience, and influenced by transplanted Europeans uninterested in helping to cultivate the nascent American school, future American composers would increasingly follow Schoenberg's dictum that 'All I know is that [the listener] exists, and insofar as he isn't indispensable for acoustical reasons (since music doesn't sound well in an empty hall), he's only a nuisance.' "

Thus Toscanini, because of his actions and the actions of those who stood with him, symbolized and indeed was partially responsible for a conscious rejection of major and important segments of the musical repertory, and therefore for the eventual atrophy of that repertory. If we take only the last part of this charge—the diagnosis of the present state of serious music rather than the account of how we got here—I think it is clear that Horowitz is right. The repertory *has* atrophied. Masterpieces, or what passes for them, are now central to concert programs and opera seasons. Great careers are now made only in old music, never in new. Despite all the performances that new works now receive, American music remains a stepchild of performers, administrators, and audiences; such new music as is scheduled is placed in juxtaposition to familiar works of proven attractiveness. In my own work as the director of a smallish music festival, I have found that the pressure in chamber and orchestral concerts to program the best-known compositions, played by the best-known soloists, is close to irresistible.

Here we are: but how did we get here? It is in attempting to answer this question that I think Horowitz most goes awry. Let me say at the outset that I think he goes so badly awry for two reasons: he vastly underestimates the role that *composers* have in deciding what kind of music they write, and he ignores the role that masterpieces of art, whether musical, literary, or visual, play in ensuring the continuation of civilization.

To begin with the role of composers in determining their own fate: there can be no doubt that most, if not all, composers mean for their music to be heard; they write for an audience that will appreciate their pieces during their lifetimes, and, I am convinced, for a posterity that will honor their memory by loving their music after they are dead. There can also be no doubt that being neglected is immensely painful for any creative figure. There can be no doubt that composers are happiest when their music is played, and played widely.

But—and here the qualification is all-important—it would be a great mistake to jump from this commonsense observation to the conclusion that the happiest composers are the greatest composers, that the existence of genius is a matter of being "stroked." For it is a fact that *what* composers write, and *how* they write, is in the most important sense determined primarily by what is *inside* them, not by what is *outside*. Some composers— Prokofiev comes immediately to mind—are extraordinarily dependent on the possibility of an appreciative audience; others—and surely Schoenberg takes pride of place here—give up assured success in one style to court disaster in another. In this way, as in every other, composers differ among themselves. The fact that composers *choose* how they shall appear to the world is what we mean by a composer's individuality or his personality. These two much abused terms are merely attempts at defining just what it is that sets one composer apart from another.

Composers—especially the most gifted composers—write what they want to write, and labor mightily to make a world for themselves where what they write can live. Unlike today's visual-arts vanguard, which seems to thrive on the gulling of a ravenous public, the musical avant-garde did not arise because there was a ready market for its products. The ready market has always been, and is now, for comfortable, familiar music. After all, Toscanini's wildly successful performances of the Barber *Adagio for Strings* hardly produced a flood of what might be called Barberian high romanticism in American music. For the best composers, the course of musical composition has been a matter of composers' choice, not of performers' or of audiences'.

The sad fact is that the shortfall in new music that so bothers Horowitz is a worldwide phenomenon and affects musical environments unpenetrated by the Toscanini magic. It is my own opinion that the seeds of the present condition of music were sown as far back as the nineteenth century, and chief among them was the ever-proliferating luxuriance of harmonic texture that marked the final development of consonant chromaticism. When music became maximally beautiful at each and every moment, as it finally did around the turn of our century in central Europe—*Verklärte Nacht* (1899) and the *Gurrelieder* (1901–13) of Schoenberg are towering examples of this culmination—sophisticated composers felt they had little choice but to react against the very idea of beauty itself. How audiences and performers reacted to this development in musical composition is a matter, if my pun may be forgiven, of record.

Let us return to Toscanini. What was he to do when he was faced, at middle age, with the prospect of there being very little new music to which he could make his full personal commitment? He did play much music written during his lifetime and in his own milieu: his services to Verdi, Boito, Puccini, and Catalani, among others, are well known. And what Toscanini played he played with his full heart and his full mind, not, as is the case with today's superstars, with one eye on the preconcert publicity and the other on the departing plane schedule. Would it have helped music if Toscanini had anticipated Leonard Bernstein at the New York Philharmonic during the 1960s, programming works that he felt himself obliged to mock and demean in preconcert introductions? Should Toscanini have concerned himself with the works of John Cage, or with Cole Porter, or with swing, or with Balinese gamelan music, to take examples from the musical areas Horowitz finds were neglected under Toscanini's baneful influence? Surely Cole Porter and swing were brilliantly successful without any help from Toscanini or from anyone like him; John Cage has triumphantly shown that one can be called a composer without composing very many notes of one's own; Balinese music, like other great expressions of distant folk cultures, remains of interest precisely to the extent it is kept distinct from alien musical influences—especially ours.

What then, I repeat, was Toscanini to do? His response, true as he was to himself as an artist, was straightforward: because as he grew older he could not make music out of the present, he chose to make music out of the past.[1] Here new questions arise. Was he culpable for this decision? Should he have performed new works in which he could not believe, rather than old works in which he did believe? Put another way, what is the responsibility of the most gifted performers, faced as they have been for some years now with a great past, a clouded present, and an unknown future? Perhaps the best way to begin to answer this question about musical responsibility is to talk about two duties rather than one: the duty to the old, and the duty to the new.

We might begin with the matter of duty to the old. The great period of Western musical composition, by which I mean the writing by individuals of extended works of permanent and well-nigh incontestable value, took place from the last years of the sixteenth century to just after World War I, or, in other words, from the time of Monteverdi to perhaps the time of Ravel. In these little more than four hundred years, the music that had originated in individual expression, particularism, and contemporaneity became marked by universality, widespread relevance, and timelessness. This completed phenomenon can justly be called the creation of a major part of our civilization.

A sizable portion of this aspect of civilization is the music written for the symphony orchestra and the opera company; its heroic figures, I need hardly say, are Haydn and Mozart, Beethoven and Schubert, Schumann and Brahms, Wagner and Verdi. These are the geniuses, and theirs is the achievement, that Toscanini honored throughout his long career. In zealously concentrating on this music of the past and in educating his audience in it, he paid the greatest tribute to the civilization that is by definition made up of the validated accomplishments of a former time. If we as a society—and if great musical executants as the representatives of art—have the duty to make the corpus of civilization available to everyone, then in giving engrossing performances of the highest masterpieces Toscanini was undertaking a vitally necessary activity—not just for himself and for his own career, but for us all.

But what of the duty to the new? How is that duty to be fulfilled? There are those who think that the salvation of music as a whole lies in the indiscriminate programming of *all* new music. On this analysis, it is precisely the duty of performers—and by extension the duty of audiences—*not* to make distinctions among different genres and qualities of music. Instead, the proper mode of advocacy and response is to be all-inclusive and all-accepting.

It is this kind of thinking that sees the future of chamber music in the Kronos Quartet's combination of John Zorn and Béla Bartók, the future of opera in the New York City Opera's combination of Sigmund Romberg and Arnold Schoenberg, and the future of orchestral music in the New York Philharmonic's combination of Gerry Mulligan and Beethoven. Also, according to this school of thought, there is nothing wrong with placing the rawest new music on programs cheek by jowl with the greatest masterpieces of the tradition. Such a juxtaposition is meant to demonstrate that the new is fully the equal of the old, and at the same time to cut the old down to proper size. Unfortunately, this misguided effort to advance the unfamiliar only succeeds in creating an affirmative-action ghetto for new music, a ghetto richly funded and utterly unattended.

It is hardly surprising that this state of affairs seems intolerable to living composers; it is also difficult for those music lovers who cherish the excitement of the unfamiliar. If mere numbers of first performances were all that mattered, we would now have no problems, for never have so many new works been played. But it is clear that the more new works are played, the worse is the situation in which composition finds itself.

Earlier I tried to make the case that composition is a matter of the will of the composer, not the performer. But to say that the composer rather than the performer most importantly determines what is written is not to absolve the performer of all responsibility for what the listener hears. The performer's responsibility is primarily, I think, to the musical composition, and thus inferentially to the art of music itself. However well or ill our performers of today are discharging their responsibilities to past masterpieces, it seems to me incontestable that the best new music, or more exactly the best music of the entire twentieth century, is now being poorly served.

It is not that our most successful performers and institutions totally ignore this music; in fact, many of them program it: the star-studded Metropolitan Opera double bill of *Bluebeard's Castle* and *Erwartung,* and the New York Philharmonic's contemporary music festivals of recent years, come immediately to mind. But the resulting performances are in the great majority of cases without penetration, without commitment, and without the kind of total absorption in the task that is necessary for doing *any* music. Above all, there is an absence of taking responsibility sub specie aeternitatis for what has been chosen and how it is done. The results of this easy and demeaning catholicity are all too palpable: frequent poor intonation, weak rhythm, and slack ensemble. Even when the mechanics are in place, there is a pervasive emptiness of character and spirit, and finally the communication of a not very subtle travesty of the original artworks. Is it any wonder that after such performances even sophisticated audiences cry "Send in the tunes!"?

It seems to me inescapable that new music requires of its performers the very same totality of dedication as old music, and that the newest work requires the same qualities of talent, character, and soul as the most acknowledged and familiar masterpieces. Here Toscanini's single-mindedness, so far from rendering him culpable for the present state of music, can provide a sure guide. For what really emerges from any study of Toscanini's work and life is not his undoubted ego, not his penchant for concentrating attention on himself, not his supreme irascibility, not his pleasure in living well, but rather the completeness of his commitment to his musical tasks. Proofs of this almost obsessive dedication abound, and they can be substantiated in the recollections of his orchestra players and in the recorded rehearsal excerpts now available. It is in the context of this dedication that we must hear, and I believe we must admire, Toscanini's frequent cries to the orchestra of *Vergogna!* ("Shame!")

It would be wrong to conclude without remarking that the other side of Toscanini's readiness to find failed music performance shameful is the radiant quality that always impelled him to strive for the realization of his own best idea of perfection. This quality in Toscanini is love, the quality that, directed toward God, shapes, and finally closes, the *Divine Comedy* of his transcendent compatriot, Dante. I have quoted Dante earlier, and I hope it will not seem presumptuous of me to quote in this context the last lines of the culminating *Paradiso*, written in the flowering of medieval Christianity:

> All' alta fantasia qui mancò possa;
>   ma già volgeva il mio disiro e il *velle*,
>   sì come rota ch' egualmente è mossa,
> l'amor che move il sole e l'altre stelle.
>
> [To the high fantasy here power failed;
> but already my desire and will were rolled—
> even as a wheel that moveth equally—
> by the love that moves the sun and the other stars.]

In the last analysis, it is clear that what distinguished Arturo Toscanini was the burning quality of the love he demonstrated in his work, not the pleasure he took or the self-satisfaction he found in it. We can agree or disagree with his choices of repertory, as we can disagree with the way in which he performed that which he chose. What cannot be disputed, and what is so evident from his many recordings, is the strength of the tie that bound him to his music-making. In that strength, and in that tie, must be our model. To understand Arturo Toscanini is to know something of the love he felt for music.

(*The New Criterion*, 1989)

15

ROGER NORRINGTON

AND

AUTHENTIC PERFORMANCE

In the past decade or so, the whole question of musical performance has become a matter of contention in a way it has not been since the rise after World War I of pianist Artur Schnabel, violinist Joseph Szigeti, harpsichordist Wanda Landowska, and, especially, conductor Arturo Toscanini.

Although each of these immensely successful performers had his or her own characteristic personal style, they all were perceived as in some sense "modern" rather than "romantic." In this battle, "modern" came to stand for a literal and cool (if, for many, austere) approach to the music, with an emphasis on playing each note, and realizing each performance instruction, as written by the composer. The result was an imposing presentation of the overall outline of every composition and a corresponding refusal to exploit particularly affecting individual moments.

By contrast, "romantic" connoted an approach to the music sometimes perceived as imaginative and warm (for example, in the cases of violinist Fritz Kreisler and conductors Serge Koussevitzky and Leopold Stokowski), and sometimes merely brilliant (in the cases of violinist

Jascha Heifetz and pianist Vladimir Horowitz). Whether thought to be imaginative and warm or merely brilliant, the result was a musical effect created by treating the notes as clay in the performer's hands, with a corresponding refusal to sacrifice individual features to considerations of architectonic structure.

It quickly became clear that the battle between the "moderns" and the "romantics" was not a battle between mind and heart, between science and emotion, but rather a battle among different kinds of sentiment and different means of conveying sentiment. By the 1970s, however, instead of a fierce contention among schools of performance, the struggle had degenerated into a generalized cult of personality, with each increasingly less individual performer measured artistically by commercial success in concert halls and in record stores.

One of the main efforts to fill the resultant vacuum has been the authentic-performance movement. This movement has been many years in the making and goes back at least to the beginning of our century. It is an offshoot of the early-music revival—the pushing back of the chronological frontiers of the performed repertory from Bach to the Middle Ages and even before. But while the early-music revival was concerned first with the rediscovery of unknown works, and only then with their performance, the currently fashionable authentic-performance movement concentrates on finding a different way to render music that is already widely known, and indeed much loved.

The authentic-performance movement has three components. First, there is the required employment of original instruments—instruments resembling as closely as possible those on which the music was to be played at the time of its composition. Second, there must be a reliance on what remains of the composer's original text, freed of all inadvertent error in transmission and publication, and of all subsequent editorial emendation. Finally, as currently defined, authentic performance necessitates the use of original performance styles—the complete observance of the composer's explicit indications and an untiring attempt to recover all that can be known of the unwritten, customary, and taken-for-granted methods of deciphering and implementing the written notation.

Thus, superannuated instruments are sought out and, if unavailable (or too far gone to restore), are closely copied: these extend from early organs, harpsichords, and pianos to discarded and often difficult-to-play winds, brass, and drums. Even new string instruments are not exempt from replacement by old; for though there has in fact been little, if any, development in the basic design of the instruments themselves since the time of the great seventeenth-century Italian craftsmen, in music written before 1750 or thereabouts forms of the viol family were called for that are now obsolete, and the shape and weight of the bows, as well as the materials from which strings are made, have also greatly changed over the years.

In the area of texts—the notes from which musicians play—the emphasis is on discovering the composer's intentions. To do this, it is necessary to separate, in as rigorous a fashion as possible, the composer's bare notes and directions—very much including his tempo indications—as well as the additions and modifications his earliest performers have supplied unbidden, from what later generations of editors and performers alike might provide in the way of explication, amplification, and deciphering.

Authentic-performance specialists are aware, as musicians always have been, that notes, to live, must be interpreted. The rules that guide and control this transition from printed symbols to vibrant sound make up what is called style. In authentic performances the sought-after styles, including details of rhythmic execution, instrumental techniques, and concert pitch, are those contemporaneous with the composer—the exact way a composer might have heard his works when they were first rendered, at the time of their composition or shortly thereafter, by the best and most representative executants of the day.

What I have just written, schematic as it is, is enough to suggest just how vastly different the authentic-performance movement is from what has until how been the accepted method of musical performance. Whereas the new approach is based on the use of scholarship to recapture a lost material reality of physically existing instruments, written texts, and definable styles, the best that has gone on over the past century and more in concert halls and opera houses has stressed spiritual insight—the empathic projection of the minds and talents of performers into the creative souls of great composers. In an older day, the greatest of performers were regarded, and regarded themselves, as quasi-divine beings who knew no rules to guide their instinctive furthering of the essence of the music and therefore could not be bound by them; now, despite many glib references to inspiration, for the most active of the new breed of performers, just as for the academic historians whom they so much resemble, everything is facts and rules of evidence.

The authentic-performance movement gained its first foothold in the compositions of Johann Sebastian Bach. This body of immortal music qualified in every way as a subject for scholarship: it was great; it was vast; it was well documented; it was intellectually complex; it was successful both with an educated nucleus and with a larger public. The beginnings of authentic Bach performance go back as far as the monumental late-nineteenth-century German editions of his works; the movement took a quantum leap forward after World War I, when Wanda Landowska's concerts and recordings on a specially built Pleyel harpsichord, with a tonal power and a timbral flexibility previously unknown, severed the century-old linkage of Bach's keyboard music to the formerly ubiquitous piano.

Another leap in the number of authentic performances of Bach solo and ensemble works occurred with the post–World War II explosion in electronic technology, when the introduction of magnetic tape and the LP made possible easily produced, cheap, and noise-free recordings—often by little-known artists—of the entire musical corpus. The surest sign of the triumph of the historical approach in Bach performance (in addition to the highly visible increase in the number of putatively authentic performances) has been the use of traditional instruments—in particular the piano—to sound bright, dry, and in every other possible way like the historical instruments which they so long ago replaced.

Once Bach performance had been colonized by the authenticists—and this process was essentially complete in the 1960s, by which time Bach-playing on the piano or by large orchestral forces, with the inevitably heavy dose of "feeling," was already seen as intellectually infra dig—it was only a short step to rolling the new historico-scholarly approach forward to classical and early romantic music: Haydn, Mozart, Schubert, and Beethoven.

As far as Haydn is concerned, a veritable ocean of research, much of it done by the American scholar H. C. Robbins Landon, has affected the performance of all the areas in which this composer worked, including his operas, symphonies, and string quartets. The musical effect, which can be noticed by comparing the spacious recordings of the past with the emblematically tight-sounding new recordings of Haydn symphonies by the Academy of Ancient Music under the English conductor Christopher Hogwood, has been to replace the traditional idea of the conductor as musical visionary with the up-to-date figure of the conductor as historical researcher, administrative agent, and time-beater.

Mainstream performances of Mozart, though perhaps not quite so taken over by the imperatives of scholarship, now increasingly display a thinness of sound, a stiffness of rhythm, an avoidance of sentimentality—and a laboriousness of instrumental execution—directly traceable to the new intellectual currents. For their part, the historically authentic Mozart performances now available fully demonstrate the new rationality. Once again Hogwood (who has recorded all the Mozart symphonies) is illustrative of the trend; another is the Dutch early-music specialist Frans Brueggen. To understand the immense changes in Mozart-playing that these contemporary versions document, one need only compare them with the pre–World War II recordings, at once sprightly and weighty, of the inimitable Sir Thomas Beecham.

In Schubert's music, the new development these days is the use of the fortepiano, a predecessor of the modern concert-grand piano that flourished in the last quarter of the eighteenth century and the first quarter of the nineteenth. The fortepiano, often mechanically inefficient and unreliable, is now widely praised as rich in color and vibrant in tone. As played on new recordings by one of its foremost contemporary exponents, the Singapore-born Anglo-Chinese pianist Melvyn Tan, this instrument brings to Schubert keyboard works all the spuriously fruity twangs characteristic of generations of poorly maintained upright pianos. Even if Tan is not to be held responsible for the sound of the instrument he has chosen, his performances remain flat, unfeeling, and clumsy; in this music, the pre–World War II recordings of Edwin Fischer and Artur Schnabel, for all their lack of modern scholarship, remain touchstones.

Though the conquests of the authentic-performance movement in the music of Bach, Haydn, and Mozart have been undeniable, it is the application of this new ideology to the playing of Beethoven that seems to me to raise the most important issues for our musical life. Now, more than two centuries after his birth in 1770, Beethoven has become the central composer of our Western musical tradition. In purely chronological terms, Beethoven occupies a position, looking at once backward and forward, in the middle of Western musical development from 1600 or thereabouts to the present day. It is highly likely that in concert programs his music is played more than that of any other composer. And beyond mere popularity, there can be no doubt that Beethoven's compositions, as individual works and as a total achievement, form both the basis and the very definition of three fundamental musical genres: with his nine symphonies Beethoven created our idea of the symphony, and the same can be said, mutatis mutandis, of his thirty-two piano sonatas and his sixteen string quartets (to which must be added the *Grosse Fuge* Op. 133).

Opinions may differ as to why this primacy of Beethoven in our musical life should be so universally accepted. The simplest answer will stress his unique greatness as a composer, but this explanation hardly suffices. For whatever the exact nature of his greatness, there can be little doubt that in complexity of workmanship Beethoven stands a distant second to Bach, and in refinement of expression, a distant second to Mozart. By contrast, the cynical will no doubt say that Beethoven is so popular because he is so much played, but surely this easy answer only begs the question. Others will point to the historical connection between the rise of Beethoven's popularity and the rise of the European middle classes in the nineteenth century and after, but this confuses temporal association with cause, and in any case runs the risk of reducing truly great art to mere sociology. Still others, arguably closer to the mark, will speak of the atmosphere of courage, heroism, and frequent triumph that Beethoven's music breathes and exudes. For the advocates of this position, even Beethoven's rapt and contemplative lyricism only completes the marvelous strength with which his music abounds.

But whatever the reasons for the place we accord to Beethoven, the fact of his primacy remains. And so any movement in performance that itself strives to be central must offer a convincing solution to the ever-recurring riddle: how is Beethoven's music to be performed?

Not surprisingly, given the close relationship that has always existed in England between intellectual and musical activity, many (though not all) of the new Beethoven performance currents have come from London and from there have made their way, mostly via recordings, to America and the rest of the world. To date, there are two complete recorded versions of the Beethoven symphonies (and many of individual symphonies as well) satisfying the present criteria of authenticity. They come from Roy Goodman and the Hanover Band[1] and Roger Norrington and the London Classical Players;[2] a third complete version, not yet available as a set, is by Christopher Hogwood and the Academy of Ancient Music.[3] All these recordings use period instruments, texts purged of later editorial accretions and zealously followed, and performing styles determined by the latest scholarly reports of what the available documents reveal of the codified and/or merely understood practices of Beethoven's own time.

On the whole, the critical reaction to this approach has been ecstatic. Here, we have been told in publications from the prestigious English record magazine *Gramophone* to the equally prestigious *New York Times*, is Beethoven's music *wie es eigentlich gewesen* (as it really was). Still, there are distinctions drawn among those praised, and the clear critical winner thus far in the authentic-performance derby has been Roger Norrington.

Now fifty-five, and for many years the musical director of Kent Opera, Norrington (in addition to his work with the London Classical Players) is currently chief conductor of the Bournemouth Sinfonietta, and also a busy guest conductor in England and abroad. He has been discussed in the *Gramophone* in the company of Toscanini and Karajan; for the now defunct *High Fidelity*, too, he was "the most talked-about Beethoven conductor since Toscanini"; for the *New York Times*, "No one is more admired in this [Beethoven] repertory than Mr. Norrington"; the musicologist Richard Taruskin, writing in the also defunct *Opus* (and despite his many reservations about authentic performance in general), has no doubt "that Roger Norrington is to be the next great Beethoven conductor."

So enthusiastic is the praise for this new arrival on the scene, and so inevitable is the final hegemony of the movement he represents made to seem, that the music lover may well feel he has no other recourse than to learn to like what is being offered. There is no better cure for such intellectual conformity than a bit of tough-minded listening.

As one makes one's way through Norrington's recordings of the Beethoven symphonies, one soon recognizes that they indeed sum up the authentic-performance movement. Here, to begin with, are all its characteristic tonal features: string sounds, especially when unaccompanied by the other sections of the orchestra, reminiscent of what is produced by a harmonium; raucous wind playing, marked not just by shrill tone but by gross unevenness and unpredictability; clumsy brass playing, by turns muffled and shrieking; tympani sounds resembling what happens when a beanbag is dropped on a tabletop. Overall balance between sections, assisted by the weakness of the string playing and by the brute force of (especially) the trumpets and the horns, so favors the winds and the brass that essential melodic features when played by the strings (the opening theme of the Eighth Symphony is a case in point) are often blotted out. Taken together, these attributes produce a choked, clipped sonority dependent on the booming acoustics of the recording space and on the addition of electronic resonance for any life whatsoever.

Though difficult to separate from the sound-ideal of authenticity, all the now much-admired features of the new phrasing are on these records as well: short note durations; much attention to detached playing in fast passages; strident accentuation; over-regular organization by bar-lines as a substitute for the natural flow of melodies. Tempos, as always proudly fulfilling Beethoven's own metronome markings, seem most strikingly to be chosen from a range restricted to fast, faster, and fastest. The use of the ritardando—the predictable slowing-down at ends of phrases and sections, omnipresent in romantic musical performance—is limited to the relatively few occasions when explicitly required by the composer; elsewhere—which means almost all the time—the foundation of the performance, in a way Beethoven could hardly have desired, or even imagined, is the tick-tock of the metronome.

So prevailingly headlong is the pulse in these Norrington records that Beethoven's music is made to seem a perfect representation of the sign in

Barnum's circuses, "This way to the egress." Everywhere there is a lack of breadth and space. Though the performances are short-winded, the music does not breathe. Because the music does not breathe, this quintessentially passionate music conveys no passion. All the reviewers, it is true, speak of the coruscating excitement they seem to get out of Norrington's work, but this verdict only proves how indistinguishable in modern criticism true excitement is from mere panic.

These performances are, in short, consistently bad—and what is bad about them is precisely the result of the fleshing-out of all the absurd musico-intellectual pretensions of the authentic-performance movement. Instruments existing only as copies of broken-down originals, and made with modern materials and by modern techniques, are seen as authentic; they are played by musicians trained on modern instruments, and not by the very best musicians either; implicit reliance is placed on texts of varying reliability; performing directions are taken from conflicting treatises written in many cases by pedants.

What is striking about the badness of these performances, however, is not their inadequacy as music-making or their relative inferiority to many other available recordings of the Beethoven symphonies, but rather the sameness that is made to suffuse these very different works. In Norrington's performances, there is not a jot of aesthetic or affective difference between the First Symphony (1800) and the Ninth (1822–24); for this conductor, evidently, everything must sound as if it comes out of the same hurdy-gurdy. The impression of consistency is remarkable in that it constitutes a total rejection of the principle of development in Beethoven's music. In our formerly benighted age—the period, that is, from Beethoven's life to the coming of authenticity and, now, of Roger Norrington—the composer was thought to have begun as a young man infusing classicism with the stirrings of heroic romanticism; in his middle period he was thought to have shaken his fist at the world, substituting for its rejection of him (and, in turn, for his rejection of *it*) his own will; as he approached death, it was thought that he had come to embrace life and the world, writing the unforgettable closing movement of his last great work, the String Quartet in F Major, Op. 135, under the motto *Muss es sein? Es muss sein* (Must it be? It must be).

If one finds the miracle of development in Beethoven to lie at the core
of his musical persona; if one expects performance to fulfill the duty of
making this development explicit in all its scope, variety, and depth—
then these Norrington performances are not merely bad but scandalous.
Of course, to call any artistic product a scandal today is, I am well
aware, to run the risk of paying what will be taken by many as the highest compliment. But the scandal I have in mind is nothing less than Norrington's all-out attack on the foundations of Beethoven's greatness.
Thus, in an interview in the *Gramophone* in April 1989, he spoke of the
pleasure he takes in the widespread recognition that he has succeeded in
adding humor to Beethoven's seriousness:

This is something Victorians and puritans and followers of the Ayatollah just can't
understand: that you can be deeply serious and humorous at the same time. It's the
heart of the matter. I think this idea that music should be *sehr ernst* [very serious] and
not a matter for humor all began in the Victorian era when music was an upper-class
activity that separated you from the trogs. Also, the time when all this heaviness set
in was the time religion was really being challenged in a major way, and for a while
music took over the significance of a religion—it acquired stained glass—and Wagner was the arch-priest. Now it was the "mystical world of German music"—it had
to be seen to be difficult, heavy, plush, an embodiment of authority—everything
that Beethoven was against. And certainly any authority that stands up and says
"We are right, my boy" I can't stand.

It is plain, then, that the source of the consistency with which these
records are suffused is Norrington's attempt to reconstitute Beethoven
not in the authentic terms of the reality of his times and of his artistic and
human persona, but in terms of the postmodern effort to humble once-
mighty artists, thinkers, and values. The musical—and, I would venture
to add, the human—result of Norrington's success in cutting Beethoven
down to size is to be found in the utter failure of his hasty and heedless
presentation of the most sublime moments of this music: the epic Funeral
March of the *Eroica,* the hushed transition to and triumphant arrival of
the last movement of the Fifth Symphony, and, above all, the pity-laden
Adagio and the hymnic finale of the Ninth.

It is no defense, either of Norrington or of his devotees, to adduce
Beethoven's metronome markings as justification for these musical
crimes. Any musician with experience in playing music by living com-

posers knows that of all their performance directions, metronome markings are the least viable, consistent, and trustworthy. The reasons, very
much applying to Beethoven, include distance in time from the work's
actual composition, inexperience with the requirements of performance,
a frequent disdain for the very fact of performance, and, above all, the
composer's preexisting and complete knowledge of the content and
structure of the music, a knowledge which no audience—and few performers either—can be expected to possess. Here, then, in the area of
tempo, is ultimately where the entire ideology of authentic performance
falls apart: ultimately, the interpreter must find the right tempo for himself.

If there is no composer-provided certainty of tempo, it remains true
that tempo in itself, in its direct ability to express mood and clarify structure, is the single most important determinant of the effect of a performance. The experience of listening to this music in Norrington's
execution, with its slavish reliance on Beethoven's metronome markings,
while at the same time remembering the performances of such conductors as Toscanini, Furtwängler, and Bruno Walter, is, in a sense perhaps
different from that which Shakespeare intended in *Henry V,* an experience of "minding true things by what their mockeries be."

If we have had the good fortune to hear Beethoven in great performances, we can indeed mind true things. But what if we have not had
this fortune? What if the prospective new audience—young, and for the
most part ill-educated and often ignorant—comes to music believing
what it reads in reputedly prestigious publications? What, in other
words, if the future audiences for these treasures of our civilization
think, as they are incessantly told, that they are being given the true
Beethoven, when it is really, in the most important sense, a mockery?

I do not know where the flood of contemporary performances may be
found that are now so needed to communicate this great music once
again. I do know that, for all their presumptive newness, the Norrington
Nine are merely the latest version of an old assault on the corpus of
beauty.

(*Commentary,* 1990)

PART FOUR

CRITICS AND WRITERS

16

JAMES WILLIAM DAVISON

OF THE (LONDON) TIMES

Today, we are told, is an age of criticism. In painting, both friends and foes of the new tell us that what we see cannot be comprehended without our studying the critic's notion of the art. In literature, the various flavors of structuralism and deconstruction have managed to replace the text with the exegesis. Across a wide spectrum of the arts, the whole situation curiously resembles the world of what used to be called haute cuisine: for every mouthful of the real thing, one must eat a thousand words.

In music, however, criticism does not quite occupy this exalted position. Here, paralleling the general torpor of a commercially entrenched and artistically routinized establishment, music criticism serves as the handmaiden of a celebrity-oriented audience, at its best applying academic musicology to the rationalizing of box-office success. Where critical writing is able to escape this state of elegant lackeydom, it soon finds itself boosting the new solely for the sake of its newness—even in situations where the critic himself is clearly aware of the ephemeral and trivial nature of that which he feels compelled to praise.

It was not always so. Back in the nineteenth century, when even intellectual journalism could be yellow, music critics saw themselves as passionate advocates of their own tastes, and equally passionate scourges of that which—at least according to their lights—sullied the holy shrine of art. Of course, there were consequences attendant on this extravagant willingness to praise and damn: for every friend a critic made there inevitably arose two enemies looking to get even. But there was another, more important, consequence. When one looks back a century ago at musical journalism in Berlin, Vienna, Paris, and London (or even New York and Boston), one finds polemics, controversy, anger—in short, vitality. It is hardly necessary to add that in criticism, as in art, vitality excuses nearly every sin.

A book published last year in England, and now available in this country, makes clear just how interesting and alive this music criticism was. Charles Reid's *The Music Monster*[1] is a biography of James William Davison (1813–85), the impulsive and outspoken music critic of *The Times* of London from 1846 to 1878. Reid is the author of biographies of several notable English conductors, among them Sir Thomas Beecham (1961), Sir Malcolm Sargent (1968), and Sir John Barbirolli (1971). He has also served as a music critic for several English publications, including the *Observer,* the *News Chronicle,* the *Spectator,* and *Punch.* So that the reader might form an idea of Davison as expressed in his own words, Reid has appended to his biographical material some amusing and effective, though tendentiously chosen, examples of Davison's critical writings.

Like every other critic, Davison of *The Times* did not write in a void. During the years of his journalistic career, romantic music was flourishing in Germany, Austria, and France. It was the time of Mendelssohn, Schumann, and Brahms, of Liszt and Wagner, and of Chopin and Berlioz. The past, that bugbear of our own musical life, was already a potent factor in contemporary taste; the recently dead Beethoven and Schubert, no less than the somewhat more distant Mozart and J. S. Bach, were already casting their long shadows across the decades. Among the living greats, there were major conflicts of personality and aesthetics. Early in Davison's reign the disciples of Mendelssohn and Schumann, and later the followers of Wagner and Brahms, were busy carving up the musical landscape in the names of their masters. And in the world of opera, the new winds associated with Wagner and Verdi were chasing out the musty remains of Donizetti and Meyerbeer.

Across the channel, England was still little more than a customer—the best one, to be sure—for the finest products of European composition and performance. Since Handel there had been no incontestably great composer resident and composing in England; since Purcell some hundred and fifty years earlier, no native-born composer had achieved European stature. In performance, though there were some exceptions among singers, Continental primacy seemed assured. All in all, it was as compradore auditors, impresarios, and performers that the English found their place in the world of music.

This was the situation in which Davison made his mark as a happy warrior of the pen. According to no less imposing an authority than the encyclopedist Sir George Grove, Davison "composed a great deal for orchestra, piano, and the voice, and will be remembered by some elegant and thoughtful settings of poetry by Keats, Shelley, and others." Even according to the account of the vastly less sympathetic Charles Reid, Davison was able to play the piano, read scores, and instantly identify known and little-known repertory. He was the major musical influence on Arabella Goddard, perhaps the first English pianist to make an international reputation, and became her husband in 1859. At his suggestion she brought the Beethoven Sonatas Opp. 101, 109, 110, and 111 to the attention of the English public for the first time.

Davison was a prolific writer for publications other than *The Times*. He was the editor of the *Musical World* from 1844 until his death and was also a longtime contributor to the *Saturday Review* and the *Pall Mall Gazette*. He wrote program notes for many important London concerts, producing analyses (again in Grove's words) "in support of the best and most classical taste." For Grove, Davison was a man of "keen wit and grotesque humour—often Rabelaisian enough . . . [and he was] very much of a Bohemian."

Not surprisingly, it was at *The Times*—"The Thunderer" of English newspaper history—that Davison exercised his greatest power. Like Davison, *The Times* took its duties to its readers seriously, even in music. This attitude was made explicit in a letter written to Davison by the paper's manager, Mowbray Morris, and quoted in the second volume of the magisterial *History of "The Times"*: "It is in our power," Morris wrote, "to do a great deal by way of giving the public a good musical taste, & our immense circulation, independent of any confidence that people may have in our judgment, entails upon us a very serious responsibility."

For Davison, this responsibility meant upholding the music of his youth against the encroachments of the full-blown Romanticism which, though he could hardly have known it, would find fulfillment at the end of the century and beyond in Strauss and Mahler, and even in Schoenberg. Davison's tastes were preeminently classical. Reid, though he does not give any examples, says that Davison "wrote of Handel, Mozart and Beethoven with veneration." Doubtless the late Beethoven sonatas, supreme examples of early Romanticism though they may be, were acceptable to Davison because Beethoven encapsulated their tumultuous emotions in a solid case of sonata form, fugue, and variation writing.

When Davison came to the music of Schubert, he made it clear that charm, melody, invention, and romance were in his eyes no substitute for the mastery of musical architecture:

Schubert, in some symphonies, overtures, quartets, etc., has evinced a great desire to excel in the sonata form; but he was not entirely successful. He either disdained or failed to understand thoroughly the indispensable elements of that form—clearance, consistency and symmetrical arrangement of themes, keys and episodes. Schubert, though gifted with an abundant flow of ideas, was greatly wanting in the power of concentration and arrangement. He accepted all that came to him and rejected nothing. Thus, while he is never insipid and almost always interesting, he is diffuse, obscure and exaggerated.

In discussing Schubert's C Major Symphony, Davison returned to the same point:

One important failing, it must be admitted, characterizes all Schubert's instrumental works; this is the evidence of the want of the constructive power which is the one particular quality to give value to the creative faculty. The richness of invention displayed in the symphony before us is [as] profuse as the capacity for order and arrangement is deficient; ideas crowd on one another with never-ending facility, but their purposeless repetition annuls the effect of their beauty and wearies the attention as much as their number and variety exhaust it.

In the case of Chopin, Davison oscillated between forthright criticism and cautious praise. Reid goes so far as to describe the praise as a "fib" done at a publisher's behest. In reviewing some newly published mazurkas, Davison puts his cards on the table:

The greatest art in musical composition is that which is deployed in developing or prolonging any thought that may arrive—the thought may be the result of natural ability, but the facility of using it happily—of making it give character to an extended work—or working out of it all of which it is capable—of causing it to be not only the original feature but the prevailing sentiment—this considerable faculty belongs only to the *practised* as well as gifted composer; and this faculty is utterly unexhibited by Chopin—indeed, the works of this author invariably give us the idea of an enthusiastic schoolboy whose parts are by no means on a par with his enthusiasm, who *will* be original, whether he *can* or not.

It was Mendelssohn, the musical incarnation of Victorian morality, sweetness of nature, and restraint of passion, who was for Davison the ideal of a living composer. Though Reid does mention that in 1847 Davison wrote for both the *Musical World* and *The Times* a "number-by-number analysis" of and "paean" to *Elijah*, he fails to give us any example of the formal discussion lavished on the work. But Davison's estimation of Mendelssohn, which Reid does quote, suffices to give the critic's true feelings: "Let me state my firm conviction . . . that Mendelssohn is nothing inferior to any of the most distinguished men that have influenced the progress of the [musical] art and that his name, placed by the side of Bach, Handel, Haydn, Mozart and Beethoven—the hitherto Unapproachable Five—will shine as bright and endure as long as any of them."

In the light of this praise, one can well feel the force of Davison's reaction to news of his beloved composer's death. As recounted by a French fellow music critic, the emotions ran hot:

Suddenly his looks, drawn as it were by some magnetic influence to a journal that lay half-open on the table, read these terrible words:

FELIX MENDELSSOHN BARTHOLDY IS DEAD

It is impossible to describe the cry of agony that escaped him. He rose—and fell immediately. His eyes were filled with tears, his face was ashen pale, his lips trembled, and during three hours he was attacked by successive convulsive fits, broken only by heartrending sobs and unconnected phrases, until he was brought to the verge of delirium and fever. Would that I could recount to you with the same familiar ease, the same impetuosity, all the charming traits, all the noble actions, all those details so touching and simple in the life of Mendelssohn such as I heard them one by one from the lips of my distracted friend.

If, for Davison, Mendelssohn meant perfection of spirit and intellect, Robert Schumann represented the opposite. In 1853, again in the *Musical World* (from which, curiously, most of the examples Reid gives of Davison's writings are taken, rather than from *The Times*), Davison's rejection of Schumann on formal grounds reached totality:

[W]e regret to say, bad as we consider the chamber compositions of this author, we are forced to pronounce the present orchestral work [the *Overture, Scherzo, and Finale*] still worse. Throughout the three movements, so unusually designated, we failed to recognize one musical idea. The *Overture* is the weak first movement of a symphony; the movement in C sharp a weaker *Scherzo*, and the last movement a weak *Finale*. The general style betrays the patchiness and want of fluency of a tyro; while the forced and unnatural turns of cadence and progression disclose neither more nor less than the convulsive efforts of one who has never properly studied his art to hide the deficiencies of early education under a mist of pompous swagger. The whole work is unworthy of analysis, since it has no merit whatsoever. . . .

For Franz Liszt, too, Davison had nothing but contempt. Here the attack was not strictly musical. Davison seemed to see Liszt as a betrayer of the desire for salvation and the godhead:

Turn your eyes, reader, to any one composition that bears the name of Liszt if you are unlucky to have such a thing on your pianoforte and answer frankly, when you have examined it, if it contains one bar of genuine music. Composition indeed!— decomposition is the proper word for such hateful *fungi* which choke up and poison the fertile plains of harmony, threatening the world with drowth—the world that pants for "the music which is divine" and can only slake its burning thirst at the "silver fountains" of genuine, flowing melody—*melody*, yes, melody, *absolute* melody.

Over many years, Davison linked Liszt with Wagner as what can only be called twin representatives of the Antichrist. Perhaps no other words of Davison in this book go so far as these to demonstrate the exalted theological role the artist occupied in the middle of the nineteenth century, and the extent to which that role could be seen as sacrilegious rather than sacrosanct: "Liszt has been ordered to Zurich by his master, Richard Wagner. The *Nibelungen* [sic] is rapidly progressing, and the unhappy piano-king (who has recently been perpetuating some orchestral symphonies and a festival Mass, in humble emulation of the Zukunft) is obliged to be present at the parturition. Where are the other wise men?"

Davison was hardly as unambivalent in his attitude to Wagner as he was to Liszt. Early Wagner—the operas written before the *Ring*, (1853–74), *Tristan und Isolde* (1859), *Die Meistersinger* (1867), and *Parsifal* (1882)—was anathema to Davison. *Tannhäuser* (1845) was a particular devil for him, as he made clear in an 1854 review of the passage known as "The Entrance of the Guests into the Wartburg":

As, according to some transcendentalists it is the mission of Richard Wagner to announce to the world "the music of the future," he merits attention. But for that we should have dismissed the present composition with a line, which is as much as it is really worth. A more commonplace, lumbering and awkward thing of its kind we never perused. . . .

Towards the end this puerile, Frenchified, patchy tune is resumed with all the pomp and stridency of the Wagnerian full orchestra (by which we mean one much noisier and much thinner than the legitimate full orchestra). The rest of the march is quite worthy of the above; and, at the end, the violins are screaming up to B flat in *alt* . . . as is Mr. Wagner's frequent and disagreeable custom. *There* is a "future" for you, O musicians!

Davison kept up his hostile position toward Wagner well into the preparations for the first complete performance of the *Ring* in Bayreuth in 1876. But in the summer of that year, actually on the scene as "Our Special Correspondent" for *The Times*, he began to change his mind. He still had his reservations, mainly because of what he saw as the inability of Wagner's music to possess meaning apart from the action on the stage. Now, however, for the first time Davison shows himself capable of praise for the composer's achievement:

[I]n the course of a single scene, more than one personage, incident or emotion is brought back to the mind, at times almost simultaneously; the themes, or such fragments of them as may be suitable, are ingeniously interwoven. This is accomplished by the poet-musician with consummate artistic propriety and often produces an indescribably beautiful effect.

The funeral march that accompanies the body of Siegfried is . . . impressive and sublime. The melody sung by the Rhinemaidens . . . in seven-bar rhythm is charming; and, indeed, all the music that characterizes the presence of these charming beings is as airy and elementary as themselves. . . .

Still, unlike other converts to Wagnerism, Davison retained enough distance from the wonders onstage to be able to characterize the artistic phenomenon with a sure touch:

In his anxious desire to exhibit the musician as the poet's humble slave, Wagner not only prevents him from soaring to the highest regions of fancy but, by crushing the buds of melody as they spring up, buds that might blossom into seemly flowers, cramps the manifold resources of expression which are the golden heritage of art. True, the serene arch-dramatist in the *Ring des Nibelungen,* with becoming self-abnegation, practises this to his own detriment, for he, too, possesses abundant melody, if not Orphean, like Mozart's, or coming directly from the innermost sources of his being, like the endless melody of Beethoven, is at least sufficiently frank, independent and alluring not to submit gracefully to the treatment it receives at his hands. Wagner allows his melody to awaken expectation by an opening phrase but seldom or never rounds off and finishes that phrase so as at once to delight and satisfy the ear. His principal charm, in fact, is the unexampled, almost magical colouring of the orchestra, which keeps us enthralled and spellbound to the last—though speculating rather than understanding, disposed to marvel rather than to sympathize.

Strangely, though Davison enthusiastically welcomed Wagner's London appearances in the spring of 1877 at the Royal Albert Hall, he nevertheless published at the same time—albeit under a pseudonym—skeptical excerpts from his diary written during the Bayreuth performances the preceding summer. The impression given by these random jottings was that of a bemused spectator of a zoo containing marvels of wonder, if not of beauty. Davison's final words on Wagner, at least as far as the present book is concerned—taken from a letter written after his retirement from *The Times* and just two years before his death—return to his earlier positions: "The music of *Parsifal* is simply execrable. I have entirely changed my opinion about the book. Gurnemanz is an absolute bore and Parsifal an insipid donkey—not the Parsifal of genuine romance. Kundry alone redeems the thing from hopeless inanity."

Davison's harsh words about contemporary opera were not confined to Wagner. Indeed, his words about Verdi's *Rigoletto* on the occasion of its first London performance in 1853 have gone down in the history of music criticism as a colossal error of prediction:

There is little offensive music in *Rigoletto;* the ears are seldomer stunned than in most of the composer's other works, and there is, we fancy, little pretence in the writing. Nevertheless, Verdi's sins are apparent in every scene. Poverty of ideas, an eternal effort at originality—never accomplished—strange and odd phrases, lack of colouring, and a perpetual swagger in the dramatic effects, are unmistakably true Verdi. . . . With all that has been accomplished for *Rigoletto* by the directors of the Royal Italian Opera, it cannot live. It may flicker and flare up for a few nights . . . but it will go out like an ill-wicked rushlight and leave not a spark behind. Such is our prophecy for *Rigoletto!*

Never one to let consistency hobble his writing, Davison went on to express favorable thoughts about Verdi's pot-boiling *Hymn of the Nations,* a stringing together of assorted anthems from England, France, and Italy. And the old curmudgeon even found some good words to say for Verdi when *Aida* was performed for the first time in London in 1876: "He is still, happily, the Verdi of our long remembrance, our own Verdi, and may he continue to remain so."

Throughout *The Music Monster* it is clear that Reid is out of sympathy with Davison's musical judgments; the critic's unmitigated rejection of *Rigoletto* especially excites his scorn. But the book is an indictment of Davison in other ways as well. Reid accuses him of taking bribes from musicians in return for favorable treatment. Sometimes the bribes Reid has in mind are no more than dinners and trinkets; in two other instances he provides examples in which Davison was offered cash by composers. The cash, it seems, was quickly returned. Reid makes rather more of the trinkets:

As to the "presents" that came Davison's way there is a revelatory passage in *The Times* official history. This tells us that Francis Hueffer, who ultimately succeeded him as *The Times* music critic, had to engage a four-wheeler [cab] to carry back to musicians the presents which, in accordance with previous practice, were brought to his door. It adds that under Hueffer the suggestion of corruption to which Davison had laid himself open entirely ceased.

Unfortunately, Reid neglects to inform his readers that his paraphrase from *The History of "The Times"* might have read differently had he taken into account the phrase which prefaces the anecdote: "It may not be true, as Mrs. Hueffer is reported to have said. . . . " It might be added, too, that the phrase "in accordance with previous practice" does not appear in any form in *The History of "The Times."*

Whatever the exact state of Davison's journalistic ethics, it seems difficult to convict him of behavior very much outside the norm of the critics of his day. Doubtless the practices of our own times are more subtle; cash bribes and expensive presents may well be a thing of the past in music criticism. But surely there are less *éclatant* ways in which critics' opinions are influenced in favor of composers and performing institutions. We apply to these ways the honorific names of trips, papers, seminars, and conferences. It all goes, not under the dirty flag of corruption, but under the banner of creating a favorable atmosphere in which art may be practiced. The present methods of stroking the critic cannot be called bribery because the critic is free to write against even his most gracious hosts. But when he does write negatively in the face of the hospitality he has received, he opens himself to the charge of biting the hand that feeds him; when in all good faith he writes well of occasions on which he has been entertained, his writings lack credence with a musical public that has its own good reasons for cynicism.

The gravamen of Reid's charge against Davison, however, is not moral; it is intellectual. It is that Davison was dreadfully wrong about the music he heard. Reid is quite clear about the reason for such a serious accusation:

> My opening sentence spoke of Davison as a musical monster. There were, I must allow, redeeming glints, the brightest being his adoration of Mendelssohn. . . . But a critic is to be judged by his response to the music of his own day. Davison grew up and lived to the end in parallel with the efflorescence of Romantic music, one of the most startling and joyous chapters in the history of mankind. His hatreds and deridings of the Romantic masters were equally startling but a lamentable inversion of all that is joyous.

It seems to me that two charges, not one, are contained here. The more obvious one, of course, is that Davison heard greatness and denied its stature. Schubert, Schumann, Chopin, Verdi—these were giants of Davison's musical experience, and to one degree or another, by hearing so little of the beauty in them, he rejected them all. Davison thus becomes the opposite of the critic of modern myth who successfully singles out the artistic giants of tomorrow. Instead of identifying winners, Davison found fault with everything.

But there surely is more to being a critic than making winning selections. A critic must describe the music he hears in a way that captures its essential nature. When we read today what Davison wrote about many years ago on its appearance, we cannot help but notice how often he got salient musical features right even when he missed what was beautiful—and got them right in a way that still seems to shed light. His comments, for example, about Schubert's lack of comfort in working with the sonata form strike home to any pianist who has spent years working on even the best of the composer's sonatas. Similarly, Davison's animadversions on Chopin's shortcomings in "developing or prolonging any thought that may arrive" will appear with particular force to anyone who has seriously listened to the wanderings of the central section of the first movement of the Polish composer's otherwise very beautiful B Minor Piano Sonata. The structural weaknesses in all too many of Schumann's works are so widely known as not to require mention; significantly, it has proven difficult, if not impossible, until the present day to perform his symphonies without altering, often radically, their orchestration.

Davison's remarks about Liszt's "hateful *fungi* which choke up and poison the fertile plains of harmony" catch something of the composer's restless and even morbid chromaticism. They also seem to go even further, and suggest Davison's recognition of, and antipathy to, Liszt's vision (shared with Wagner) of the unity of love and death. In this regard, it is relevant to cite the lines of the poet Uhland—from the poem "Seliger Tod" ("Blessed Death")—which Liszt used for the second of his three *Liebesträume* (1850), originally written as songs and then later as piano pieces:

Gestorben war ich	[I had died
Vor Liebeswonn,	Of love-rapture,
Begraben lag ich	I lay buried
In ihren Armen;	In her arms;
Erwecket ward ich	I was awakened
Von ihren Küssen,	By her kisses,
Den Himmel sah ich	Heaven I saw
In ihren Augen.	In her eyes.]

As for Wagner, certainly it can be said that, for all its merits, *Tannhäuser* is not a transcendent work, that it still carries with it much baggage of the composer's fustian youth. There can be no doubt at all that, were it not for Wagner's works subsequent to it (and *Lohengrin*, 1848), we would view it as an interesting work by a minor composer. Davison's description of the *Ring* at Bayreuth in 1876 fully deserves *The Times* history's tribute: "[D]espite his mistrust of everything associated with the name of Wagner, he wrote a series of accounts which are masterly on the informative side. Indeed, that dated August 20, which sums up the impressions of a first hearing of *The Ring,* is something more. It contains much just and intelligent criticism which could only have been made by one who had studied the scores and listened attentively to the performances."

Perhaps nowhere else is *The Times* history's verdict—"On the whole it may be said of Davison that he began a tendency in the paper's music criticism, noticeable ever since, to swim against the tide of popular favour"—more clearly exemplified than in this "monster's" judgment of the early works of Verdi. It goes without saying that they were, are, and doubtless will be, enormous popular successes; it is also plain that their greatness lies in their appeal to a common (in the sense of widespread and shared) taste. As with Wagner's earlier operas, today we do not judge *Rigoletto* through mid-nineteenth-century ears. Instead we judge all of Verdi on the basis of our knowledge of the incomparably more elevated and greater *Otello* and *Falstaff,* which Verdi wrote approximately forty years after *Rigoletto.*

So the charge against Davison is not that he *mistook* the works of these masters; it is rather that he didn't *like* them. This charge merges almost indistinguishably into another, and more serious, accusation. It is that Davison preferred the old to the new, and in so doing defaulted on the responsibility of the critic to the present and the future.

Here is a charge to strike fear into the heart of every critic who cares for the good opinion of his peers, and who, in the words of Macbeth, has " . . . brought/Golden opinions from all sorts of people,/Which would be worn now in their newest gloss,/Not cast aside so soon." Unfortunately, a critic who capitulates in the face of pressure to be upbeat about the new on principle becomes little more than a mirror image of the critic who, again on principle, always chooses the old. Both critics—the lover of the new and the lover of the old—treat their own tastes as arbitrary extensions of will, as if to like a particular kind of art one only had to want to do so badly enough. To say of Davison that he should have liked the new music he heard, the music that was taking Europe by storm, is to ask that he should have made his musical decisions arbitrarily rather than on the basis of his talents, his training, and his preferences. Had he done so, he would have been both less accurate as a critic and vastly less interesting to read.

We are always being told that the new, in order to survive, must be boosted. Malign consequences are everywhere seen to result from lack of critical encouragement, and whole books—most notably Nicolas Slonimsky's *Lexicon of Musical Invective* (1953)—have been devoted to documenting critical rejections of what later turned out to be great composers and their music. Reid himself makes an absurd claim for Davison's long-term influence on the taste of the musical public:

In Davison's day readers of *The Times* and the *Musical World* went to those prints as founts of truth and good sense. Nor was his spell confined to his own day. It long survived him. Until middle age I myself spurned Chopin. From Chopin recitals I stayed away, explaining to Chopinite friends that I did not wish to be smothered with scented cushions. In the case of Liszt, sedulously remembered as a "womanizer" and nothing else, I substituted for "scented cushions" the phrase "scented pillow slips." Both gibes were reflections of Davison animosities which, dutifully cultivated and spread, continued to hold sway during much of the following century.

From Reid's words one could form no idea that the composers most reviled by Davison were, and are, the great staples of the musical repertory, or that our problems in finding a viable new music stem not from the rejection of greatness but from its very triumph. More important—at least in evaluating Reid himself as a critic—is the curious phenomenon of a writer on music being so easily beguiled, not by music, but by words written about music.

Just because we do seem to lack both successful new music and a fresh stock of old masterpieces, it could be said that most of what we have in music today *is* words—measured words, scholarly words, judicious words, and, above all, printed words. What all these words about music add up to can be seen from even a cursory perusal of the pages of the *Gramophone,* England's grand old auntie of a record-review magazine. Here, in balanced tributes to old composers from Albinoni to Zandonai, twentieth-century composers from Malcolm Arnold to Bernd Alois Zimmermann, and performers from Ashkenazy to Zukerman, one can catch a sufficient whiff of the boredom from which music criticism suffers today; nothing is the greatest, nothing is the worst, but everything is heart-warming and hopeful. Faced with all this good feeling, a mere music lover might be pardoned for preferring that old music monster, J. W. Davison.

(*The New Criterion,* 1985)

JAMES HUNEKER

AND AMERICA'S MUSICAL

COMING-OF-AGE

Imagine a small child, said by some to be musically precocious, as he sat at a Steinway grand piano more than forty years ago, vainly attempting to show interest in practicing some small pieces of Chopin. The California sun was shining outside, the day was short, and the practice hours long. The demands of a doting mother and of a piano teacher of the old Russian school were strict even when not severe, and to the child the prospect of a lifetime of practice just possibly someday making perfect seemed dull indeed.

But wait. As the child stared sadly at the music before him, he found something more in those assorted yellow-bound volumes published by G. Schirmer than mere notes, the uninvited causes of his labors; there were words, too, enchanting descriptions of the Polish composer's music. Indeed, the greatness and romance the child could hardly find emerging from his own exertions he found in the words the kind publisher had provided:

During the last half of the nineteenth century two men became rulers of musical emotion, Richard Wagner and Frédéric-François Chopin. The music of the Pole is the most ravishing in the musical art. Wagner and Chopin; the macrocosm and the microcosm. Chopin, a young man, furiously playing his soul out upon the keyboard, the soul of his nation, the soul of his time, is the most individual composer who ever set humming the looms of our dreams. . . . Chopin is not only the poet of the piano-forte, he is the poet of music. . . .

There were exciting words, too, for the child about the individual pieces that sat so resistantly on the music-desk of the piano. Descriptions of the pieces the child was attempting to play were understandably the first sought out; here, alas, the child was disappointed, for the commentator's major efforts were devoted to those works of Chopin's which lay beyond the child's technical command and physical grasp. But what magical comments there were for other, indubitably more exciting, compositions, compositions which, with practice, might well be performable when weak fingers were stronger and small hands were larger. Of the C-sharp Minor Waltz, Op. 64, No. 2, for example, the child read: "The veiled melancholy of the first theme has seldom been excelled by the composer. It is a fascinating lyric sorrow, and the psychologic motivation of the first theme in the curving figure of the second theme does not relax the spell. A space of clearer skies, warmer, more consoling winds are in the D-flat interlude; but the spirit of unrest soon returns. The elegiac note is unmistakable in this veritable soul dance."

The reader need remain in suspense no longer. The child so eager to read that the practice hours might pass more quickly was I; more important, the writer of the delicious and educative words that caused my time to move so profitably was James Huneker, a critic not just of music but of literature, drama, and painting, and one whose historical position as our leading evangelist of the arts remains as firm today as it was at the time of his death in Brooklyn in 1921 at the age of sixty-four.

The coming of intellectual age which Huneker's florid notes in the Schirmer Chopin edition helped to hasten for me parallels, in a small way, the major contribution he is credited with making toward the maturity of American cultural taste in the years before World War I. Indeed, the present received opinion of Huneker was voiced by H. L. Mencken, who liked to see himself as a prophetic figure in America's passage from provincialism to cosmopolitanism. In 1917, Mencken wrote of Huneker: "If the United States is in any sort of contact today, however remotely, with what is aesthetically going on in the more civilized countries—if the Puritan tradition, for all its firm entrenchment, has eager and resourceful enemies besetting it—if the pall of Harvard quasi-culture, by the Oxford manner out of Calvinism, has been lifted ever so little—there is surely no man who can claim a larger share of credit for preparing the way. . . . " Mencken's claim is a large one, one that invites consideration of its truth in its own time. It also invites consideration for its relation to our putatively different musical life today. And so my task here will be to examine Huneker's critical career, chiefly with reference to music, but with examples drawn from his writings about the other arts as well, to see just how far forward he did indeed bring our attitudes toward high culture; I shall be concerned also to evaluate just what this artistic coming-of-age meant for the exact nature of American musical taste then—and now.

James Huneker was born in Philadelphia in 1857, the son of middle-class parents, German or Hungarian on his father's side, Irish on his mother's. Part of his inheritance was Fenian, for his maternal grandfather was a prominent Irish patriot who had emigrated from County Donegal in 1820; part was music-loving and art-loving, for his father knew the pianists Sigismond Thalberg and Louis Moreau Gottschalk and the violinist Henri Vieuxtemps. The senior Huneker also owned a large collection of mezzotints, line engravings, etchings, and lithographs, including work by Lucas van Leyden, Dürer, and Rembrandt. His mother, a devout Roman Catholic who had been a schoolteacher before her marriage, wrote well and read omnivorously. Encouraged by his mother, from his earliest days the young Huneker got on well with Jews, studying Hebrew toward a possible future vocation as a priest. In much later life he responded to an Irish streetcar conductor who described an attractive and hilly neighborhood through which the vehicle was passing as "Kike's Peak" with the words, "God was ever good to the Irish and to his own."

The young Huneker did not have an easy time in school, and made abortive attempts at becoming a railroad engineer, a lawyer, and a piano salesman. He had more success reading literature, quickly becoming acquainted with the work of Poe, Baudelaire, Gautier, and Flaubert. In the spring of 1878 Huneker visited Walt Whitman in nearby Camden, but his father, aware of Whitman's dubious reputation, quickly put an end to the relationship. He was fascinated by the theater, which was in lively shape in Philadelphia in those prefilm and pretelevision days. But his real love was music. He took piano lessons and reveled in the locally produced chamber-music evenings, during which professional musicians played to an enthusiastic audience of amateurs. And while still in his teens, he started to write. His first effort, published in the *Evening Bulletin*, was a report of one such concert.

The 1876 Centennial Exposition in Philadelphia whetted the young Huneker's appetite for travel and experience of the wider world. To his already remarkably cosmopolitan upbringing he now added a year of piano studies in Paris at the end of the 1870s. Though later in life he taught piano in New York at Jeannette M. Thurber's National Conservatory of Music (upon the recommendation of Rafael Joseffy, the Chopin authority and pupil of Liszt), as a student Huneker wasn't good enough to gain admittance to the Paris Conservatoire; instead he had to content himself with auditing the class of Georges Mathias, a student of Chopin himself. As it has done for so many susceptible young Americans in the past two centuries, Paris opened Huneker's mind even further to the new in music, literature, and the visual arts.

Huneker, of course, was hardly cut out by either nature or nurture to be an expatriate. But when he returned to the United States he found Philadelphia dull, despite its many musical activities. By now a writer for Theodore Presser's *Etude* magazine, Huneker cast longing eyes toward New York, then as now the center of American music. Finally, in 1886, he moved to New York, there to embark on the career of free-lance critic, which was to describe his way of life and thought for the next thirty-five years.

In New York, Huneker was caught up in a musical maelstrom. The new Metropolitan Opera House on Broadway and Thirty-ninth Street had opened in 1883 with a performance of Gounod's *Faust*; by 1892 all of Wagner's major works (save *Parsifal*) had been given there, and in the 1890s Metropolitan casts for both German and Italian operas reached a level of international distinction only rarely equaled since. In orchestra life, there were numerous and regular concerts by the New York Symphony under the leadership of the Damrosch family, and by the New York Philharmonic under Theodore Thomas in the 1880s and Anton

Seidl in the 1890s. After 1887, the Boston Symphony played as many concerts annually in New York as did the Philharmonic. The opening of Carnegie Hall in 1891 was marked by a visit from Tchaikovsky, who conducted there his *Marche Solonnelle*, the Third Orchestral Suite, and the B-flat Minor Piano Concerto. European artists were beginning to live in New York as well. Joseffy, who was born in Hungary, settled in New York after his 1879 debut under Leopold Damrosch; in the early 1890s the great Lithuanian-born pianist Leopold Godowsky established residence in New York, where he taught at the New York College of Music; from 1892 to 1895 the Czech composer Antonin Dvořák was the director of the celebrated National Conservatory.

In the year of Huneker's arrival he attended the American premiere of Wagner's *Tristan und Isolde* at the Metropolitan Opera House, paying for a top-gallery ticket by pawning his overcoat. For all his many literary interests, music was his life. Soon after coming to New York he told a story in the *Etude* of a pianist on his deathbed who, asked by a priest whether he was a Catholic or a Protestant, answered: "Father, I am a pianist." In recounting this story, Arnold Schwab, Huneker's invaluable and indefatigable biographer, remarks that Huneker's reply "illustrates his own attitude toward religion"; it seems at least as likely that it illustrates Huneker's own attitude toward music and the piano.

For the next decade and more Huneker bathed in the heady cultural waters of a New York now beginning to combine the economic progress of a century of American independence with the contributions of the successive waves of immigrants—Irish, German, central European, Balkan, Mediterranean, and Jewish—who were now placing their imprints on our nation. He reveled in the life of the little family hotels, where excellent table d'hôte dinners could be found in the company of artists and intellectual dreamers. Always a lover of Pilsener beer, he was a great saloon-goer, and there too he sampled New York's melting pot. As Huneker's biographer writes: "At Justus Schwab's greasy saloon near the German neighborhood of Tompkins Square, Huneker hobnobbed with French communards, Spanish and Italian refugees, German socialists, and Russian politicals."

All this time Huneker continued to write prolifically for newspapers and periodicals, as he was to do for the rest of his life. By 1899 he was ready to publish *Mezzotints in Modern Music*, his first of some twenty-one books. Two of these books were collections of previously published short fiction; three (among them a short history of the New York Philharmonic) were journalistic hack jobs; one consisted of two volumes of memoirs; and one was a remarkable novel, published shortly before he died. The remainder of Huneker's books were collections of essays on European subjects, based upon his free-lance articles, many of them on recent and romantic music but many also on the new dramatists of the 1890s, modern and classical painters, French and English literature, and the philosophy of Nietzsche.

Echoing in its title his father's collection of black-and-white art, *Mezzotints in Modern Music* established the framework for a critical career of remarkable intellectual consistency. It begins with a ringing article called "The Music of the Future." Curiously for a hotheaded lover of the new in art, but significantly for his critical development, Huneker's projected future seemed to belong to Johannes Brahms, not Richard Wagner. In praising Brahms, then perceived as Wagner's archenemy and artistic opposite, Huneker put his facility for purple prose at the service of an unwavering classic position: "Brahms reminds one of those medieval architects whose life was a prayer in marble; who slowly and assiduously erected cathedrals, the mighty abutments of which flanked majestically upon mother earth, and whose thin, high pinnacles pierced the blue; whose domes hung suspended between heaven and earth, and in whose nave an army could worship, while in the forest of arches music came and went like the voices of many waters."

Elsewhere in *Mezzotints in Modern Music* Huneker is nothing if not eclectic. He writes at length about Tchaikovsky, Richard Strauss, and Nietzsche, Chopin, Liszt, and Wagner, mixing praise and reservations. Even when his reservations are quite severe, the prevailing tone is one that encourages the reader to seek out the music for himself. Thus, in the case of Tchaikovsky, when Huneker finds himself unable to understand the second and third movements of the "Pathétique" Symphony—he describes the five-four meter of the second as "a perverted valse, but one that could not be danced to unless you owned three legs"—he still can find the movement "delightfully piquant music," and call the "touch of

Oriental color in the trio . . . very felicitous." And for the famous last movement, Huneker pulls out all the stops of exalted fin-de-siècle literary morbidity:

Since the music of the march in the Eroica, since the mighty funeral music in Siegfried, there has been no such death music as this "adagio lamentoso," this astounding torso, which Michel Angelo would have understood and Dante wept over. It is the very apotheosis of mortality, and its gloomy accents, poignant melody and harmonic coloring make it one of the most impressive of contributions to mortuary music. It sings of the entombment of a nation, and is incomparably noble, dignified and unspeakably tender. It is only at the close that the rustling of the basses conveys a sinister shudder; the shudder of the Dies Irae when the heavens shall be a fiery scroll and the sublime trump sounds its summons to eternity.

Huneker waxes enthusiastic about Richard Strauss's 1896 tone poem *Also sprach Zarathustra*, clearly relishing the linkage between Strauss's music and Nietzsche's iconoclastic philosophy. For Huneker the composition is

the gigantic torso of an art work for the future. Euphony was hurled to the winds, the Addisonian ductility of Mozart, the Théophile Gautier coloring of Schumann, Chopin's delicate romanticism, all were scorned as not being truthful enough for the subject in hand, and the subject is not a pretty or sentimental one. Strauss, with his almost superhuman mastery of all schools, could have written with ease in the manner of any of his predecessors, but, like a new Empedocles on Aetna, preferred to leap into the dark, or rather into the fiery crater of truth.

Overall, Huneker stresses Strauss's achievements in gaining control over "the indefiniteness of music," and in giving "an emotional garb to pure abstractions." In the end, Huneker is under no illusion that in the union between the superman-poet and superman-composer there can be any winner but the music. His words once again emphasize a belief in the primacy of music: "Poor, unfortunate, marvelous Nietzsche! But it is Strauss mirroring his own moods after feeding full on Nietzsche, and we must be content to swallow his title, 'Also sprach Zarathustra,' when in reality it is 'Thus Spake Richard Strauss!' "

From Strauss, Huneker moves back to Chopin, thus embarking on a course he was to take often in his life. Always determined to defend Chopin against charges that he was a sentimental miniaturist, Huneker looks for "the greater Chopin," the classic master of noble forms and large emotions. This Chopin he finds in such then less-played works as the F-sharp Major Impromptu, the three Polonaises (those in F-sharp Minor, A-flat Major, and the Polonaise-Fantasy in A-flat Minor), the Preludes, and the Scherzi. Quick to find the equivalents between creators in different arts, Huneker compares Chopin with Poe. For him they both were "[e]xquisite artificers in precious cameos . . . of a consanguinity because of their devotion to Our Ladies of Sorrow, the Mater Lachrymarum, the Mater Suspiriorum and the Mater Tenebrarum of Thomas de Quincey. If the Mater Malorum—Mother of Evil—presided over their lives, they never in their art became as Baudelaire, a sinister 'Israfel of the sweet lute.' Whatever their personal shortcomings, the disorders of their lives found no reflex beyond that of melancholy."

If Huneker loves Chopin, he only likes Liszt. Somewhere he sees Liszt as a mountebank both spiritual and musical. Even when describing the B Minor Sonata, the Liszt piano work he most admires, he cannot help remarking on the composer's insincerity. This insincerity is shown in the appearance of "the sigh of sentiment, of passion, of abandonment which engenders the notion that when Liszt was not kneeling before a crucifix, he was before a woman." Huneker is fascinated by Liszt's path-breaking Transcendental Etudes and Concert Etudes, but it is significant that he ends his *Mezzotints* chapter on etudes for the piano by advising pianists to "play the Chopin études, daily, also the preludes, for the rest trust to God and Bach. Bach is the bread of the pianist's life; always play him that your musical days may be long in the land."

Finally, of course, there is Wagner. Huneker is at great pains to separate the composer from his literary utterances: "Keep in your mind that Wagner the artist was a greater man than Wagner the vegetarian, Wagner the anti-vivisectionist, Wagner the revolutionist, the Jew hater, the foe of Meyerbeer and Mendelssohn, and greater than Wagner the philosopher." Huneker finds Wagner "a poet of passion," though he does not admire the composer's librettos. In a mixed tribute to the composer, Huneker closes *Mezzotints* with a kind of surrender: "We are the slaves of our age, and we adore Wagner because he moves us, thrills and thralls us. His may not be the most spiritual art, but it is the most completely fascinating."

Huneker's second book is devoted to Chopin. Called *Chopin: The Man and His Music*, the book, published in 1900, attempts to serve as biography, study of the composer's psychology, and brief description of each piece in his oeuvre. What Huneker achieves in this book is not scholarship, reasoned consideration of his idol, or even a real book; rather he is here the piano aficionado, the worshiper at the sacred fount of the keyboard. For him, the Etudes are "Titanic Experiments"; the Preludes are "Moods in Miniature"; the Nocturnes describe "Night and its Melancholy Mysteries"; the Ballades are "Faëry Dramas"; the Polonaises are "Heroic Hymns of Battle"; the Mazurkas are "Dances of the Soul"; the Scherzi are "Chopin the Conqueror." The end of the book is a tribute to the immortality of art and the artist, thrown into the void of the future: "He did not always succeed, but his victories are the precious prizes of mankind. One is loath to believe that the echo of Chopin's magic music can ever fall upon unheeding ears. He may become old-fashioned, but, like Mozart, he will remain eternally beautiful."

Huneker's two books of short fiction, the 1902 *Melomaniacs* and the 1905 *Visionaries,* convey by their titles something of the overheated, extravagant, and bizarre atmosphere of the stories they contain. The most significant influence on Huneker's style—in addition to Poe—was Joris Karl Huysmans, whose 1884 novel *A rebours* still seems, a century later, the most important example of *l'esprit décadent.* To the classic symbolist—and later decadent—brew of voluptuousness, febrile nervosity, indulgence in drugs and alcohol, obsessive seeking after sensation, and satanism, Huneker adds the triumph of music as queen of the arts by putting in melomania—a crazed involvement in music whereby the art of tone becomes an all-consuming, destructive passion.

In these forty-four stories (several more are scattered through the books of essays), Huneker presents an asylum gallery of artists, along with the trapped members of their families. His protagonists are varied, though curiously repetitive. A composer creates a music so emotionally powerful that its performance in Paris causes a conflagration that destroys the city. A pianist, now surviving by playing in a cheap restaurant, tells of his drunken and botched debut, caused by his awareness the evening before that his coming failure would kill his parents. A soothsayer creates a new art—the eighth deadly sin—out of perfumes. A mad

Russian scientist uses fireworks to make a world-conquering beauty, but the fireworks go out of control and kill the watching thousands. An Irish priest is taken to a Greek Orthodox baby who turns out to be the Antichrist; by baptizing the child the priest destroys the creature's spell. Perched between the mock-serious and the dead-serious, these stories now seem too artificial to compel attention, but in their day they must have caused many a maiden—and bachelor, too, for that matter—to shiver. Again, they testify to the gathering strength of art as a religious mania. Despite their slight value as literature, Huneker's stories do make clear an important change in turn-of-the-century opinion about the significance of music and the other arts: from merely expressing tragedy, they have progressed to causing it.

Increasingly, the word *anarch* becomes central for Huneker, who lays stress upon the idea of the great artistic creator as totally self-governing. Thus *Overtones*, his 1904 collection of essays, is dedicated to Strauss, whom Huneker calls in the dedication "An Anarch of Art." Strauss's overlordship is shown in his "cold, astringent voluptuousness." Huneker goes on to write: "He himself may be a Merlin,—all great composers are ogres in their insatiable love of power,—but he has rescued us from the romantic theatric blight; and a change of dynasty is always welcome to slaves of the musical habit." Once again it is curious that in the foregoing quotation Huneker rejects Wagner's unification of the arts in favor of that expression in music alone for which he admired Brahms, and for which he now credits Strauss. This quotation is of interest, too, for its comfortable Nietzschean division of the world into master and slaves—in this case, the master who composes and the slaves who have the musical habit.

It is no surprise when, in *Overtones*, Huneker goes on to reject Wagner's *Parsifal* as absolute music and to find in the opera a "lack of absolute sincerity . . . the work of a man who had outlived his genius." In this judgment of *Parsifal*, Huneker is only walking in the footsteps of Nietzsche, who followed a period of Wagner idolatry with the most vitriolic rejection of *Der Meister* on record. In Nietzsche's condemnation of Wagner's causing music to be taken over by the drama, Huneker finds corroboration for his own conviction that "music pure and simple, for itself, undefiled by costumes, scenery, limelights, and vocal virtuosi, is the noblest music of all."

Elsewhere in *Overtones* Huneker scorns Mendelssohn as a writer of "Bach watered for general consumption." Continuing the fight of the nineties over Max Nordau's *Degeneration*—a rejection of modern art (and artists) as depraved—he asserts that "there are no sane men of genius." He rejects Verdi's music written before *Aida* as brainless, though promising and potent—but he praises *Falstaff* to the skies. He admires Debussy's new *Pelléas et Mélisande,* though without finding it successful as absolute music. He ends with a plea for "intellectual music" without "metaphysical meanings," and his proffered model is Mozart's G Minor Symphony: "in its sunny measures is sanity."

Neither the 1905 *Iconoclasts* nor the 1909 *Egoists* deals with music at all. *Iconoclasts* is concerned with the contemporary European dramatists—first among them Ibsen—and in particular with plays containing a social message. Because my main concern here is with Huneker as a music critic, it is perhaps only necessary to remark that in his fulsome praise for Ibsen he seems to have one standard for drama—realism—and another for music—beauty: "Love me, love my truth, the playwright says in effect; and we are forced to make a wry face as we swallow the nauseous and unsugared pill he forces down our sentimental gullets."

Egoists carries the subtitle "A Book of Supermen," and is chiefly interesting for its articles on nineteenth-century French writers, including Stendhal, Baudelaire, Flaubert, Anatole France, Huysmans, and Maurice Barrès—in addition to Nietzsche and Stirner. The book treats these disparate creatures as supreme individualists, and though it gives them high praise for their ability to follow their own way, Huneker seems to be making an attempt to gain rational control of an artistic movement all too easily allowed to luxuriate, as it had in his own short fiction, in its own willfulness. Thus, in the essay on Baudelaire, he attacks the idea that artists are dissipated creatures:

What the majority of mankind does not know concerning the habits of literary workers is this prime fact: men who work hard, writing verse—and there is no mental toil comparable to it—cannot drink, or indulge in opium, without the inevitable collapse. The old-fashioned ideas of "inspiration," spontaneity, easy improvisation, the sudden bolt from heaven, are delusions still hugged by the world. To be told that

Chopin filed at his music for years, that Beethoven in his smithy forged his thunderbolts, that Manet toiled like a labourer on the dock . . . is a disillusion for the sentimental.

And with Nietzsche, too, Huneker, if not actually changing his opinion on the philosopher's stature as a superman and an "anarch," seems to qualify his position: "No longer is he a bogey man, not a creature of blood and iron, not a constructive or an academic philosopher, but simply a brilliant and suggestive thinker who, because of the nature of his genius, could never have erected an elaborate philosophic system, and a writer not quite as dangerous to established religion and morals as some critics would have us believe."

The 1910 *Promenades of an Impressionist* is concerned with painting. The use of "impressionist" in the title does not refer to the painters of that school but to Huneker's characteristic device of critical impressionism, the recording of his reactions and feelings as aroused by the art he was considering. The book opens with a discussion of the post-Impressionist Cézanne, whom Huneker respects but cannot warm up to. As would happen when he came to face the new music of Arnold Schoenberg, Huneker is careful to make the distinction between truth and beauty: "Stubborn, with an instinctive hatred of academic poses, of the atmosphere of the studio, of the hired model, of 'literary,' or mere digital cleverness, Cézanne has dropped out of his scheme harmony, melody, beauty—classic, romantic, symbolic, what you will!—and doggedly represented the ugliness of things. But there is a brutal strength, a tang of the soil that is bitter, and also strangely invigorating, after the false, perfumed boudoir art of so many of his contemporaries." In *Promenades*, Huneker gives a sign that, as the appreciator of the new, he is increasingly conscious that a critic can in his life represent only one moment of artistic revolution, and that the critic's role, too, will be superseded. Thus, he compares Cézanne's still lifes to those of the eighteenth-century painter Chardin: "Chardin interprets still-life with realistic beauty; if he had ever painted an onion it would have revealed a certain grace. When Paul Cézanne paints an onion, you smell it. Nevertheless, he has captured the affections of the rebels and is their god. And next season it may be someone else." Huneker's lurking rejection of the new in art becomes clear when he writes of Frans Hals: "How thin and insubstantial modern painting is if compared to this magician. . . . "

From this point on, it is difficult not to feel that, with one glorious exception at the very end of his life, Huneker's remaining books mark a downward curve. The 1911 *Franz Liszt* is a congeries of quotations from contemporaries of the composer and lists of his pupils and descriptions of their playing. Despite praise for Liszt's emancipation of instrumental music through his contributions to the symphonic poem, much of the book is merely a hymn to the piano, Liszt's graceful contribution to which, Huneker realizes, "will die hard, yet die it will." Of Liszt's arrangements and paraphrases, Huneker writes: "One may show off with them, make much noise and a reputation for virtuosity, that would be quickly shattered if a Bach fugue were selected as a text."

The very title of the 1913 *Pathos of Distance,* taken from Nietzsche, admirably conveys the tone of retrospection which would now increasingly characterize Huneker's writing, and marks, along with the consideration of Schoenberg two years later in *Ivory Apes and Peacocks,* the limits of his wholehearted acceptance of the new. In *The Pathos of Distance,* Huneker admires post-Impressionism, but without paying it the ultimate honor: "Rhythmic intensity is the key to the new school; line, not colour is king. Not beauty, but, as Rodin said, character, character is the aim of the new art." While Huneker could find room in his pantheon for Cézanne, Gauguin, Van Gogh, and Matisse, he could find no such place for the Cubists: "The catalogue of the Tenth Autumn Salon [Paris, 1912] shows . . . few masterpieces, much sterile posing in paint, any quantity of mediocre talent, and in several salles devoted to the Cubists and others of the ilk any amount of mystification, charlatanry, and an occasional glimpse of individuality. I am in sympathy with revolutionary movements in art, but now I know that my sympathies have reached their outermost verge."

In the 1915 *Ivory Apes and Peacocks* Huneker seems willing to accept the music of Schoenberg's *Pierrot Lunaire* as something the future may embrace, though it is plain that his tolerance of it is owing entirely to the demands of reason and not to love:

I fear and dislike the music of Arnold Schoenberg. . . . the aura of Arnold Schoenberg is, for me, the aura of subtle ugliness, of hatred and contempt, of cruelty, and of the mystic grandiose. He is never petty. He sins in the grand manner of Nietzsche's Superman, and he has the courage of his chromatics. If such music-making is ever to become accepted, then I long for Death the Releaser. More shocking still would be the suspicion that in time I might be persuaded to like this music, to embrace, after abhorring it. . . . I have been informed that the ear should play a secondary role in this "new" music; no longer through the porches of the ear must filter plangent tones, wooing the tympanum with ravishing accords. It is now the "inner ear," which is symbolic of a higher type of musical art. A complete dissociation of ideas, harmonies, rhythmic life, architectonic is demanded. To quote an admirer of the Vienna revolutionist: "The entire man in you must be made over before you can divine Schoenberg's art." . . . Cheer up, brethren! Preserve an open mind. It is too soon to beat reactionary bosoms, crying aloud, Nunc dimittis! Remember the monstrous fuss made over the methods of Richard Strauss and Claude Debussy. I shouldn't be surprised if ten years hence Arnold Schoenberg proves quite as conventional a member of musical society as those two other "anarchs of art."

Unfortunately, this laudable optimism that a new generation will make up its mind favorably about currently problematic art rings false in the light of Huneker's own unwillingness to praise any new music as he had praised the new music of his youth. The new music was not what he loved; he did not love Stravinsky, Kodály, and Bartók, of whom Huneker could say no more than that they "are not to be slighted." Even more clearly, his beloved music was not that of Prokofiev: Huneker, though he later was to find some of the composer's miniature piano pieces "piquant," in a 1918 review (quoted in the Arnold Schwab biography) thought his music "volitional and essentially cold," marked by "intrinsic poverty of ideas," and written by a "psychologist of the uglier emotions—hate, contempt, rage—above all, rage—disgust, despair, mockery, and defiance." Even in the case of his once-adored Richard Strauss, Huneker is unable to go beyond *Salome*, *Elektra*, and *Der Rosenkavalier*. *Ariadne auf Naxos*, the premiere of which in the original Max Reinhardt version he attended in Stuttgart in 1912, he found a misfire, and for the probable success of Strauss in the future he is forced to fall back upon the composer's undoubted success in the past.

Although in *Ivory Apes and Peacocks* and the subsequent 1917 *Unicorns* Huneker is still capable of praise for new literature—he admires Conrad, Wedekind, the now-forgotten Russian novelist Michael Artzibashef, and Joyce—his musical world seems to have closed in. He has nothing to say in his books about any American composer save Edward MacDowell, and only in the case of a few performers—the pianists Godowsky and

Vladimir de Pachmann, and the singer Mary Garden—can he manage something like the old enthusiasm.

Indeed, what I have earlier called Huneker's increasing mood of retrospection comes to a climax in his last book, the posthumously printed *Variations,* which appeared in 1921. In a chapter entitled "A Mood Reactionary," presciently anticipating today's sophisticated musical opinion, Huneker writes in his own name what he had only written before as a spoof under the pseudonym of "Old Fogy":

Berlioz, Tchaikowsky and R. Strauss are not for all time.

The truth is that musical art has gone far afield from the main travelled road, has been led into blind alleys and dark forests. . . . [W]ho has "improved" on Bach, Handel, Haydn, Mozart, Gluck, Beethoven, Schubert, Schumann, Chopin? Name, name, I ask. What's the use of talking about the "higher average of today?" How much higher? You mean that more people go to concerts, more people enjoy music, than fifty years or a hundred years ago. Do they? I doubt it. Of what use all our huge temples of worship if the true gods of art no longer be worshipped therein? Numbers prove nothing. . . . The multiplication of orchestras, opera-houses, singing-societies, and concerns [is] not indicative that general culture is achieved. Quality, not quantity, should be the shibboleth. The tradition of the classics is fading, soon it shall vanish. We care little for the masters. Modern music worship is a fashionable fad. People go to listen because they think it is the mode. Alack and alas! that is not the true spirit in which to approach the Holy of Holies, Bach, Handel, Mozart, and Beethoven. Oremus!

And lest the words I have just quoted be taken as no more than the passing mood of a prolific writer, the final words of *Variations,* in all their simplicity, convey all too well the mood of Huneker's musical last will and testament: "A good comrade, a loving husband and father, the giant tenor of his generation, Enrico Caruso is dead. But to his admirers, he remains the dearest memory in this drab, prosaic age."

Two books more of James Huneker remain to be considered: *Steeplejack,* the memoirs which appeared in book form in 1920 after their newspaper publication two years earlier, and *Painted Veils,* his 1920 novel. *Steeplejack* is a charming book, full of reminiscences and amplified gleanings from previously published material. The anecdotes it contains are wonderful, and one of them at least deserves immortality:

I made Monsignor laugh [on a visit to the Vatican in 1905] when I retailed that venerable tale about Liszt's repentance and withdrawal from the world to the Oratory of the Madonna del Rosario on Monte Mario, an hour from Rome. Pope Pio Nono conferred upon the Magyar pianist the singular honor of personally hearing his confession and receiving the celebrated sinner into the arms of Mother Church. (Perhaps the delightful old Pope was curious.) After the first day and night, Liszt was still on his knees, muttering into the exhausted ears of the unhappy Pontiff the awful history of his life and loves. Then, extenuated, Pio Nono begged his penitent: "Basta! Caro Liszt. Your memory is marvellous. Now go to the piano and play there the remainder of your sins."

But even more important than *Steeplejack*'s anecdotes are the revelations it contains about Huneker's own approach to work as a critic. In an attack upon Swinburne's statement that the chief attraction of the profession of criticism should be the possibility of giving noble praise, Huneker points out that the poet "had the most vitriolic pen in England," and then goes on to remark: "Neither praise nor blame should be the goal of the critic. To spill his own soul, that should be his aim. Notwithstanding the talk about objective criticism, no such abstraction is thinkable. A critic relates his prejudices, nothing more. It is well to possess prejudices. They lend to life a meaning."

But Huneker's mature thoughts on criticism are concerned with more than his own individual impressionist style. He knows, too, and marvelously expresses, the universal truth that a critic is at the mercy of the artistic quality of that about which he writes: "I was slowly discovering that to become successful, a critic can't wait for masterpieces, but must coddle mediocrity. Otherwise, an idle pen. Big talents are rare, so you must, to hold your job, praise conventional patterns. And that way leads to the stifling of critical values."

Huneker's novel, *Painted Veils,* begins with a fin-de-siècle epigraph, redolent of the diabolism with which he had played for so many years: "Now the Seven Deadly Virtues are: Humility, Charity, Meekness, Temperance, Brotherly Love, Diligence, Chastity. And the Seven Deadly Arts are: Poetry, Music, Architecture, Painting, Sculpture, Drama, Dancing."

The novel tells the story of an American opera singer, greatly gifted in voice and ambition, and a rich American expatriate. The opera singer, meant to suggest Istar, the Assyrian goddess of love, knowing nothing of virtue, chooses the deadly art of music and lets nothing human or divine stand in the way of her career. The American expatriate, her lover and a sometime music critic whose life in many ways parallels Huneker's, knows the good but allows himself to be the cause of the ruin of others. The opera singer, after a lifetime of sexual license, remains "the greatest Isolde since Lilli Lehmann . . . Istar, the Great Singing Whore of Modern Babylon." Her American lover dies in Paris in the final stages of syphilis. Long after the novel's many bawdy incidents have been forgotten, the reader retains a strong and moving impression that for Huneker, as for so many Catholics on the Continent, art has been the other, and reverse, face of God. In this, his last book published during his lifetime, Huneker returned, in symbolic expression if not in actual observance, to the devout Catholicism of his family.

As this consideration of James Huneker comes to its end, the real nature of his contribution to the cultural taste of his America, and to the cultural taste of our America, becomes clear. There can be no doubt that he was a vivid and effective messenger, not just for the various arts of the 1890s, but in a wider sense for the European gospel of art and aestheticism. Whatever may have been his contribution to the advancement of American taste in literature and drama, it seems that in the visual arts he recoiled personally from the implications of much of the new painting from post-Impressionism onward. The fact that in the service of the gospel of the new he felt it necessary to praise that which he could not love suggests an earlier origin for today's spurious doctrine of the artistic "cutting edge." It also suggests the importance of Huneker's role, and that of his historical reputation, in fostering that doctrine.

In the case of music, his recoil from the avant-garde very likely returned him to a taste that went little further than Chopin. In this he functioned not to bring American opinion over to the side of the new music of the eighties and nineties, which in any case had achieved wide popularity on its own by the coming of the twentieth century, but rather to solidify that antecedent worship of the classic German composers and Chopin which to this day marks the orientation of cultivated music lovers.

A word is in order, too, about Huneker's literary achievement. Unlike his music-critic colleagues (and friends) H. E. Krehbiel, Richard Aldrich, and Lawrence Gilman, Huneker was an exciting writer. In this day of the increasing penetration of criticism—especially music criticism—by the academy, Huneker's work strikes me as possessing, and conveying, the golden value of artistic involvement. In the best sense, his style was always oriented to action, leading the reader toward ever more vital thought about and experience of art.

It must not be forgotten that James Huneker began his critical career as a musician and pianist, and a musician and pianist he remained to the end of his life. When Mencken's philistine-bashing boosterism of Huneker's contribution to advanced taste in America is properly forgotten, I hope that I at least, in tribute to my childish hours of attention to Huneker while sitting at the piano, will remember his words from the closing paragraph of *Steeplejack*:

I can't play cards or billiards. I can't read day and night. I take no interest in the chess-board of politics, and I am not too pious. What shall I do? Music, always music! There are certain compositions by Chopin to master which eternity itself would not be too long. . . . I once more place the notes on the piano desk. . . . How many years have I not played that magic music? Music the flying vision . . . music that merges with the tender air . . . its image melts in shy misty shadows . . . the cloud, the cloud, the singing, shining cloud . . . over the skies and far away . . . the beckoning cloud. . . .

(*The New Criterion*, 1987)

18

EDWARD SAID, MUSIC CRITIC

Edward Said is a man of parts. Born in Jerusalem in 1935 to Christian Arab parents, he spent his adolescent years in Cairo and then was educated in the United States at Princeton and Harvard. A specialist in English and comparative literature and an advocate of the new textual approaches in literary studies, he has taught at Harvard, has been a visiting professor at Johns Hopkins and Yale, and the Christian Gauss lecturer in criticism at Princeton; at present he is Old Dominion Foundation Professor in Humanities at Columbia. He is the author of several acclaimed books, including *Beginnings: Intention and Method* (1975), *Orientalism* (1978), and *The World, the Text, and the Critic* (1983). He has received numerous awards, including a Guggenheim Fellowship (1972–73) and the first Lionel Trilling Award at Columbia (1976).

Said is also the most prominent political spokesman for the Palestinians in the United States. He has written widely on the Palestinian and more general Arab causes; these writings include *The Question of Palestine* (1979), *Covering Islam* (1981), and *After the Last Sky: Palestinian Lives* (1986). His journalistic commentary on the Middle East appears frequently in this country and in England, and for some years he was a member of the Palestine National Council.

But Said is more than a literary critic and an Arabist. He is a dedicated amateur musician and pianist, with a particular interest in the great classics of Western music, from Bach to Richard Strauss. For several years he has been writing lengthy articles on the New York musical scene in the.

left-wing *Nation*. These articles have generally been of a severe cast, and quite elitist in their high standards and unsparing demands.

Now Said has brought the three parts of his life—the new literary studies, the Arab political cause, and the music he loves—together. Through the good offices of the Columbia University Press, he has recently published *Musical Elaborations*,[1] his 1989 Wellek Library Lectures at the University of California at Irvine. Although the subject—perhaps it might better be called the object—of these lectures is the music Said knows and loves, the critical approach he has taken is very much in keeping with the prevailing postmodern attitude of the Wellek Lectures, which have included presentations by such avatars of the new deconstructionist sensibility as Perry Anderson, Jacques Derrida, J. Hillis Miller, and Jean-François Lyotard.

At the outset, Said makes his purpose clear. He wants to treat music as he and others have treated literature, and though it is only *playing* (his italics) that fully satisfies him, he urges upon his readers the identification of the social, historical, and cultural factors that have given great music its currency. He praises recent academic musicology but finds it "reverential," one assumes because musicology still finds music too pure to be discussed in terms of sociology, anthropology, and politics. He does find value in the willingness of such younger scholars as Rose Subotnik and Carolyn Abbate to examine music from outside music itself, but he finds these studies, including their use of deconstruction, narratology, and feminist theory, only in their infancy. He tells us that we have learned much about how culture operates from Roland Barthes and Michel Foucault, about how to examine a text from Derrida, Hayden White, and Fredric Jameson, and about gender from Elaine Showalter, Germaine Greer, and Gayatri Spivak; but he laments that, despite the existence of these rich insights, we have few who write about music in the way that Raymond Williams wrote about literature.

Accordingly, Said points out that the roles played by music are extraordinarily varied and include the linkage between music and privilege, music and nation, music and religious veneration. He is a great, though not total, admirer of the German Marxist sociologist and music critic Theodor Adorno. He accepts Adorno's idea of the "regression of hearing," the notion that the level of the musical audience has been lowered by the substitution of passive listening in concerts and to recordings for active participation through amateur performance and score-reading. He does not, however, go along with Adorno's Hegelian conception of music as teleologically mirroring the emptiness and destruction of the capitalist world. Said prefers to see music as existing geographically and spatially, bound to its origins in place and the physical surroundings in which it is performed. He cites the Italian Marxist philosopher Antonio Gramsci's opinion that music plays a part in the conquest of civil society, but he finds that not all music is a part of the domination of others; some music dissents, addressing issues of what Said calls "solitude, memory, and affirmation."

All this is contained in the introduction to *Musical Elaborations* and prefigures the longer discussion that follows. In "Performance as an Extreme Occasion," the first of the book's three chapters, Said cites the literary critic Richard Poirier's conception of the performing self and quotes him to the effect that "Performance is an exercise of power, a very anxious one." For Said, these words apply with special force to musical performers, who for him have used their virtuoso abilities and their single-minded concentration on their work to distance themselves from the listener, who is thereby placed "in a relatively weak and not entirely admirable position." He goes on to acknowledge "the listener's poignant speechlessness as he/she faces an onslaught of such refinement, articulation, and technique as almost to constitute a sado-masochistic experience."

As an example of this phenomenon of dominance, Said cites the playing of Chopin etudes by the Italian pianist Maurizio Pollini, whom he accuses of using his technical mastery to "completely dispatch any remnant of Chopin's original intention for the music, which was to afford the pianist, any pianist, an entry into the relative seclusion and reflectiveness of problems of technique." Performance, thus separate from composition, "therefore constitutes a special form of ownership and work."

Said is particularly concerned with the practice of transcription, whereby music written for one instrument or combination of instruments is, through a kind of alchemical virtuosity, transmuted into the property of a performer on another instrument. He talks about Glenn

Gould's marvelous playing of transcriptions of Beethoven symphonies and complicated Wagner excerpts, and calls this mastery a wish "to reassert the pianist's prerogative to dominate over all other fields of music."

Noting that concert performers no longer play much contemporary music, Said finds Western classical-music concerts are now

highly concentrated, rarefied, and extreme occasions. They have a commercial rationale that is connected not just to selling tickets and booking tours but also to selling records for the benefit of large corporations. Above all, the concert occasion itself is the result of a complex historical and social process . . . that can be interpreted as a cultural occasion staked upon specialized eccentric skills, upon the performer's interpretive and histrionic personality fenced in by his or her obligatory muteness, upon the audience's receptivity, subordination, and paying patience. What competes with these occasions is not the amateur's experience but other displays of specialized skills (sports, circus, dance contests) that, at its worst and most vulgar, the concert may attempt to match.

Said does not go so far as to castigate the conductor Arturo Toscanini, in the fashion of Joseph Horowitz's recent biography. Indeed, though he recognizes the disturbing (to him) fact of Toscanini's corporate success, he greatly admires the conductor's unsentimental 1938 performance of the Beethoven Symphony No. 3, the *Eroica,* in which he finds the conductor "trying to force into prominence, or perhaps enforce, the utterly contrary quality of the performance occasion, its total discontinuity with the ordinary, regular, or normative processes of everyday life."[2]

Once again, Said returns to his much admired Gould, who for him attempted, both through the genius of his playing and his decision to give up the routinized existence of a touring artist, to integrate his music with the world—without relinquishing its "reinterpretive, reproductive" aspect. For Said, this is "the Adornian measure of Gould's achievement, and also its limitations, which are those of a late capitalism that has condemned classical music to an impoverished marginality and anti-intellectualism sheltered underneath the umbrella of 'autonomy.' "

The second chapter of *Musical Elaborations* is called "On the Transgressive Elements in Music." Here Said uses the word "transgressive" to describe the ability music has "to travel, cross over, drift from place to place in a society, even though many institutions and orthodoxies have sought to confine it." But he quickly embarks on an elaborate discussion of the late deconstructionist literary critic Paul de Man, much in the news lately for his anti-Semitic, pro-Nazi sympathies during World War II. He treats, but does not resolve, the question of whether de Man's later intellectual work is to be held hostage to his earlier political views. These early views seem particularly offensive to Said, not simply because of their anti-Semitic and pro-Nazi character but because de Man entertained the idea of "the creation of a Jewish colony isolated from Europe." For Said, this means that de Man had joined the Zionists in advocating Jewish domination over the Palestinians, and thus provided "dramatic confirmation of the links between right-wing and even fascist European thought and Zionism itself." For Said, these links include scholarly evidence of "connections between right-wing Zionism— whose most famous living representative is Yitzhak Shamir—and officials of the Third Reich, including Adolf Eichmann."

From this it is a quick jump back to music, as Said points out that in the *Ring* Wagner created the villain Alberich, modeled on an anti-Semitic stereotype and at the same time displaying, in his "willing acceptance of lovelessness and damnation . . . [an] unremitting desire for world conquest [that] adumbrates the appalling designs of the 1000-year *Reich*." Even the novelist Thomas Mann, whose *Doctor Faustus* (1949) is at once the greatest work of fiction ever written about a musician and a chilling indictment of Germany in the first four decades of the twentieth century, cannot escape Said's net: for him, the novel, in its characterization of a whole people and a whole culture, unpleasantly displays the European imperial drive to "judge, theorize, and totalize simultaneously."

Consistent with the importance Said gives to the notion of domination, he sees music performance, only a "little" dramatized, as "a police regime of the signifier." Even Mozart, on this view, was aligned at Salzburg with Nazi *völkisch* ideology. For Said, the repertory everywhere displays the power of this "police regime." At the Metropolitan Opera, Italian *bel canto* and *verismo* operas have crowded out Czech, French, British, Russian, and most German operas; in orchestra concerts, Austro-German compositions have crowded out French, Czech, Spanish, and

Russian music. Bach, too, is not exempt from criticism: according to Said, the great length of the B Minor Mass is an example not only of Bach's "authorial productivity" but also of his "ambition to win a place of noticeable importance in the entourage of a prince."

As Said moves from his second to his third and final chapter, he discusses music that transgresses the role it has been allotted in society. This music includes the cynical and witty *Così fan tutte* of Mozart and the abstruse variations on *Vom Himmel hoch* of Bach, which, writes Said, "dangles pretty much as pure musicality in a social space off the edge." He devotes many words to his own reaction to the pianist Alfred Brendel's Carnegie Hall performance of the Brahms Variations Op. 18. This is music that emphasizes what Said once again calls, in the title of his third chapter, "Melody, Solitude, and Affirmation." From Proust he takes a notion of melody as the distinguishing feature of a composer; this characteristic melody then speaks directly and privately to the listener, communicating what Said calls the music of the music. He has a particular affinity for pieces written as variations rather than in sonata form; they are timeless, elaborative, and free; by contrast, sonata form is goal-driven, masterful, and thus hegemonic. The chief function of Brendel's Brahms performance in Said's life was to send him back to the piano, himself to play what Brendel had played. Thus the highest compliment Said can pay to music is that it inspires him to his own amateur performance.

More widely, he finds that Beethoven freed music to be ruminative and exfoliative, and that Richard Strauss set an example in his late works of doing without the assertion of a "central authorizing identity." *Musical Elaborations* ends with a tribute to Strauss's *Metamorphosen* (1944–45), an elegy mourning the destruction of the German musical world Strauss had helped to create, and based on intricate transformations of a fragment from the Funeral March of the Beethoven *Eroica*:

[M]usic thus becomes an art not primarily about authorial power and social authority, but a mode for thinking through or thinking with the integral variety of human cultural practices, generously, non-coercively, and, yes, in a utopian cast, if by utopian we mean worldly, possible, attainable, knowable.

I have thus far attempted a dispassionate statement of Said's arguments. I have done so, and at length, because his work does not lend itself to easy summarization. Considered for its literary style, it may charitably be called discursive. In fact it is rambling and woolly. The three chapters of the book are but a wordy recapitulation of the introduction, with the leading ideas not so much amplified as repeated at greater length. As assertion follows assertion, and qualification follows qualification, the reader must feel that he is watching a revolving barber pole, not following an argument. Everything Said thinks of reminds him of something else; put another way, the reader cannot see the mosaic for the tesserae.

The hand of postmodernist lit-crit jargon hangs heavy over every page: in a splendid example of this embracing of every terminological trend, Said calls the film made of Gould playing and talking about the Bach *Goldberg Variations* just one year before his death "an act of closure"; anyone not so with-it intellectually would simply have called it a farewell. Passage after passage must be read several times over to tie clauses together, and even to unite verbs with subjects. The fruit of rereading is little more than the reader's awareness that once Said as critic has said the words "domination" and "authority," he has said it all.

Le style est l'homme même—style is the man himself—Buffon told us in the eighteenth century. It is impossible not to feel that Said's stylistic divagations are but the presenting face of his own complicated critical program—though I suppose that after reading his book, I should refer not to his program but to his agenda.

Said cannot allow us to forget that he is a Palestinian Arab living in exile, though exactly why he has chosen this exile—other than to show us the error of our ways—he never states. To convict the hated Zionists, he must drag in Paul de Man, for no other reason than to illustrate the connection between art and life, and as an example of Jewish complicity with the Nazis; similarly, he cannot resist the temptation to associate Yitzhak Shamir with Adolf Eichmann. So obsessed is Said by the subject of Zionism that even his praise for Marcel Proust as an artist seems suspect, for was not Proust the greatest twentieth-century chronicler of the unassimilability of the Jews, Zionists in spite of themselves, to society?

Here Said has really written two books about music, or rather one book about two kinds of music. There is the music he sees—or hears—from outside, and there is the music he plays and loves. The music he experiences from outside is the great music of the repertory, the masterpieces kept alive by virtuoso performance. This music he sees as a part of the European oppression of societies and peoples, both their own and foreign; not only does he reject the appearance of this music in concert, but, following Adorno, he rejects it even more ardently when it is available on recordings.

And yet it finally emerges that Said has a soft spot for even this public music, and for its performers. He is a great admirer of the Beethoven *Eroica*, surely a touchstone of public music; a passage in the Brahms Variations he heard played by Brendel reminds him pleasurably of the noble "Nimrod" variation in the *Enigma Variations*, the most famous work by the arch-imperialist Edward Elgar. It is true that Said has kind words for the music of the French Catholic and musical modernist Olivier Messiaen, as he has for the Jewish political radical Frederic Rzewski's Variations on the Chilean workers' song "The People United Will Never Be Defeated!" But in fact, his taste, to judge by the music he discusses at length, is foursquare and safe; like every other music lover these days, he likes Bach, Mozart, Beethoven, Chopin, Wagner, Brahms, and Richard Strauss, most of them German, and all safely situated in the dominative and hegemonic Eurocentric canon.

Looked at in this way, Said's second kind of music—the variation writing he admires so much in Beethoven and Brahms—seems only a special case of the public music from which he affects to keep his distance. For Said's private music, intimate, contemplative, and speaking to the individual, is but an offshoot of the truly dominating structures in Western music: harmony and counterpoint. It is these structures, with all their explicit rules and accepted, though no less formative, conventions, that make possible both the sonata form that Said finds dominative and the variation form he finds so privately appealing.

It is tempting to see in Said a frustrated concert pianist, a man who but for the grace of God would be traveling around the world from concert hall to concert hall and recording studio to recording studio. Unfortunately, there is no way of knowing from Said's writing, despite his many words about his Polish-Jewish piano teacher in Cairo, at just what level of proficiency he actually plays; what is clear is that, in his enthusiasm for going home after the Brendel recital to try the Brahms piece for himself, just as in his comment at the beginning of this book that it is *playing* the music that gives him the greatest pleasure, he has identified himself as someone hopelessly hooked on making music for himself.

We should make no mistake about it: making music for oneself, and not relying solely on the work of others in concerts and recordings for musical experience, is good and praiseworthy. What one learns about the music as one plays it, or attempts to play it, is invaluable. It is also true that this ability seems to be dying out as modern life values great music as a normative cultural pursuit ever less. There can be no doubt that Said, unlike so many who write about music, actually loves the art and is willing to give up a major portion of his life to his pursuit.

It is difficult indeed to quarrel with Said's preference for experiencing great music as a private pleasure. It has been clear for many years now that true music lovers—those who are interested in music, not in glamour—are increasingly leaving the world of public concerts. However, they are only to a limited extent going back to Said's desideratum of making the music for themselves; instead, they are more and more relying on cheap, technologically satisfactory, and virtually indestructible recordings. The reasons for this flight from the public sphere are many and difficult to weigh. They include the enormous number of possibilities, provided by the late capitalism Said finds so repellent, for using leisure time; the lack of a solid educational background in the greatest materials of Western civilization, among them music; the overwhelming competition, and the resulting corruption of taste, which high culture faces from popular culture. Perhaps this situation can be summed up by saying that we are facing a triumph of markets, not just in the production of economically useful goods but in the provision of culture as well. People the world over now know that it is possible for them to get what they want, and that they need no longer accept what a once dominating elite thinks is good for them. Thus the musical woes Said describes as being caused by patterns of domination and hegemony are actually the result of system-wide breakdowns in such domination and hegemony.

Furthermore, the praiseworthiness of Said's commitment to music should not blind us to the fact that in his approach to the body of musical masterworks he has pulled off a neat trick. It is not too much to say that he has found a quite ingenious way to kill his music and have it too, to attack its social and cultural basis politically and intellectually, and then to cherish it in his private hours of self-contemplation.

It is all very well to inveigh, as Said so often does, against virtuosos for distancing the audience from the music through the dominative—there's that word again—force of their performances. But all the composers whom Said admires were virtuosos: Bach was a virtuoso organist and harpsichordist; Mozart a virtuoso harpsichordist and fortepianist; Beethoven, Chopin, and Brahms virtuoso pianists; and Wagner and Strauss virtuoso conductors. The music of all these geniuses was written by them in the knowledge of their own great talents as executants; their greatest music was not written for amateurs but for themselves, or for virtuosos like themselves.

Even more, the sad fact is that the music Said loves exists (as he must know) only as a development inseparably tied to modern European history, in all its religious, economic, and social triumphs. That there exists a music for him to write about, and a music whose fate he can bewail, is owing to the very cultural matrix he resists and undermines in so many intellectual and political ways. In this, his attempt to question for others what he cleaves to himself, Said is only replicating the course of his eminent academic colleagues in their literary and cultural studies of the classics; like them, he knows the great works and spends his time with them, in literature as in music. If the price of being allowed such a closeness to masterpieces is that they be destroyed for students—well, that's just the way the cookies of scholarship crumble.

(*The New Criterion*, 1991)

19

BUT IF THE ARTIST FAIL?

It may be taken as a rule that the public, able to judge only from outward signs, knows little about the inner lives of artists. Nowhere is this more true than in the case of the great musicians. Here, in conceiving its heroes, the public mixes a weak perception of biographical reality with a strong dose of bathetic sentimentality. Thus, for the nineteenth century, Beethoven's storming of the heavens was produced by, and was a triumph over, deafness; Schubert's flood of melody was so inextricably linked with his having died at an early age as to seem by some happy miracle its inevitable outcome; Chopin's wistful harmonies and poignant climaxes could only have been produced by a weakened consumptive. Perhaps most striking in this litany of satisfyingly maudlin outcomes was the image of Mozart's purity mocked—but also made ever more pure— by his failure to earn even a modest living from his divine music.

In our now almost bygone century, while the scale on which great musicians work has been seen to change, the sentimentality has remained. As the stage and film triumph of Peter Shaffer's *Amadeus* makes clear, Mozart, now portrayed as a loudmouthed, childlike genius, remains fair game for the spinning of psychological romances. Moving on to more recent art, we treat the powerful emotional effect of Mahler's music as the ineluctable manifestation of a life in which he was doomed to be a success as a conductor but a failure as a composer. Schoenberg's greatness—indeed the very survival of his music at the present time—is seen as the moral rather than the musical result of his refusal to write the lush and passionate compositions for which he had an undeniable talent. Bartók's music is made vastly more accessible by the memory of his poverty-ridden death from leukemia in an uncomprehending wartime America. Webern's brief and often uncommunicative works gain in meaning from the fact of his innocent death at the hands of an American soldier just after the end of World War II. Shostakovich's greatness is made even greater by his political tribulations in Stalinist and post-Stalinist Russia.

It will not have escaped the reader that all these easy conflations of historical fact and musical reality, despite the real sufferings they recount, belong to that hoary literary genre known as the artistic success story. For the devotees of this brand of melodrama, an artist can only be at his greatest when his greatness rises from the ashes of suffering, and the survival of the artist's oeuvre, to be rightly honored, must be grounded in that suffering. Though in all these cases the extent of the misfortune may be debatable, the success must be real: the consideration of such painful cases would hardly occur were it not for the victories that have brought them to our attention. And so, because the suffering of the artist becomes merely a cog in the wheel of success, the inner life which produces and embodies the suffering becomes a matter of no importance, a demonstration of necessary sacrifice and perhaps even of necessary psychopathology.

What has been true for the public image of the great creators of the past remains true for today's musicians as well. Now that the public seems to have decided that the age of the great primary creators of music is over, the popular idea of musicians has changed. Recent books about successful living musicians, for example, are almost always about performers, not composers. Whether these books deal with great careers or the trials and tribulations of the hopeful, the note struck is not one of triumph rooted in tragedy, or even of triumph and tragedy separately. Instead, the books tell of essentially limited artistic achievements rewarded, if at all, by the normal satisfactions of daily life. On a deeper level, moreover, these books are about outward events distantly observed. Whether the artist thinks great thoughts, or whether he thinks at all, we are not told; all we know is that he is providentially there to be written about.

Three examples of such books, appearing in recent years, display this trend of making the artist just like you and me, only more so. Not surprisingly, they have their origins in *New Yorker* profiles, and are nicely within the tradition of that magazine's long-time department, "Onward and Upward with the Arts." All three are written by *New Yorker* editor and contributor Helen Drees Ruttencutter. The first, *Pianist's Progress* (1979), attempts to be a heartwarming and frequently bittersweet chronicle of the career strivings of Robin McCabe, a young pianist who had attended the Juilliard School; the second, *Quartet* (1980), is a rather more unrelievedly optimistic account of the Guarneri Quartet, one of today's most prosperous American string quartets; the third, *Previn* (1985), is a short life-and-times of André Previn, the new music director of the Los Angeles Philharmonic.

The opening section of the second chapter of *Pianist's Progress* captures well the tone of this very modern attitude toward the artist, an attitude that manages to find good in all things, even in the bad:

I first became interested in the problems of student pianists, and how they go about trying for a career, in the fall of 1973, when I met Robin McCabe, one of Juilliard's two hundred. Juilliard has no dormitory facilities, and a pupil from out of town either pairs up with another student to rent an apartment or lives in a residential hotel or takes a room with kitchen privileges in a private apartment—preferably somewhere in the vicinity of Juilliard. Robin and another Juilliard pianist, Richard Fields, each rented a room in the duplex apartment of Jane Harris, a pianist friend of mine who lived off Central Park West two blocks north of the school. I lived in the same building, and sometimes caught glimpses of Robin—usually on the run. . . . I rarely saw Richard. . . . Richard was a shy young man, and a talented pianist. A preschool [?] student at the New England Conservatory, in Boston, where he grew up, he'd come to Juilliard fresh from high school—he was younger than Robin—and he was unhappy with his teacher, who overwhelmed him in general and verbally scalded him when he did not live up to her expectations. Richard frequently slept half the day away in escape from the trauma awaiting him at school.

Robin and Richard used the upstairs door of Jane's apartment, and sometimes when I was there Robin would come downstairs to tell us something funny that had happened at school or talk about a concert she was going to give. . . .

As *Pianist's Progress*—a weighty title, perhaps, for so unassuming a book—goes on to describe what the book's dust jacket calls the "rigors and joys of study, practice, and performance," it becomes clear that we are being presented not with great artistic events and accomplishments but only with halting personal steps and outcomes. The author's conclusion, as she discusses Robin McCabe's decision to move permanently from her birthplace in Puyallup, Washington, to New York City, makes clear that neither the book nor the life it describes has in any large allegorical sense been a progress; rather it has been an increasing accommodation of art to personal emotion: "I asked Robin whether—now that she had her final degree—she still wanted to live in the Northwest and teach, and have Barrett [Herbert Barrett, a New York concert manager] book concerts for her from there. She thought for a minute, and then she said, 'This past year has made me realize that my center of gravity is here. This is where I belong, where I ought to be. To put it more accurately, this is where I *want* to be.' "

By contrast, Ruttencutter's book on the Guarneri Quartet deals not with a struggling young pianist but with a busy chamber-music ensemble, a group that she begins her book by describing, perhaps not quite accurately, as "the preeminent string quartet in the world today." The group is seen rehearsing, traveling, playing, and, above all, succeeding. The success is limited musically by the sad fact that the music the quartet plays—no matter how well it plays—is music which has been played innumerable times in the past by historically significant ensembles and is today played all over the world by groups more or less equal to the Guarneri in skill and earning power. But this is all grist to Ruttencutter's *New Yorker* approach of finding everything wonderful even when—or precisely because—it isn't great. And so the book ends on the highest note the author can manage, a description of a Guarneri concert at the White House during the Carter administration. But it is an apotheosis of the media, not of the spirit:

Even in their dark suits—the required dress for the evening—Beall [the group's manager] would have seen them as "four handsome devils," and they played with tremendous energy and excitement the lushly beautiful quartet [Dvořák's "American" Quartet], which gives all of them, a number of times, showcase solos that display their great talent and the beauty of the instruments they play. The audience gauchely and wonderfully applauded between movements. Most American audiences, no matter how good a concert is, seem reluctant to show their pleasure. If people stand, chances are it's a prelude to a fast exit. This night, when the quartet finished, the audience leaped to its feet and applauded thunderously. The President,

But If the Artist Fail?

precluding an encore—it had been a long night—stood and shook hands with each man. Then he turned to [Menachem] Begin and the audience and, with a broad smile, said, "Aren't they the greatest?"

Ruttencutter's new book on André Previn is yet another study in the trivial worship of art and the artist. For her, everything about her hero is the greatest; but greatest means fame and success, not the majesty of a life in art. Nowhere is this more clear than in her description of Previn in a chamber-music rehearsal at Tanglewood with three principal players of the Boston Symphony:

> At two on Friday afternoon, Previn rehearsed the Mozart piano quartet with [the violinist] Silverstein, the cellist Jules Eskin, and the violist Burton Fine in the Shed. It was their second, and final, rehearsal. The first one had amused Previn. He told me, "I was prepared to really dig in, but we just played through it, and then Joey [Silverstein] said, 'Now let's tell jokes.' Well, they work so hard up there, and they're so good. . . . "
>
> On Friday afternoon, when they'd finished the first movement, Previn turned his part back to page 1, in anticipation of working out certain spots, but the others seemed eager to get on with it. When they had finished the last movement, Previn went backstage with Silverstein, and while Silverstein was wiping the rosin off his violin and carefully tucking it into its case they discussed what they might play next summer. Silverstein said, "How about one of the Brahms trios?" and Previn said fine, he liked all of them. Maybe the B Major. Silverstein nodded.

In a similar vein of good feeling, we have been provided in recent years with a spate of books by great and near-great singers, the overwhelming majority of which tell us of what we ought to think it feels like to live the life of career triumph. A noxious example of this particular kind of foolishness is *Full Circle* (1982), Dame Janet Baker's putative diary of the last months of her operatic career. No better and no worse than what has come from her colleagues, these diary entries cover a broad range. There is the trivially descriptive:

> It's always the petty, silly irritations which mar a day. This morning began with post, the usual conglomeration of adoring letters, unwanted advice, and abuse. The latter I can tell just by the writing on the envelopes, and usually the first sentence confirms my suspicions; into the waste-paper basket they go! I slept very badly last night, never a good prelude to the following day. The telephone rang incessantly; I looked at the diary for the month of May which we have tried to keep as quiet as possible to give me a breather before Glyndebourne begins; it is an horrific sight,

not from the number of engagements but from all the surrounding commitments to people who must positively be seen and attended to before we disappear to the seclusion (I hope!) of Sussex for six weeks.

And the trivially philosophical:

My working years may be shorter than those of most people, but the fulfilment I have always felt will, I truly believe, remain with me in retirement, giving me a sort of "permission" to enjoy the last part of my life to its utmost. Middle and old age are special times. They are Nature's way of preparing us for the last stages of our development. If things have gone as they should during the other stages of life, the final section is all set for the most important phase of all—the spritual [sic] one. It seems to me that the body does its best to release us for this phase by its own ageing.

The result of all this soft-minded self-indulgence is that we can make happy contemplation for ourselves out of the suffering and pleasures of others. Thus pleasured, we can conceive of the artist according to the new gospel of arts advocacy, as the only truly happy being, the explorer whose lucky fate it always is to find a fresh and excitingly stocked continent.

But as we all know from our own traversal of life, there is such a thing as failure without success, and it is failure, rather than success, which is the normal condition of man. What is true for humanity in general is doubly true for the struggling artist; for this aspiring creature, the unhappy ontological reality is that one fails in the first instance not because one's art is rejected but because one isn't an artist at all.

There are sadly few chroniclers of the desperation—quiet or otherwise—of the would-be artist. In literature, the English fin-de-siècle writer Max Beerbohm is a noble example of a writer who took the fate of even the failed artist seriously. Though often perceived as a mere aesthete, Beerbohm demonstrated—in "No. 2, The Pines," an account of the last years of the poet Swinburne and his keeper Watts-Dunton—a deep understanding of the living tomb which the last years of a great artist often are. And in "Enoch Soames," the classic story of an artist who sells his soul to the devil for nothing, Beerbohm described the life of an author whose failures were unredeemed by success or by any achievement, no matter how unappreciated. Significantly, Beerbohm's own reward for the comprehension he showed of the artistic predicament has been to have his literary achievement taken at face value—as merely an elegantly refined form of parody.

In the literary consideration of music, there is another remarkable, though now little-discussed, exception to this rule of sentimentally transmuting the dross of failure into the glory of art. That exception comes from Somerset Maugham, a writer whose very success with the reading public over more than the past half-century is all too frequently taken as the sign of a deeper artistic failure. It could be said that one of Maugham's preoccupations as a writer was the artist—as success (in the case of El Greco), as ruin (the Gauguin-like Charles Strickland in *The Moon and Sixpence*), or as the object of the manipulation of others (the aging Edward Driffield, modeled on Thomas Hardy, in *Cakes and Ale*).

Maugham's greatest—or at least most harrowing—account of the fate of a hopeful artist was contained in "The Alien Corn," a 1930 short story first printed in book form in *First Person Singular* (1931) and then made into a film in *Quartet* (1948). At first glance, "The Alien Corn" is a simple story about the scion of a rich and highly assimilated Anglo-Jewish family, a febrile young man who, much against his family's wishes, wants to be a concert pianist.

Speaking in the voice of Ashenden, his fictive alter ego, Maugham tells this simple story on two levels, the first social and the second personal. On the social level, Maugham describes in painful and pitiless detail the efforts of the Bland family, originally Bleikogel, to become, through adroit use of their immense fortune, an accepted English county family. Accomplishing this task is not easy: Sir Adolphus ("Freddy") and Lady Muriel, née Miriam, must hide in their racial closet not only the skeleton of the still living and tyrannical Dowager Lady Bland, who speaks with a German accent, but also that of Ferdinand Rabenstein, her dashing brother.

It is Rabenstein—"Ferdy" to family and friends alike—who provides the link between the old world of the Bleikogels and the new world of the Blands. He is a curious figure, on the one hand eager to play the role of a courtier in gentile high society, and on the other secretly proud, if not quite of his origins, then at least of himself. Vastly rich and highly cultured, he collects art and plays Viennese waltzes on the piano with the skill and suavity he displays in life. Clearly modeled by Maugham after the rich Jews of German origin newly acceptable at court in the reign of Edward VII (1901–10), Rabenstein is welcomed everywhere, save by the younger Blands: to them he is an embarrassment because of his doubly foreign past.

On the personal level, "The Alien Corn" presents the doomed struggle of George Bland to be that which he is not—an artist. Young, handsome in a conventional English way, the heir to a great fortune, George cares not for the newly adopted life over which his parents have taken so much trouble. He has no desire to do as his father and mother wish: to be a country squire, to marry an English girl of good—i.e., gentile—stock, and some day to succeed to his father's title and his seat in Parliament. Ashenden treats the last point on this parvenu wish-list with a wryness not untinged by cynicism:

> "Is George interested in politics?" I asked, to change the conversation.
> "Oh, I do hope so. After all, there's the family constituency waiting for him. It's a safe Conservative seat and one can't expect Freddy to go on with the grind of the House of Commons indefinitely."
> Muriel was grand. She talked already of the constituency as though twenty generations of Blands had sat for it.

What George does want is to be a pianist. He conceals this desire from his parents, telling them that he wants to go to Munich to learn German when in fact he plans to study the piano there. Because he balks at coming home for the splendid party his parents wish to give on their estate to celebrate his coming of age, his parents learn the awful truth. When he does come back for the party, and good-naturedly endures the festivities, his parents hope that he has submitted to their plans for him.

But the senior Bland's optimism is dashed when George makes it clear not only that he intends to return to Munich to continue piano studies but that he is willing to forsake even his parents' hard-won Englishness. Again, the narrator's cynicism, this time not excluding a certain genteel anti-Semitism, makes clear the gulf between parents and son:

> Freddy was peremptory. He forbade George to go back to Germany. George answered that he was twenty-one and his own master. He would go where he chose. Freddy swore he would not give him a penny.
> "All right, I'll earn money."

"You! You've never done a stroke of work in your life. What do you expect to do to earn money?"

"Sell old clothes," grinned George.

There was a gasp from all of them. Muriel was so taken aback that she said a stupid thing.

"Like a Jew?"

"Well, aren't I a Jew? Aren't you a Jewess and isn't Daddy a Jew? We're all Jews, the whole gang of us, and everyone knows it and what the hell's the good of pretending we're not?"

Then a very dreadful thing happened. Freddy burst suddenly into tears. I'm afraid he didn't behave very much like Sir Adolphus Bland, Bart., M.P., and the good old English gentleman he so much wanted to be, but like an emotional Adolph Bleikogel who loved his son and wept with mortification because the great hopes he had set on him were brought to nothing and the ambition of his life was frustrated. He cried noisily with great loud sobs and pulled his beard and beat his breast and rocked to and fro. Then they all began to cry, old Lady Bland and Muriel, and Ferdy, who sniffed and blew his nose and wiped the tears streaming down his face, and even George cried. Of course it was very painful, but to our rough Anglo-Saxon temperament I am afraid it must seem also a trifle ridiculous.

At this point the Dowager Lady Bland intervenes to suggest a compromise: since clearly George should not throw away all the treasures the world counts important unless he has genius as an artist, he must agree— after two further years of study—to an independent evaluation by (in Ashenden's words) "some competent and disinterested person." If that person were to say that George "showed promise of becoming a first-rate pianist, then no further obstacles would be placed in his way." If not, then George would have to come home and take up the life his parents wanted for him.

George accepts Lady Bland's compromise and returns to Germany. Unvisited (at his own request) by his family, he lives the life of a student. When Ashenden, on a pretext, comes to Munich, he hears George play, and finds his playing peculiarly unsatisfactory: "He sweated profusely. At first I could not make out what was the matter with his playing, something did not seem to me quite right, and then it struck me that the two hands did not exactly synchronize, so that there was ever so slight an interval between the bass and the treble; but I repeat, I am ignorant of these things; what disconcerted me might have been merely the effect of his having drunk a good deal of beer that evening, or indeed only my fancy. I said all I could think of to praise him."

After the two years are up, George returns for the verdict, and it is Ferdy Rabenstein who now provides the means of the story's horrifying denouement. He brings the renowned concert pianist Lea Makart to the Blands' for the purpose of judging George's future. The entire family (with Ashenden) assembles with her to listen, and the verdict is what they must have feared. For as Ashenden makes clear, despite all the attempts at accommodation to an essentially philistine world, every one of them—even Freddy and Muriel Bland—was capable of recognizing artistic distinction, or its absence:

He played Chopin. He played two waltzes that were familiar to me, a polonaise, and an *étude*. He played with a great deal of *brio*. I wish I knew music well enough to give an exact description of his playing. It had strength and a youthful exuberance, but I felt that he missed what to me is the peculiar charm of Chopin, the tenderness, the nervous melancholy, the wistful gaiety and the slightly faded romance that reminds me of an early Victorian keepsake. And again I had the vague sensation, so slight that it almost escaped me, that the two hands did not quite synchronize. I looked at Ferdy and saw him give his sister a look of faint surprise. Muriel's eyes were fixed on the pianist, but presently she dropped them and for the rest of the time stared at the floor. His father looked at him too, and his eyes were steadfast, but unless I was much mistaken he went pale and his face betrayed something like dismay. Music was in the blood of all of them, all their lives they had heard the greatest pianists in the world, and they judged with instinctive precision.

After this, Lea Makart's verdict does not come as a surprise. It is only a confirmation:

At last he stopped and turning round on his seat faced her. He did not speak.
"What is it you want me to tell you?" she asked.
They looked into one another's eyes.
"I want you to tell me whether I have any chance of becoming in time a pianist in the first rank."
"Not in a thousand years."

Now it is Maugham's turn, in the voice of Lea Makart, to speak to the vocation of the artist, to the role of money and power in art, and to the relationship between the artist and the world which makes his art possible:

"Ferdy has told me the circumstances," she said at last. "Don't think I'm influenced by them. Nothing of this is very important." She made a great sweeping gesture that took in the magnificent room with the beautiful things it contained and all of us. "If I thought you had in you the makings of an artist I shouldn't hesitate to beseech you to give up everything for art's sake. Art is the only thing that matters. In comparison with art, wealth and rank and power are not worth a row of pins." She gave us a look so sincere that it was void of insolence. "We are the only people who count. We give the world significance. You are only our raw material."

Perhaps to soften her presumption, Lea Makart plays for the group she so plainly sees as but one more audience among the many to whom she has presented her art. Her playing is exquisite, but the admiring Ashenden is not quite lost in its beauty:

With another part of me I watched the others and I saw how intensely they were conscious of the experience. They were rapt. I wished with all my heart that I could get from music the wonderful exaltation that possessed them. She stopped, a smile hovered on her lips, and she put on her rings. George gave a little chuckle.

"That clinches it, I fancy," he said.

What had "clinched it" for George Bland was for Lea Makart just another event in the crowded daily life of a great musician. As she and Ashenden drive back to London, all the talk is of career—her career— and not of the inner life, sometimes grand and sometimes tragic, of the artist: "She told me of her early years in Manchester and of the struggle of her beginnings. She was very interesting. She never even mentioned George; the episode was of no consequence; it was finished and she thought of it no more."

For George, too, the matter was finished. "The Alien Corn" ends with a short, deadpan paragraph, perilously close to the superficiality of efficient journalism, describing a routine tragedy:

Perhaps because the shooting season was about to open he took it into his head to go into the gun-room. He began to clean the gun that his mother had given him on his twentieth birthday. No one had used it since he went to Germany. Suddenly the servants were startled by a report. When they went into the gun room they found George lying on the floor shot through the heart. Apparently the gun had been loaded and George while playing about with it had accidentally shot himself. One reads of such accidents in the paper often.

One of the great strengths of "The Alien Corn" is its skillful interweaving of two themes, the social and the personal, the atmosphere of

Jewish assimilation and the tragic fate of a young man who could not become the artist he wanted to be. But Maugham does more than tell a seamy and fairly trite story of social climbing and the desire to pass. He also suggests that, in their desire to no longer be seen as Jews, the Blands also have willingly given up the secular civilized culture which they, like Ferdy Rabenstein, had found as part of their birthright. Before the final crisis, this cultural renunciation seems already to have been made. Thus when George sits down at the piano to play a Chopin nocturne, just before the family council at which Lady Bland offers her compromise, his father expostulates: "Stop that noise, I won't have him play the piano in my house." But when the chips are down in George's moment of truth before Lea Makart, the Blands in fact turn out to need no professional advice; they know enough to know that their son will never be an artist—not because they don't want him to be, but because he lacks the gift.

And so, strangely enough, the Blands' deracination leads directly from the abandonment of their past, through the abandonment of their culture, to the final tragedy of their son's lonely failure. As penetrating as Maugham's description of the fate of the Blands as Jews is, the true subject of "The Alien Corn"—and the cause of the story's impact—is the lonely fate of the artist. This loneliness, and this fate, is of course a general matter, not confined to Jews, or to the rich, or indeed to the young. It is rather the normal destiny not only of the artist who fails to be an artist but, eventually, of the artist who succeeds and then finds—as all artists must—that the permanence he has sought is subject to his own mortality. In this respect, the fate of the fictional and ungifted George Bland is not so terribly different from that of the very real-life great musical artists who find themselves faced by the inevitable decline and destruction of their powers in what they must see as a kind of living death.

Here, it seems to me, is the reality of the inner life of the artist. This life is a constant—and constantly losing—battle to keep at bay, on one side, the permanent shortfall of physical and mental abilities in the context of the perfection that art strives to be, and, on the other side, the inevitable arrival of silence and death. One can catch something of this dual struggle in the well-known words of Sergei Rachmaninoff, both a great composer and a great pianist, as he lay on his deathbed: "At my age one can't miss practice. . . . My dear hands. Farewell, my poor hands. Farewell, my poor hands."

Just now, treated to the latest electronic marvels of small, portable cameras and digital recording, the musical public has been given a new and infinitely poignant account of the autumn years of a supremely great musical performer. *Vladimir Horowitz: The Last Romantic,* a film soon to be a compact disc, was shown to large audiences of the pianist's admirers in Carnegie Hall in the middle of November. Here, in shots of the eighty-one-year-old artist at home performing a varied program for his wife and talking with her and members of the technical crew about himself, his past, and music in general, one saw vividly (in de Gaulle's memorable phrase) the shipwreck that is old age.

From the moment of the film's opening—a shot of the pianist plainly worried, as he rode with his wife in a limousine, about his present capacities to play in public—to the end more than an hour later, when he finished a harried and smashed performance of the famous Chopin Polonaise in A-flat Major by turning to the camera and saying with an anxious grin, "Just like old days!" the viewer was conscious of greatness in irreversible decline. It is true that along the way the film presented musically breathtaking Horowitz performances of slow pieces by Bach-Busoni, Schubert, and Scriabin. And scattered among the more technically demanding works which he also played—and which he palpably failed to master as he once had—were moments, again in lyrical passages, of surpassing reflective beauty. But overall, whether in music or words, the mood was one of fatigue and weakness, of lessened powers and energy.

Through it all, Horowitz seemed conscious, indeed all too conscious, of what was happening to his body and his mind. Not only did he ask many times, in a childlike way, for compliments and reassurances on his playing from the film and recording personnel. Not only did he say time and time again how he knew all of music, and could play any piano piece. Not only did he repeatedly speak, like some modern-day Baron Charlus announcing the death of all his friends and his own survival, of colleagues of yesterday (among them Rachmaninoff and Toscanini) who had died, leaving only himself alive. Even more tellingly, he pointed out half-sadly, half-quizzically, "The world is sinking now. . . . The world is not so good." And he made clear, by immediately playing the haunting Scriabin Etude in C-sharp Minor, Op. 2, No. 1 (1887–89), that in perfectly re-creating a moment of Russian culture before the Revolution he was intoning a requiem for our own world, and for himself.

For many, of course, there may appear to be a way out of this gloomy situation. Despite the artist's own professionalism, he can always remain at heart an amateur, a lover of the art who finds a greater personal satisfaction in witnessing beauty than in struggling to create it. Indeed, the great Franz Schubert himself wrote a song, always a sentimental favorite of musical people the world over, that makes precisely this point. In *An die Musik* ("To Music"), the words of the poet Franz von Schober provided Schubert with an opportunity to capture, and even inspire, the mood of a century that took the deepest satisfactions from music:

> Du holde Kunst, in wieviel grauen Stunden,
> Wo mich des Lebens wilder Kreis umstrickt,
> Hast du mein Herz zu warmer Lieb' entzunden,
> Hast mich in eine bess're Welt entrückt,
> Bess're Welt entrückt.

> Oft hat ein Seufzer, deiner Harf' entflossen,
> Ein süsser, heiliger Akkord von dir,
> Den Himmel bess'rer Zeiten mir erschlossen,
> Du holde Kunst, ich danke dir dafür,
> Du holde Kunst, ich danke dir.

> [You dear art, in how many gray hours,
> When the wild commotion of life ensnared me,
> You have fired my heart to warm love,
> And carried me away to a better world,
> Carried me away to a better world.

> Often a sigh, escaped from your harp,
> A sweet holy chord from you,
> Unlocked for me the heaven of better times,
> You dear art, I thank you for this,
> You dear art, I thank you.]

But lest one take undue comfort from these reassuring thoughts—and from the beautiful music which clothes them—there exists powerful evidence that, for those most deeply involved in the propagation of the music which *An die Musik* so emotionally celebrates, musical satisfactions are not enough, and the reality of music-making is hardly so reassuring. On the recording of Lotte Lehmann's Farewell Recital[1] in Town Hall in February of 1951, the great *Lieder* singer ended the concert (and her major performing career) with an encore expressing her gratitude to the blessed music which gave life to her being. The encore, of course, was *An die Musik,* sung with all the resonance of an almost half-century-long career on the German and Austrian lyric stage. The performance of the song is beautiful and infinitely touching—until the last repeated and final *Ich danke dir.* These three words Lotte Lehmann could not bring herself to sing, or even speak. Consumed by emotion, she left the stage. To listen to the record today is to find part of the true reality of a musical career, the part ignored by those who hanker after the stories of artistic beatification and failure redeemed after death, and by those who relish the trite success stories of the Pavarottis and their like that infest today's literary world of artist biographies. It would be a pity if the harsh interior reality that artists face in their daily lives were forever to be ignored by those who, in reading about these artists, prefer enjoyment to understanding.

(*The New Criterion,* 1986)

PART FIVE

CULTURE AND SOCIETY

20

IVY LITVINOV

The Commisar's Wife

On its face, the long life of Ivy Litvinov (1889–1977), the little-known wife of a famous man, combined decided improbability with curious irrelevance. So unlikely was what happened to her, and so resolutely minor a figure did she remain, that one can only admire John Carswell, her new and loving English biographer,[1] for attempting to make everything sensible and significant. Why he has essayed the task at all is perhaps a subject for Carswell's own biographer; our concern here must be with the heroine herself.

She was born Ivy Low, the part-Jewish daughter of a second-rate intellectual jack-of-all-trades who had the good fortune (for his reputation in the eyes of the world and for the esteem of his daughter) to die young. She had, not surprisingly, an unhappy and confined Victorian childhood, which she nevertheless managed to ride into a youthful literary career as a novelist whose most fully imagined subject was herself. Her first novel, *Growing Pains* (1913), was a sentimental codification of the process that prepared her for adult childishness. It was followed by *The Questing Beast* (1914), a torrid (for its time) account of office life and the sexual pitfalls of loneliness. Neither book became a best-seller, but *The Questing Beast*, because of its depiction of scandal, did become a succès d'estime.

In 1916, the twenty-seven-year old Miss Low married Maxim Litvinov, a Bolshevik revolutionary detailed to London for semiclandestine political and financial activity. After the October Revolution of 1917, Litvinov emerged as the official spokesman in England for the new regime in Russia and soon was in a position to put his fresh diplomatic credentials to the tasks of winning international respectability for the Soviet Union and bringing on the collapse of capitalism.

Soon after, the Litvinovs (now the parents of two children) moved to the Soviet Union, he first and she a bit later. Maxim's activities now centered on the creation of the *Narkomindel*, as the People's Commissariat of Foreign Affairs was known. At first his flair was for administration, with an occasional trip abroad for negotiation thrown in. In 1930, he became Commissar, or foreign minister, and in 1933 he negotiated the recognition of the USSR by the new American administration of Franklin Roosevelt; two years later he negotiated a pact on behalf of Stalin with Pierre Laval and the French government.

As the early 1930s—the locust years, in Churchill's memorable phrase—wore on into the prelude to World War II, Litvinov became the chief international marketer of Stalin's Popular Front against Hitler & Co. His evident sincerity, combined with his rumpled and unpretentious appearance, served to guarantee his master's bona fides among those formerly hostile to the USSR as well as among those always eager to believe. But once Stalin had decided on a deal with Hitler, the all too Jewish Litvinov had to go, and in the spring of 1939 he went, relieved of his duties (so the official story went) at his own request. In February of 1941—just four months before Germany's invasion of Russia—he was stripped of his membership in the Party Central Committee. But the wily Stalin had one last use for the discarded salesman: in late 1941, five months after Hitler's invasion of Russia, Litvinov was appointed Soviet ambassador to Washington, once more to cultivate his old friend and diplomatic partner FDR. By 1943 he was through, not just in Washington, but as a functioning personage; his death on the last day of 1951 was remarkable only in that it took place in Moscow in his own bed, rather than at the hands of a firing squad.

High-level Soviet wives are semipampered phenomena of whom little is known and from whom nothing, save on the rarest of confected occasions, is ever heard. Because Ivy was foreign by birth (and by citizenship), she remained a creature slightly apart from the usual run of childbearing dormice required by the standards of socialist morality. She was, after all, a writer, made so as much by design as by talent; she thought and wrote in English, bringing to her work, even when she wrote on Soviet themes, a distinctly foreign mentality and literary style.

Her major completed literary project during her Soviet years was a detective novel written (with the aid of hypnotherapy to start the creative juices flowing) in the late 1920s. The story she wrote was set in the petty underworld of Moscow during the period of the New Economic Policy, that cynical Bolshevik use of capitalism and capitalists to provide just enough economic growth to ensure a base for the collectivization of agriculture and the extermination of millions. Ivy called it *His Master's Voice*, after a phonograph record that constituted one of the most piquant elements at the scene of the crime. Favorable though the book was to the progressive direction of Soviet life, it was too realistic to be publishable in the USSR; Ivy had to be content with a modest edition in English, brought out by Heinemann in 1930. Just how complaisant was the behavior required from even a foreign-born Soviet ambassadorial wife may be gathered from Ivy's utopian words at the front of the 1943 American edition of her book, now entitled *Moscow Mystery*:

[The book] opens on a "bitter night in February, 1926," beneath the walk of the Kremlin; it ends before the ballet season closes for the summer. That was seventeen years ago. February nights are still bitter cold in Moscow, and the ballet season runs from September to June. But almost everything else has changed. . . .

The buildings which have changed the streets of Moscow have changed the lives of the people in the streets. For these buildings were not merely the first modern architecture in Russia—their very functions were new. Their operation brought to the city a new population—office workers to staff the new government departments, bus drivers to drive the new motor-buses, teachers for the new schools, students from all over the Union for the new colleges.

Environment can affect the lives of adults, as well as children. Seventeen years ago it was normal for a night watchman and his entire family to inhabit one room in an old house, and for the night watchman's wife to get up in the morning to make her lodger's tea on a primus stove in the same room. Now it would be normal for them to have street-level apartments with a modern kitchen, in a tall apartment house. . . .

Her one venture in the style of a fellow-traveling Agatha Christie aside, most of Ivy's energies during the period of her husband's rise and subsequent downfall were employed in translating from the Russian, teaching Basic English in the face of the opposition of school administrators, raising her children in what she could manage of an English manner, and indulging a somewhat wayward sexuality. On this subject, Carswell, quoting Ivy, leaves little room for modesty or perhaps even for romance. In Berlin, she met a German doctor named Kurt, and felt

sort of happy. Had something I never had before. Beginning with an "o,"and now I feel serene, domestic and self-respecting. . . .

[For a later tryst] Kurt arrived at 3. He came straight up to me and we simply fell upon each other with delight. He thought he had never seen me looking so nice and loved my hair. And I thought him ever so much more attractive. . . . [T]here is something clean and compact about him that is almost irresistible. We went together to Friedel's hotel at 6.30 and found her with her friend Beatus and to my dismay an "orgy" all fixed up for us 4. . . .

I couldn't say anything as they all seemed to want it, but of course what I really wanted was Kurt all to myself. They all agreed that my hair was an enormous improvement and of course Friedel found it "a little perverse" so that was all right. We had a nice dinner and coffee together and I liked Beatus very much. A fat man, distinctly Regency, with an eye glass and soft white hands. Then we went up to Friedel's really huge room and all undressed and I may say tho' it was rather amusing at moments (especially the eyeglass of Beatus, to which he clung) I got no satisfaction out of the whole evening, tho' Kurt had me at least 4 times and at incredible length. He only had Friedel once and that made me frankly unhappy. . . .

[And on another occasion she observes that] Beatus is infinitely more subtle and intelligent than Kurt. . . . He has not Kurt's marvelous potency and it is obvious that this could not be expected. You can't have everything. Besides he was not bad. . . . What I specially like about Beatus is that he made me feel I was wonderful for him and said he could never forget me, while dear Kurt always makes me feel that it is *he* who is so wonderful. Of course Kurt would hardly have understood a dozen words of mine, our minds are so different. . . .

Despite Maxim's deathbed words to Ivy—"Englishwoman, go home!"—she stayed in the USSR, remaining close to her children (and to theirs: Pavel Litvinov, the celebrated dissident, is her grandson) and cultivating her personal life. Again, Carswell leaves little to the imagination: "Even as seventy approached she was not beyond the reach of passion, but now it was unhesitatingly homosexual. She made a note on 'Thursday 5th or 6th or I know not what of Feb 1959,' from which it is clear that she was having an affair with a woman younger than herself. 'Fantastic day ended. Wild, sweet love. My only desire—that any moment of it should go on for ever. Any—doesn't matter which. With her, not so simple.' "

In 1960, she made an extended visit to England. Many of her contemporaries, including the sometime Communist sympathizer, fine printer, and advertising whiz Francis Meynell and the stalwart Stalinist cum natural scientist J. D. Bernal, were still alive, as was a small but comforting English bank account her thoughtful husband had arranged during the early 1930s. Though she felt compelled to return to Russia in 1961, she began to be published as a short-story writer, at first in the as always leftist *New Statesman*, and then after 1966 in *The New Yorker*. In subject matter, her sentimentally cast stories alternated between memories of a turn-of-the-century childhood and personal accounts of the shabby world of shanty dachas and crude vacation rooming houses available to the superannuated widow of a half-disgraced and totally discarded diplomat. Many of these stories, with all their echoes of other—and better—women writers, were collected and published in 1971 under the title *She Knew She Was Right*.

In the 1970s Ivy went home to England to die. There, in a tiny apartment outside London, she was surrounded by various émigré members of her family, indulgent friends, and uncounted scraps of disorganized reminiscences. Some words of hers, written in New York in 1943, are used by Carswell as a motto at the front of his book; in themselves they give an adequate account of the quixotic side of Ivy's life and the shallowness and indulgency of her self-image: "For many years I was obsessed with the idea that God had sent me to Russia for the purpose of being the only English subject in the Soviet Union who could write. By writing I mean doing it so that people wanted to read it all the time they were reading it; they wanted to go on reading it simply for pleasure." Carswell ends his book with an ultimately unsatisfying verdict on Ivy: "She was dealt a high card in life, but it was in the wrong suit."

It can hardly be said that Carswell's work is a brilliant accomplishment in biography. Unfortunately, he often seems unsure in dealing with simple details of twentieth-century political and cultural history. Thus he gives the impression that George V was king of England (rather than Prince of Wales) in 1905, when in fact he did not ascend the throne until

1910. Similarly, Carswell writes of the "charm of Russia's imperial ballet (which captivated London and Ivy in 1911)"; but this landmark in the evolution of English taste was occasioned not by "Russia's imperial ballet" but by the privately financed and run Ballets Russes of Serge Diaghilev. Carswell also manages to be off by one year in dating Maxim Litvinov's agreement with FDR about restoration of US-USSR relations in 1934 (not 1933); he is unclear, too, about the year the Litvinovs both came to Washington for his ambassadorial stint, getting it correctly in one place as 1941 and then suggesting six pages later that Ivy arrived in 1942.

More important by far than these mere details is Carswell's inability to connect in any evidential way what was going on around Ivy in England before her marriage with her life, her thought, and the actions she took. There are, for example, many pages in the book on the English socialist Zionist physician David Eder, who married Ivy's Aunt Edith. For Carswell, Eder was the great influence on Ivy: "It would hardly be an exaggeration to say that David Eder was Ivy's second father, more real than Walter [her father], and the very converse of Sandy [her stepfather]. . . . The Eders, husband and wife, stood for all the lost Walter could have offered his bounding daughters." All the more pity, then (given how strongly Carswell thinks this influence on Ivy), that not one fact based either on Ivy's testimony or on the recollections of intimates is given to support Carswell's claim.

Although there is much in this book about the exile Russian revolutionary movement in London and about Maxim's place in it, there is no material connecting Ivy in any real way either with the movement or with her future husband's life. Instead we are given, time and again, suppositions:

One wonders if Ivy ever bargained for a husband whose chief resolve was now [1917] to return to Russia in the certainty that he was destined to play an important part in its revolution. She believed in freedom and progress, she was glad the Tsar was overthrown, but she had no deeply rooted political convictions. Her ambitions were literary. Yet if she wanted to keep the stability Maxim represented for her, with his maps, his neatness, his caution about money, his devotion to their children, she would have to follow him into the fearful adventure of the Revolution.

It is clear that rather than provide an intellectually coherent and disciplined biography, Carswell has given us a personally written and influenced (his mother was one of Ivy's closest friends over many years and he himself knew Ivy in her last years) life-and-times based on linkage by speculation rather than on evidence. The result of all this suggestive writing is that we emerge from the book no wiser about the real significance of this impulsive and often foolish woman who, though failing to be a major writer, has nonetheless much to reveal as a mirror to her times.

One aspect of her—and her husband's—mirroring function derives from the simple fact of their physical survival during the Soviet nightmare. On this score Carswell gives fascinating material about Maxim's disillusionment with Stalin's regime, a disillusionment he put into action by setting up an English bank account and by talking against Soviet policies to State Department official Sumner Welles in 1943 and to the American journalist Richard C. Hottelet in 1945. Even more damningly, he arranged for Ivy to place some of his papers in a numbered New York safe-deposit box in 1943.[2] As to why the Litvinovs survived, Carswell advances several explanations he himself calls "all equally speculative and unconvincing." These range from Stalin's affection, his reward for faithful service, and his desire to keep Litvinov, as it were, in cold storage for future use, to his desire not to destroy "a Bolshevik of the first generation who had a unique understanding of the West" and with whose policy, in any case, Stalin himself had been associated.

Toward the book's end Carswell adds another and more compelling reason why Litvinov (and his wife) survived:

In the Bolshevik system, even in the bloody mind of Stalin, there lay a calculation that the possibility of Western approval must never wholly be discarded. Total isolation, absolute defiance, were positions to be avoided, and the destruction of Litvinov would have violated this instinct. . . . Almost alone among the Soviet leadership he had a constituency in the West which had come to associate him personally with disarmament, resistance to fascism, and collective security; and it was a constituency which extended to the highest levels among senior statesmen who felt he would keep his word. His opinion may not have counted for much in the high policy of the Kremlin, but his standing abroad was a factor in its calculations.

Since Carswell has gotten as far as identifying world opinion as a "factor in [Soviet] calculations," it is a pity he does not go on to identify just what segments in the West were considered to be most important in the Kremlin scheme: the world of progressive opinion that shades gradually

from fellow-traveling on the left to the high-minded liberalism of what
passes for the center of democratic societies. For this motley cast of political half-thinkers, Maxim Litvinov was, and, to judge from the evidence of William L. Shirer's recently published volume of memoirs,[3]
remains, a personal symbol of a proper former revolutionary. Unmistakably Jewish but never a Zionist, dedicated to principle but cannily
tough-minded, personally nonviolent but a loyal representative of massive military power, an enemy of right-wing fascism who could put the
best face on its Communist analogue, Litvinov sublimely represents the
addled idea that one can run a bloody revolution and immediately there-
upon love mankind forever after. That Stalin and his successors have
understood how to appeal to this large political grouping outside the
walls of their own prison has been clear from the palmy days of the
Popular Front to the present nuclear-freeze movement; the Litvinovs'
survival is but one more example of the old truth that the USSR is a
devoted respecter and follower of public opinion—always abroad,
never at home.

More complicated to assess is the way in which Ivy Litvinov as a
woman and a writer reflected the worlds in which she grew up and in
which she chose to live. Carswell quite properly devotes much space to
an account of her family background, with its not unusual example of
mid-nineteenth-century Jewish émigré seriousness channeled at one and
the same time into capitalist business activity and philosophical rational-
ism. Ivy's grandfather, Maximilian Löwe, was both a speculator in the
City of London and a founder, along with Charles Darwin and two
members of the Wedgwood family, of a heretical free-thinking congre-
gation led by Charles Voysey, an important mid-Victorian dissenter.
That such a movement away from what might have been thought traditional English religious beliefs was not incompatible with outspoken imperialism and patriotism needs no more demonstration than a quotation
from the entry on Maximilian's son (and Ivy's uncle), Sidney, contained
in the *Concise Dictionary of National Biography*:

LOW, Sir SIDNEY JAMES MARK (1857–1932), author and journalist; educated at King's
College School and Balliol College, Oxford; first class, modern history, 1879; brilliant editor of St. *James's Gazette*, 1888–97; ardent imperialist and friend of Rhodes,

Cromer, Curzon, Milner [qq.v.], &c.; works include *The Governance of England* (1904) and *A Vision of India* (1906); knighted, 1918.

But late-nineteenth-century England, and not just Tsarist Russia, was of course the scene of a great battle between fathers and sons—and daughters too. Ivy did not follow the path of her Uncle Sidney. Instead, like so many intellectually inclined young women of the day, she chose to follow the path of literary self-expression. Carswell notes at some length the possible roots of this self-expression, among which he lists her father's forebears, her mother's Anglo-Indian military background, the interest of the educated English public at the turn of the century in foreign and especially Russian literature, and the general presence of progressive ideas in the air. Unfortunately, Carswell does not really press on to document in Ivy's own words the extent to which she became a purposeful carrier of what was enlightened progressive opinion just before World War I, and what remains so today as well.

Certainly evidence for Ivy's opinions *before* her encounter with Maxim is hardly lacking. Just because her lifelong literary product was always so autobiographical, her two novels[4] of 1913 and 1914, respectively, provide much material about how she viewed herself and her world; it is perhaps the major flaw of Carswell's book that he gives little consideration to these basic documents.

Growing Pains, the first of these two novels, is a curious amalgam of complaint and self-satisfaction, of protest and sentimentality. The story of a girl who is, at the beginning of the novel, still a small child, the novel charts an orphan's course through the ministrations of an aunt, a puritanical nanny, and an intellectually disreputable and blindly authoritarian boarding school, and the delicious tortures of first encounters with potential suitors and other men. Here, in the first large literary canvas of a woman in her mid-twenties, are set out all the discontents and fantasies that, without being cast in political form, are the necessary personal foundations for a politics of utopian protest.

This, for example, is the six-year-old Gertrude's experience of adult morality and the attempt to teach it:

"Well, you do as I tell you, and pop into that there drawer, and bring out that there small paper-bag!"

She broke out into triumphant laughter at the sight of Gertrude's bewildered face.

Gertrude duly went through the process described by Ada as running into her drawer, and produced the small bag. She laid it on the table in front of Ada, and walked slowly towards the kitchen door, trying to look unconscious. At the door she was summoned by Ada's voice, as she had expected to be.

"'Ere!" said Ada, "I arst you to bring me that bag, but I never arst you to 'elp yourself."

"I didn't!" said Gertrude indignantly. "I never touched one of them!"

"Never touched one of what, miss? You tell me that!"

"Never touched one of the sweets!"

Delighted at the success of her little ruse, Ada pointed a menacing finger at her charge.

"Well, then, you tell me this," she said, "if you never took one of them, 'ow did you know as they were sweets in the bag?"

Gertrude hung her head miserably.

"I never touched one of them!"

"If you did," said Ada, "kindly remember that over my dressing table is the words 'Thou God seest me,' and nex' time I sees them words I shall know whether or not you're telling the truth, young lady!"

Gertrude was alarmed. She really had not taken a sweet, but she had a nasty feeling that the text might play her false.

From this account of the deceit of those in power it is hardly far to a discovery of hypocrisy at work even in Gertrude's contemporaries:

Someone struck up a tune, and the *Veni Creator Spiritus* was begun.

"Come, Holy Ghost, our souls inspire" ("Oh, *please*, Holy Ghost!" whispered Gertrude, under cover of the music), "and lighten with celestial fire."

Gertrude looked at her schoolfellows as they droned out the majestic words. The same expression of bored submission was apparent on every face.

"They don't believe in it any more than I do," she thought. "If the Holy Ghost really *did* come into the dining-room, I believe they'd be horribly shocked."

The hymn was over, seats were resumed, and Bibles produced. The resemblance to the usual weekly Scripture lesson was marked. References were looked up, and the meaning of the original Hebrew for various words carefully explained. Gertrude, who had vaguely hoped for some soothing of the perpetual dull ache at her heart, was scarcely disappointed. She had only faintly hoped.

The result of all this was alienation, not just from her peers and the world, but also from herself: "When the girls were filing out of the room, Mademoiselle laid a detaining hand on Gertrude's arm. In a miserable state of defiance, fear, and disgust, Gertrude remained rigid. Her throat became suddenly dry. She had an overpowering sense of *inward failure* [emphasis in the original]. She described it to herself as 'feeling as if she had no inside.' The sensation was so strong that she wondered how it was she did not double up like a paper doll."

Growing Pains gives us, too, a picture of that drive to sisterhood which is a natural concomitant of feminine disquiet: "Her new passion, together with the slow awakening of adolescence, burned as a consuming fire in the breast of Gertrude. The very sight of Madge was enough to set her senses reeling, and when she came upon that sight unexpectedly, she would feel giddy and faint and often be forced to sit down very quickly." Not surprisingly, given the surpassing aestheticism of the years just before World War I, art comes to Gertrude's rescue. But this is art not as craft, but as feeling:

"If you won't work, Gertrude, it's no use your ever hoping to draw," [her art teacher] said decisively.

"It isn't won't—it's can't," protested Gertrude.

"Nonsense! You've far more talent than Amy Nelson, and yet she's always ahead of you. Besides, when you choose you can do very well indeed."

"You don't understand. It's not when I *choose*—it's if I can *feel* like it. I can't ever feel those silly old melons and loaves and things, so it's useless my trying to draw them. [Emphasis in the original.]

Despite her inability to see art as anything but self-expression, for Gertrude the power of the gospel of beauty was all-conquering:

It was a bright day in June, and the sun flooded her bedroom through the blind, and aroused her earlier than usual. Her eyes fell on the jug and basin on her washing-stand.

"Well, I never noticed that before!" said Gertrude rubbing her eyes. "That jug is beautiful! What a glorious color! How happy it makes me! But how silly! Why should a beautiful jug make me happy?"

Now the turning point of Gertrude's life—and of the novel as well—is at hand. It comes—surprise!—through art. An older man to whom she is already attracted invites her to an art exhibition where some of his paintings are on view. Gertrude is drawn inexorably to his picture of a flower; here, through the experience of art, she reaches maturity:

As Gertrude looked, memories rushed back upon her of a morning in spring when for the first time she fell in love with Beauty. . . . Gertrude sat down; she felt a little faint with happiness. She saw in a dream her darkened, sordid life lit up, ennobled, and made significant by the pure light of visible beauty. She felt purged, as by a coal from the Altar of Heaven, as she realized what scales had fallen from her eyes. . . . Gertrude knew that she was at last in touch with the Real in human relations, and the solemnity of that knowledge compelled sincerity with herself.

Growing Pains ends with an enthusiastic descent into conventional sentimentality. Gertrude marries her artist, finds married love in his arms "immeasurably dear." On the next to last page of the book, the following treacly exchange between husband and wife takes place, ever so delicately hinting at pregnancy:

"Won't you sit down?" said Don. "You're looking *very* well. Been to many theatres lately?"

"No," said Gertrude primly. "I hardly ever go out at night. My husband doesn't care for it, and, besides, I have to take care of myself now."

"Darling!" said Don, suddenly serious, "are you *really* well? Do you really take care of yourself?"

"Old silly! Of course! 'Yes' to both."

Ivy's next novel, *The Questing Beast*, published just one year later (1914) by Martin Secker, is modeled closely on the writer's own experience as an employee at the Prudential Assurance Company. Despite the fact that the Prudential was one of the most humane and enlightened employers of its time, Ivy's reaction to her work was one of revulsion, which she described in "Pru Girl," a story printed in her 1971 collection:

Eileen was even unhappier at the Pru than she had anticipated. The girl clerks were utterly uninteresting to her, and as for niceness they were mostly the daughters of small tradesmen and bank clerks. They thought Eileen a mass of affectation with her unmanicured hands and her poetry books and high-brow novels. They themselves scarely noticed the names of authors and eagerly followed the serial in the daily paper their fathers took in; they even discussed the heroines in Sweetheart Novelettes and other orange-covered booklets that until now Eileen had never seen anywhere but in the drawer of the kitchen dresser. For six months the only work entrusted to her was the copying of names, addresses, and policy numbers out of dirty ledgers into clean ones, omitting heavily erased canceled policies. If she made the slightest slip, the supervisor tore the whole page out of the ledger without a word. Later she was given letters to type, teaching herself as she worked from the company book of instructions. For one week a month everyone had to take a turn at the loathed addressograph.

Like the much later short story, *The Questing Beast* carries the private discontents of *Growing Pains* into the wider world of the workplace. Now the heroine is Rachel Cohen, a desperately lonely girl who turns out from the beginning of the novel to be a true literary intellectual. Like Ivy, she doesn't like her job. The first chapter of the book is called "Late!" and the second "Penal Servitude"; it seems that Rachel can't manage to get up early enough to get to her jail-like work on time. The atmosphere in the novel is the same as in "Pru Girl":

At about twelve o'clock the menu for the day was passed round the desk, amid derogatory remarks.

After eating her lunch, Rachel kept apart from her colleagues. She found a small volume of poetry in her desk, and with this she retired to a warm and comfortable seat in the lounge. She did not read, however, but stared into the fire in sullen misery. She had been two years in the office now, and was not yet used to it, nor reconciled to her fate. She was, if anything, a shade more miserable than she had been at first, because she felt more dully hopeless. The first month had been one of such wild torture that she had not believed it could last. She had felt like a child who is being punished by being made to stand in the corner, and who turns round every minute, expectant of release—but now, having endured for many months, she began to see no reason why it should not go on for ever. It gradually sank into her, too, that many of her colleagues had been over thirty years in the office, and among them were some who must have minded as much as she did at first. . . .

A new element is added. For the causes of Rachel's habitual tardiness at work (she is otherwise, by all accounts, a highly competent employee) are literary: she reads passionately—*Anna Karenina* and other serious things—and she writes. For her, the act of writing is indeed all-absorbing:

She wrote steadily for nearly an hour and a half. Somewhere in the house a door banged perpetually. Each report smote her senses. Rachel frowned nervously, but the reason of the annoyance did not penetrate her consciousness for a long time. When it did, she started to her feet to go out and shut the door. In the middle of the room she stood quite still and wondered why she had got up. She looked about the room for suggestions, but finding none, sat down again and took up her pen. The door banged again. "Of course!" said Rachel, and starting up again ran to close it.

She came back and went on writing. A passing breeze shook the wind-bell, and at its sweet, faint music Rachel looked up and smiled.

It is an ill thing for your night's rest to write until a late hour, and by the time Rachel had "written herself out" she knew that she could not hope to sleep for many hours. "I shall be lucky if I don't hear it strike three," she told herself.

Over her supper of bread and milk she read what she had written. It was a short story, about five thousand words in length. . . . The central idea was just what might have been expected from a young girl in Ray's position—in fact it was inspired by her constant and enthusiastic reading of Tolstoi, Dostoevsky, and Turgenev. (She was just like all the other intellectual young people of to-day.) . . .

The story . . . was neither ineffective nor ill-written. (It was noticeably free from clichés.) It left its author exhausted and exalted, but little prepared for the tiring morrow. Now, however, her aching limbs and inflamed eyes were no longer a grievance.

Is not the soul more than the body?

Suddenly, about a third of the way through the book, Rachel meets a man to whom she is attracted—the first (for there are in fact three in all) Questing Beast of the title. Beast number one is a quintessential cad named Giles Goodey, a married man who (under the cover of intellectual friendship) brings something new to Rachel's life:

Rachel was giving herself surprises. She was discovering weaknesses in herself—one in particular. This particular weakness was a tendency to enjoy having her hand held by a man whose conversation bored her and whose mind she despised, and this and kindred but infinitestimal [sic] favours were sufficient to keep Giles in attendance on her. Subconsciously he knew what Rachel was to learn in conscious bitterness, that there was a bond between them and a plane on which they could meet with perfect sympathy, a plane on which nature was striving to place them. Rachel, after her first shock at the revelation of this weakness in herself, treated it rather as another woman would treat in herself a sudden desire for a cup of tea with her lunch: the approved treatment is to say: "I mustn't become dependent on it," and to continue in the indulgence. And after all, was it an indulgence, or was it simply that is was rather less boring to submit to mild caresses than to have to respond to Giles's conversation?

Giles and Rachel have an affair, complete with (as the affair seems to be coming to an end) his copying out a sonnet for her. But it is her decision to break off relations, and when she does so Ivy's description of Rachel once again strikes the note of female ascendancy so characteristic of all her writing: "But because he [Giles] was an incurable *poseur*, it must not be imagined that he did not suffer. In the end he suffered more than Rachel, because he loved her, body and soul, and she, as she said, had never loved him."

Though the couple soon meet again—when in Ivy's tremulous words, Rachel "only caught one terrified breath and submitted"—a new affair is now at hand. Noel Young, a brother of one coworker and the fiancé of another (and himself an employee in the insurance office), appears on the horizon, and once more Rachel is attracted. This time it is not only the man who, for Rachel, is the Questing Beast: this time it is also Rachel herself who engages on the great quest. She attempts to give Noel up, not viewing the renunciation as a total loss:

But Rachel was not altogether unhappy. What had once seemed a tragedy—the necessity of her daily attendance at the office—became an unnoticed part of her life, and she was upheld by the knowledge that Noel loved her and that she had acted unselfishly in leaving him. She had begun to write regularly now. It had once come to her to think: "I believe I could write a novel." At first she had put away the idea, believing that greater leisure and quiet than she enjoyed must be necessary for such a stupendous achievement. She began the first chapter once, but destroyed it a week later. She was in no doubt as to her literary gift, but what she had written down seemed to her so unlike the novels she had read that she decided it would not do. She knew that she had some ideas to express. . . . It became a strong obsession, this longing to write in the first person, and to describe herself in detail. . . . She knew, now, that she was going to write about herself. . . .

Finally what had remained until that moment an *affaire blanche* is consummated—but not until Rachel reads Noel the early part of her manuscript. With a friend's counsel, Noel finds a way to rationalize going back to his betrothed on the grounds that Rachel has had a lover before him. Ivy's contempt for traditional male morality couldn't be clearer: "Alas, for chivalry! Noel began to feel quite differently about Rachel, when he saw the attitude that a decent man like Humphreys adopted. He began to think that the fact of Rachel having had a lover before did make all the difference. What had happened would have been impossible with some girls. With Frances, for instance. Never had Frances seemed so far-away, so unapproachable. Oh, let us give it a name! So desirable!" Rachel is in despair. Once again, her literary vocation points the way:

"I will not go under," she said defiantly. "No man on earth is worth going to pieces over."

She took out her manuscript again. . . . Once she had got to work her pen flew over the paper for hours at a time, and she was able to forget the heaviest part of her grief, and to recover some of her self-respect in the spectacle of her industry and the quality of some of the work that she did in those dark hours.

Now, too, she is pregnant. Her new landlady befriends her, and with the help of the women in the office, who type her manuscript, the novel is made ready. It is accepted by a publisher, and soon Rachel is looking forward to twin blessed events: "My two babies," she tells her landlady, "will be born in the same month." Soon she has both a child and a literary success.

In the epilogue of *The Questing Beast*, Noel comes several years later to visit Rachel at the seaside. He is greeted by a small boy named Noel, and when he asks Rachel where her husband is, he is soon made to realize that the child is his. But far from asking for sympathy, Rachel makes clear her desire to raise the child herself without a father as she pursues her literary vocation. The novel ends with a strong demonstration of sisterhood by Rachel and her landlady, leaving Noel an unwanted intruder in a community of women. As Noel walks away, the book ends with these words: "Presently a motor-horn began to sound incessantly, and he guessed that young Noel was investigating the car. He felt bitterly that it was hard on a man to have no right to tell his own son to shut up making such an infernal row."

For all their defects of tone and literary construction, these novels remain, even seven decades later, implicit with life. The life they contain was never matched by Ivy Litvinov in her later writing, which at its best seems a stale rehash of old memories of an England now foreign or a retelling of scenes from Russian life better done by native practitioners. Just because of the pulsing vitality that marks these two early novels, one cannot help asking one question: what happened to this spirit when Ivy Low married?

It is tempting indeed to answer this question as Carswell does: Ivy Low as Ivy Litvinov was a person in the wrong situation. To answer the question in this way, however, is to place all the burden of explanation for what happened to this writer on her experiences and fate in the Soviet Union after her marriage. But this answer, comforting as it may be for those who think that the demonic name of Stalin can explain all the evil in what would have otherwise been a noble experiment, fails to take account of the cul-de-sac inherent in the ideas from which Ivy first wrote and which she espoused with so much energy.

Ironically, what must have seemed before World War I as the freeing of the human spirit ended in a creative drought. The Victorian emphasis on moral uplift and the progress of, and through, science was succeeded by a belief in what would now be called human potential. The particular contribution of the intellectual figures of the 1890s and later to the discussion of values was to place uplift, scientific thought, and the future of the individual in opposition, not just to the state, but to the very idea of a traditionally established order.

For Ivy Litvinov, as for so many of the best and brightest of the day, life as a social process was defined as a struggle against obscurantist, even where not actually vicious and exploitative, repression. For her (despite some strong early positive inclinations), religion was a sham, bourgeois morality was a farce, marriage was a legal union in which the man did not love and the woman could not trust, work as it must be done by the millions was drudgery and boredom, and sexual passion was transitory and incomplete. Politics, as we know both from Carswell's book and from the evidence of Ivy's writing, was a matter of little importance.

What, then, remained? Only self-expression. But even for an artist the self cannot be taken for granted; self-expression, after all, must have something to express. That something, though mediated by the self, is nonetheless the world of people and things. To construe it, as a whole generation of educated writers at the turn of the century did, as the destructive encounter of the self with society is to deny the author the only subject matter he can communicate to others. To say this is not to ask for socialist realism or for the support of any particular established order; it is only to suggest that a writer who does not go toward the world cannot in the long run continue speaking to it.

Doubtless we shall never know just why Ivy Low married Maxim Litvinov. Surely she must have found the new world of her husband's revolutionary activities and friends an attractive change from the English society at whose hands she felt she had suffered so much. Unfortunately, the Soviet world that Ivy soon encountered was a world even less attractive to her than the one she had left. All the promises of human liberation that sounded from every Bolshevik organ soon metamorphosed into not just sham, but murder.[5] For Ivy, the result was twofold: on the physical level, a descent into aimless, tortured sexual promiscuity; and on the literary level, a flight into hackwork and the endless reworking of old memories. All that was left to her in the Soviet Union was thus to cultivate the weaknesses, both personal and literary, which had marred even her prerevolutionary work.

Carswell has chosen to begin the title of his book with the word "Exile." Whether or not he intended it, in the case of Ivy Litvinov, exile has two meanings: flight from her land, and alienation from her own social world and even from her own deepest self. In our time the profession of exile is an honored one, and its favorable associations should not be allowed to obscure the fact that Ivy Litvinov was an exile from a democratic England by her own choice; that this condition robbed her later writing of contact with her own world; that by an irony of fate she was to become an exile even in a social system she must, however fuzzily, have once in potential admired. Because the notion of survival is so closely linked with exile, we should be careful, too, to avoid seeing her long life as a simple validation of her existence. Vyacheslav Molotov, after all, has also survived, in his case into an honored and indubitably old age.

For those who, like John Carswell, must look for a rationalization of the troubled life and ugly times of Ivy Litvinov, perhaps the simplest formulation is the best; she reflected the forces that made her what she was. A wiser choice, made early, might have averted the evil decree for her, as for so many of our century's other lost souls.

(*The New Criterion*, 1984)

21

THE MUSE UNDER MUSSOLINI

Whatever may be said about the lack of centrality of serious music in twentieth-century culture, there can be no doubt that it has engaged the attention of the dictators for whom our epoch is so infamous. Though none of us can be sure of the precise connection between art and life, for totalitarian regimes that connection has been always absolute, and often bloody.

Nearest to us in this dismal record of the manipulation of art for the aggrandizement of illicit power is the China of Mao Tse-tung, especially the Cultural Revolution of the 1960s. Mao's campaign against the arts was crafty in the extreme, for it was based on the suppression of the same artists who, only slightly earlier, under the rubric of "Let a Hundred Flowers Bloom," had followed the demands of their own aesthetic goals. While most Western attention was concentrated on the torture of writers, music, too, was given the benefit of Mao's loving thought. Western intellectuals, quick to defend literature, seemed hardly to react when performers of European music had their hands broken, or when the classic Peking opera was redirected by force to embody the dictates of Maoist social doctrine. Indeed, many of our own avant-gardists showed a thoroughgoing concern for the new at the expense of the old; the English composer Cornelius Cardew, for example, proclaimed himself on the side of Mao Tse-tung's thought, and to our own John Cage, zany as ever, it seemed as if the (to him) admirable old fellow might well be responsible for "the bringing together of the family."

A bit farther back in time there was the chilling fate of the USSR under Stalin, and before him, Lenin. These two monsters and the system they created subjected the Russian musical tradition of Glinka, Borodin, Mussorgsky, Tchaikovsky, Rimsky-Korsakov, and Rachmaninoff to the demands of proletarian agitprop and socialist realism. Prokofiev and Shostakovich, the first having come to maturity before 1917 and the second trained by products of the ancien régime, were alternately treated as Communist stars and as petit-bourgeois villains. Fortunately, Shostakovich's tragic story—thanks to the work of Solomon Volkov—is well known in the West; that of Prokofiev, who had the misfortune not to outlive his tormentor Stalin, is still curiously muffled. The emigration of Soviet performers from their once-promised land has produced at least three major accounts of life under tyranny. In Valery Panov's *To Dance* (1978), Jasper Parrott's *Ashkenazy: Beyond Frontiers* (1984), and Galina Vishnevskaya's *Galina* (1984) we learn in sordid detail what it was like for a dancer, a pianist, and a singer to experience the terror of Bolshevik artistic success.

When we go still farther back to musical life in Adolf Hitler's Germany and Austria, we encounter a paradoxical situation. For Jews, and for those non-Jewish musicians too closely associated with the despised twelve-tone compositional techniques of the proudly Jewish Arnold Schoenberg, life was a living (and usually a dying) hell, in which even total capitulation was unavailing. But for most non-Jewish musicians, normal musical life went on under Hitler and even flourished. Scarce resources were always made available, and gifted performers, even when concert halls and opera houses were nightly being destroyed, were favored beings, uninterfered with as long as they continued to entertain their audiences. Some of these remarkable artists—one thinks immediately of Wilhelm Furtwängler, Herbert von Karajan, and Elisabeth Schwarzkopf—went on to become constitutive influences on postwar musical life. While major controversy has often swirled around these artists and their colleagues, there can be no doubt that, in the absence of any evidence of specific criminal acts, their art has been allowed to triumph over their political pasts.[1]

There is another twentieth-century regime which in this respect deserves our consideration. Mussolini's Italian fascism, more than a decade before Hitler's conquest of power in Germany, was deeply concerned with art in general and music in particular. Now, with Harvey Sachs's *Music in Fascist Italy*, the first serious treatment in English of music under Mussolini has appeared.[2] The story Sachs tells is both deeply interesting and highly inconclusive. In any case, he has put us in his debt for giving us such a thorough account of music and politics in fascist Italy and for relating this sorry spectacle to the wider panorama of Italian music from the turn of the century to the end of World War II.

There is a note of bygone glories present from the very outset of Sachs's book. He begins with the death of Giuseppe Verdi in 1901, an event which marked the end of a career that had taken the art of opera from his early masterpieces to the artistic heights of *Otello* (1887) and *Falstaff* (1893). For a half-century, Verdi had carried not just Italian opera but Italian music as a whole on his broad shoulders. Despite the one-opera successes of Mascagni, Leoncavallo, Giordano, and Cilea, only one true successor to Verdi was to emerge: Giacomo Puccini (1858–1924). While one would hesitate to place the less musically and dramatically profound Puccini on the same level as Verdi, the fact remains that in the operas from *Manon Lescaut* (1893) through *Turandot* (completed in 1926, after Puccini's death, by Alfano)—and very much including *La Bohème* (1896), *Tosca* (1900), and *Madama Butterfly* (1904)—he created a body of highly popular repertory works, and that in so doing he was the last composer, of whatever national origin, to accomplish the feat.

But whereas Verdi had in all ways been an innovator, Puccini was an autumnal figure, content to provide beautiful Italianate melodies, richly harmonized and orchestrated with touches of French impressionism, all in the service of theatrically effective, well-made, and heart-wrenching plots. With Puccini's death, Italian musical leadership—at least as measured in critical esteem—passed from the composers of opera to those of instrumental music. New operas continued to be written, but the old level of mass success was nowhere to be found.

Even more disastrous for opera as a living art form was the sad fact that much of opera's traditional audience went over to film. At the same time, the new instrumental music hardly proved able to take up opera's slack. Of all the composers writing symphonic works and chamber music, only Respighi managed to find a secure place in the repertory, at home or abroad. And even his three popular and gaudy symphonic poems, *Fountains of Rome* (1917), *Pines of Rome* (1924), and *Roman Festivals* (1929), have won little respect from critics or other composers. The only other important Italian instrumental composer of the period, the modernist Alfredo Casella (1883–1947), now seems quite forgotten, even in his homeland.

This dismal picture of Italian music must not be allowed to obscure one simple fact: the Italian people have for centuries been, and remain to this day, one of the most musical peoples in the Western world. Such composers as Palestrina and Monteverdi, Vivaldi and Domenico Scarlatti, Rossini, Donizetti, and Bellini—and Verdi and Puccini—have shaped our very conception of melody and form. Italian singers have for centuries given us our idea of the musical use of the human voice. The families Guarneri and Stradivari have defined for us what string instruments should sound like. In our own time one Italian conductor in particular, Arturo Toscanini (1867–1957), has determined for us how Italian as well as German music should be performed. And we must not forget, either, the contribution of Italian émigré instrumentalists in forming American symphony orchestras at the turn of this century, and for many years thereafter.

It was this paradoxical situation of glory and desuetude that Benito Mussolini inherited just after World War I. As a political figure he was part magician, part mountebank, part fool, and part monster. Entering politics as a socialist of the left, he soon developed a winning socialism of the right, and made his own person the symbol of the revival of Italian national greatness. Even worse for music, he was a reasonably competent violinist, a sometime music critic, and, in general, a music lover.

What made Mussolini and his fascism so suicidally attractive to so many Italians also endeared him to musicians. Undoubtedly his first and greatest appeal was the promise of order. World War I had been a disaster for Italy in the loss of lives and treasure; the political and economic struggle that followed the war seemed to push the nation to the brink of anarchy. For Puccini in 1924 (as quoted by Sachs from an account of the composer's conversation), the political choice was clear:

I don't believe in Democracy because I don't believe in the possibility of educating the masses. It is like trying to hold water in a wicker basket! Without a strong government headed by a man with an iron fist, like Bismarck in Germany in the past and like Mussolini in Italy now, there is always the danger that the people, who construe freedom as mere license, will become undisciplined and wreck everything. That's why I'm a fascist: because I hope that fascism will achieve in Italy, for the good of the country, the pre-war German national model.

Such feelings were hardly confined to the pro-German Puccini. Even Toscanini, Italian patriot to the core, supported Mussolini as a means of dealing with the weaknesses of Italy's political structure: as Sachs points out, Toscanini at first admired Mussolini's "Bolshevik-like platform" enough to stand for Parliament as a (losing) candidate on the Mussolini ticket.

Closely bound up with order as a selling point of fascism was nationalism. The territorial settlements following World War I had not brought Italy the rewards that its participation in the fighting had promised: the decline of Italian power seemed to suggest a parallel decline in Italian culture. Mussolini promised a transformation of the Italian image from that of the easygoing, folk-song-loving Neapolitan layabout to that of Imperial Rome. Though in actuality the solid musical achievements of this new dispensation were to be largely confined to the Roman symphonic poems of Respighi, fascism seemed to promise a renewal of professional and general music education, a better life for performers, the revival of Italian composers of the past, and the making of a new national atmosphere in which great music could once again be written.

Finally, fascism appeared to provide a new idea of what *kind* of music should be composed. By the early 1920s, the crisis of modern music had already become manifest, and nowhere was it more apparent than among conventionally trained musicians. Opera, it was clear, had come to an end as a constantly evolving and popular art form. It was equally plain that younger Italian composers, like their colleagues everywhere, were turning away from nineteenth-century romanticism to a modernism variously associated with the atonalism of Schoenberg, the neoclassicism of Stravinsky, and the various brands of futurism, including those connected with the Italian writer Fillippo Marinetti (1876–1944). Whatever the exact nature of the new music, it was obvious to all that it would not possess the melodic and harmonic power and charm that had made Italian music so successful.

Perhaps the most succinct statement of the romantic reaction against modernism was contained in a 1932 "Manifesto of Italian Musicians for the Tradition of Nineteenth-Century Romantic Art," signed by leading Italian musicians including Respighi and Riccardo Zandonai (1883–1944), the composer of the then fairly popular opera *Francesca da Rimini* (1914). Sachs's selection from this document expresses the feelings that many musicians have harbored but few, in Italy or elsewhere, have been willing to state publicly:

One world has been hit, so to speak, by all the squalls of the most reckless "futuristic" concepts. As it grew more furious, the password truly aimed at the destruction of every old and ancient artistic ideal. . . . What have we gained from this? Atonal and polytonal honking. And what has been achieved by objectivism and expressionism? What's left of them? . . . A sense of facile rebellion against the centuries-old fundamental laws of art has infiltrated the spirit of young musicians. . . . The future of Italian music seems safe [according to the modernists] only at the tailend of all the different types of foreign music. . . . There are [also] those who wish to re-chew the cud of our distant musical past. Above all, however, the last century's romanticism is being opposed and combatted. . . .

The manifesto then goes on to speak of the specifically Italian context: "We Italians of today . . . in the midst of a revolution that is revealing, once again, the immortality of Italian genius . . . feel the beauty of the times in which we live and wish to sing of them, in their tragic moments as well as in their ardent days of glory. Yesterday's romanticism . . . will also be tomorrow's romanticism. . . . "

The problem, of course, was to put all these inchoate desires into practice. Here all the hopes were dashed. Instead of art and artists in power, there were bureaucracies and administrators arranging the thousand petty jealousies, intrigues, and incompetencies characteristic of musical life. And so under Mussolini, as Sachs confirms, nothing in music really changed, though everything became even more shabby and seedy than it had been before.

In music education, studies were written and committees met, but musicians continued to be ill-trained and Italian children were taught ever less of their country's glories. Badly needed new concert halls were not built, and some existing ones—as in the case of the acoustically excellent Augusteum in Rome—were even torn down. Beautiful and successful new music, despite numerous contests and prizes, was not written. On the positive side, performers, many of them first-rate, continued to appear, and the old operatic masterpieces continued to be put on and venerated.

At first, the worst that happened under Mussolini was that the personal politics so common in operatic and musical life were allowed to play on a national stage. Usually this meant no more than favoritism shown to party hacks, and a largely pro forma submission of policy matters to Rome, in many cases to Mussolini himself. But the potential for violence was always present, and in at least one case turned into a major embarrassment for Mussolini and a major turning point in the image abroad of Italian fascism. Sachs devotes much space to describing the regime's attempt, in 1931, to force Toscanini to begin a concert in Bologna with the fascist anthem, "La Giovinezza." When it became known that Toscanini would refuse, he was roughed up just before the concert by a fascist tough. The world outcry was tremendous, and Toscanini did not conduct again in Italy until after World War II; even before his self-imposed exile in the United States, this fiery Italian patriot became the most admired symbol of antifascist Italy.

On a less glamorous level, however, Italian music went on, and the fascists did little to discourage new developments in contemporary music. The early 1930s, for example, saw the founding of two important music festivals, the Festival internazionale di musica in Venice (from 1930) and the Maggio musicale in Florence (from 1933). Both these festivals programmed much difficult new music, including works of Stravinsky, Schoenberg, and Berg: the last two composers were thus welcome in Italy at a time when they and their music were proscribed in Germany. Similarly, Jewish performers, including Bruno Walter, Fritz Kreisler, and Otto Klemperer, were welcome in Italy well after they had become outcasts under the Nazis.[3]

The fascist regime remained surprisingly hospitable to musical modernism even after the war started. Amazingly enough, Berg's *Wozzeck*, a prime example of what Hitler called *entartete Kunst* (degenerate art), was performed in Italy in 1942. Even the dodecaphonist Luigi Dallapiccola (1904–75) was lightly treated. For Jewish artists, of course, everything changed after the strengthening of the alliance between Mussolini and Hitler after 1938. Thenceforth, Jewish composers and performers were excluded from Italian music, though physical repression was not employed against them until the German takeover of much of Italy in 1943.

More than four decades have now passed since democratic government has returned to Italy. It is perhaps the most surprising message of Sachs's book—but a message which rings true—that the trends in musical life already so visible in the early 1920s have changed little under freedom from what they were under tyranny. Grand opera has become even grander, and even less of a truly popular and organically growing form. And though Sachs does not stress this point, it is clear from his analysis that the musical avant-garde—associated with such traditionally modernist figures as Dallapiccola and Luigi Nono (born 1924, and the husband of Schoenberg's daughter Nuria), and the more experimentally inclined Bruno Maderna (1920–73) and Luciano Berio (born 1925)—has carried what passes for new music in Italy even farther away from romanticism and any possible public sympathy. And over everything—whether in opera, concert life, or music education—hangs the suffocating fog of bureaucracy, made dense with the political arrangements and accommodations that seem to form an inevitable part of massive government support. The Italians are still a musical people, and they still love music, but with every passing day the vital and particular characteristics of Italian musical culture—even in the field of opera, which they invented—grow less.[4]

For this unhappy outcome, one would very much like to blame Benito Mussolini, his lackeys, and the Italian musicians who, in order to survive and in some cases get ahead, slavishly collaborated. But while the historical record does indeed show that the fascists were swine and that many artists behaved badly, it does not prove that fascism did very much more than administer, in a confused and inefficient way, a decline that had set in somewhere around the turn of the century, and that has continued to this day.

Before we blame the Italians for this musical decline, we must recognize the sad fact that serious music, viewed as a living art, has not done well in our time. At the turn of the century contemporary music meant the symphonies of Brahms and Tchaikovsky, the late operas of Verdi and the first of Puccini, the early works of Debussy and Ravel, the tone poems of Strauss, the *Enigma Variations* and the *Dream of Gerontius* of Elgar. All those marvelous pieces—and many more—have shown an astonishing life and permanence. Now we live in an age of which the last forty and more years have seen almost no accretions to the accepted repertory. The greatest European music festivals, as always the models for America as well as for Europe, stress celebrity performers doing celebrity works in pleasing ways; indeed, it all reeks of the title of a German opera-tune LP of a few years ago: *Weltstars singen Welthits*. Whether the country under discussion is Germany or Austria, Italy or France, the Soviet Union or Japan, England or the United States, music has become an international task, and one that increasingly belongs to show business.

For those who love music, it is troubling that what they cherish has come to this pass. It is perhaps even more troubling that the problems so blatant in musical life may well be only a particularly obvious manifestation of a much wider contemporary shortfall in the creation of high culture. The fears expressed about the present and the future of music are, on this analysis, similar to the worries many involved in the other arts feel as they survey their own fields and compare what they see to the past.

To talk of these fears and worries is not to say that nothing of artistic worth has been created in our epoch. There have been marvelous things done in this century in painting, architecture, dance, poetry, fiction, and music, too; but what once seemed to be a flood has for long been a trickle, and that trickle now seems to be a drought. To talk, as so many do today, of "postmodernism," of the triumph of stylistic pluralism and diversity, or of the happy destruction of boundaries between popular and high art, is only to commit the error Matthew Arnold so tellingly identified (in *The Function of Criticism at the Present Time*) as having "the grand name without the grand thing."

It is certainly plausible to assign responsibility for what has gone wrong to the undoubted depredations of totalitarian regimes and ideologies. But even so, there can be little doubt that democratic governments and philosophies, no matter how much they are worth fighting and dying for, have done little better in the creation of art. We do not know why this should be so, and, needless to say, our commitment to liberty must not be dependent upon liberty's use-value for art. Perhaps democracies, as a historical phenomenon, are still far too young to create the greatest artistic civilizations; perhaps the creation of such an austere and not immediately gratifying culture is a demand we have yet to make of our free societies and of ourselves.

It is a measure of the importance of Harvey Sachs's study of music under Mussolini that his story destroys our easy notion that by itself democracy provides the royal road to art and civilization. As a result of *Music in Fascist Italy*, we are further than ever before from thinking that a simple solution to the problems of culture and its creation can be found in political systems, operating by and in themselves.

(*The New Criterion*, 1988)

22

SAY NO TO TRASH

Mapplethorpe and the NEA

In canceling the Robert Mapplethorpe exhibition last week, Washington's Corcoran Gallery did more than refuse to show a few raunchy photographs of what the press, unable to print them, primly called "explicit homoerotic and violent images." Because the exhibition was supported in part by public funds from the congressionally embattled National Endowment for the Arts, the Corcoran doubtless considered financial self-interest in arriving at its decision. One hopes those responsible are aware that in saying no to Mapplethorpe, they were exercising the right to say no to an entire theory of art.

This theory assumes, to quote an official of the neighboring Hirshhorn Museum, that art "often deals with the extremities of the human condition. It is not to be expected that, when it does that, everyone is going to be pleased or happy with it." The criterion of art thus becomes its ability to outrage, to (in the Hirshhorn official's words) "really touch raw nerves."

Despite its occasional usefulness, this theory ignores the vast corpus of great art that elevates, enlightens, consoles, and encourages our lives. The shock-appeal of art is questionable when it encompasses only such fripperies as displaying inane texts on electronic signboards in the fashion of Jenny Holzer; it becomes vastly more deleterious when it advances, as Mapplethorpe does, gross images of sexual profligacy, sadomasochism, and the bestial treatment of human beings.

In a free society, it is neither possible nor desirable to go very far in prohibiting the private activities that inspire this outré art. People have always had their private pleasures, and so long as these pleasures remain private, confined to consenting adults, and not immediately injurious, the public weal remains undisturbed. But now we are told that what has been private must be made public. We are told that it is the true function of art to accommodate us to feelings and actions that we—and societies and nations before us—have found objectionable and even appalling.

In evaluating art, the viewer's role is thus only to approve. We are told that whatever the content of art, its very status as art entitles it to immunity from restraint. There are certainly those who will claim that the Mapplethorpe photographs are art, and therefore to be criticized, if at all, solely on aesthetic, never on moral, grounds. Are we to believe that the moral neutrality with which we are urged to view this art is shared by its proponents? Can it, rather, be possible that it is the very content so many find objectionable that recommends the art to its highly vocal backers?

Further, there are those who would have us believe that because we are not compelled to witness what we as individuals find morally unacceptable, we cannot refuse to make it available for others. Taking this position not only ignores our responsibility for others, it ignores the dreadful changes made in our own lives, and the lives of our children, by the availability of this decadence everywhere, from high art to popular culture.

It is undeniable that there is a large market for the hitherto forbidden. Upscale magazines trumpet the most shocking manifestations of what passes for new art. A rampant media culture profits hugely from the pleasing, and the lowering, of every taste.

Just as it is neither possible nor desirable to do much about regulating private sexual behavior, little can be done legally about the moral outrages of culture, either high or popular. But we can say no, and not only to our own participation as individuals in this trash. We can decline to make it available to the public through the use of our private facilities and funds: this, the Corcoran, acting as a private institution, has now done.

There is still more to be done. Acting on our behalf as citizens, our government agencies—in particular the National Endowment for the Arts—can redirect their energies away from being the validators of the latest fancies to hit the art market. Instead, public arts support might more fully concentrate on what it does so well: the championing of the great art of the past, its regeneration in the present, and its transmission to the future. This would mean saying yes to civilization. It is a policy change that deserves our prompt attention. One hopes that the Corcoran, by saying no to Robert Mapplethorpe, has begun the process.

(*The New York Times*, 1989)

23

OPERA AND POLITICS

At the beginning of January I was invited to take part in a panel discussion at the annual meeting of Opera America, the advocacy and service association of opera companies, large and small, in the United States and Canada. This meeting, a several-day affair, was to be held at the end of that same month in Washington, D.C., scarcely a stone's throw from the headquarters of the National Endowment for the Arts, the center of so much public controversy in recent months over the proprieties of federal arts funding.

Both because of the present climate for public support and because of wider trends in opera today, the panel to which I was invited promised to be particularly interesting. On it there was to appear the controversial stage director Peter Sellars, much noticed in the more progressive precincts of the opera world for his production of John Adams's *Nixon in China* (1987), and for his audacious updatings of Mozart operas at the Pepsico Summerfare festival at the State University of New York at Purchase, as well as a similar treatment of Richard Wagner's *Tannhäuser* at the Chicago Lyric Opera a season ago. There were to be three other members of the panel: Christopher Hunt, the guiding genius of Pepsico Summerfare from 1984 until its dissolution last year; the black composer Anthony Davis, whose opera *X*, a setting of the life of Malcolm X, was much talked about on its production in the 1986 season at the New York City Center Opera; and finally my friend and teacher (at Juilliard some three decades ago) Hugo Weisgall, the composer of the classic American modernist opera (based on Pirandello) *Six Characters in Search of an Author* (1956), who is now engaged in writing a large work based on Racine's *Esther* for the San Francisco Opera. The moderator of the panel was to be David Gockley, the current president of Opera America, and for many years now the general director of Houston Grand Opera, a company much praised for its willingness to program contemporary works and for its presentation of both operas and old Broadway musicals.

As interesting as the makeup of the panel was the proposed subject for discussion: "Opera as a Vehicle for Social Commentary or Activism in Today's Society." Considered in the light of the NEA's recent troubles, this subject seemed to speak directly to the concerns of an arts world shaken by the Serrano, Mapplethorpe, and Artists Space grants; much of the defense of the NEA, after all, had been mounted, not just in support of artistic freedom, but of the idea of art as being by its nature provocative, shocking, and offensive.

As might have been guessed, I had been invited, in the light of my lack of enthusiasm for avant-garde music-theater compositions and operatic productions, to provide a suitable foil for Sellars. Unfortunately, in the event there was to be no confrontation with him, for this busy man was suddenly prevented by the press of work in Los Angeles from appearing on the panel. His place was taken by the operatic stage director Leon Major.

Hunt, Weisgall, and Davis spoke before me, Major after. I can do no more than summarize their contributions here. Hunt began by saying that we live in an age of accustomed mediocrity. Our duty is to change society. In Europe, activism in opera (and in art in general) is taken for granted; here, he avowed, "the bland [are] leading the bland." We must get rid of "old dead audience expectations" and stress in the classics "what speaks to us now." According to Hunt, all art is political; art either seeks change or is a propagandist for the status quo. For Weisgall, the question posed to the panel was meaningless: what counted was not an a priori discussion of what opera should do, but the quality of the work—and *that* could be demonstrated only in production. For Davis, there was now a new sense of opera, a sense of remembering, as he had tried to do in *X*, the forgotten historical record of the multicultural contributions to American life and art. Viewed in this way, it was clear that to ignore or demean popular culture was to be in opposition to our American selves. For his part, Major stated that opera should not be an event in the life-style of the rich. We must realize that our past had not just been influenced by Europe, but also by Africa and Asia; it was in these latter directions that we must look for the future of opera.

As for my own contribution to the panel, I spoke from notes, not a written-out text, and in preparing what follows I have relied on a transcript made from an audio tape furnished by National Public Radio.[1] My only modifications have been to smooth out syntactical infelicities and to supply necessary (albeit limited) explanatory material. I have made an exception to this rule only in pulling into the printed version responses prompted by the lengthy question-and-answer period that followed our opening remarks. Here, then, are my remarks to the Opera America panel.

When I was coming here today on the plane, I thought that I really wanted to begin with the old story of the Finnish composer Sibelius, who said that he preferred the company of bankers to the company of musicians because musicians only wanted to talk about money.

It seemed to me as I was flying in on the Trump Shuttle that the 1980s had been the decade of our talking only about money whenever we discussed the arts. It seemed to me that, now that we're in the 1990s, we've seen an enormous shift from money to politics; what's being talked about now in the arts is nothing more or less than politics. Then of course I got here to Level Three of the J. W. Marriott Hotel, and I saw that Opera America is sharing the floor with the National Council of Savings Institutions. It occurred to me that we really have to ask ourselves whether opera is in a better situation than the savings and loan business. It certainly can't be in a worse position.

On my own analysis, discussions such as the one assigned to us today should begin by making clear our own personal definitions of what opera is. For me, opera is music that sets words to be staged. I put music first because I think that what makes opera a different kind of staged words— different, that is, from theater—is music. And the power of music in opera is such that at its best it has the power to become more important

than the words, to become more important than the theater that sur-
rounds and clothes the words. And when it becomes more important
than the words and the theater, we call it opera.

Let's stay with the words for a moment, because the primary question
that was assigned to us today—"Is it appropriate that opera serve as a
vehicle for social commentary or as an exemplar or call to activism?"—
deals entirely with words, that is, with subject matter. The comments
we've heard so far, though they haven't always been about any particular subject matter, have said that subject matter is a good thing. Well, it
seems to me that what opera deals with are the great and timeless oppo-
sitions of life. You all know about them: love and jealousy; loyalty and
treachery; devotion and hatred; the individual and the family; the nation
and the world; and what used to be called—and what I shall still call—
God and man. And of course the prime subject, the greatest subject of
opera, is vengeance and reconciliation.

The organizers of this panel have given us for our consideration a
whole list of social issues that opera may possibly deal with. The list
begins with the individual versus society. Then it goes on to multicultural and multiracial society, the fate of the planet, use and abuse of
technology, distribution of wealth, AIDS, the homeless, gender, abuses
of power, and censorship. Well, my guess is that these questions will
only have importance for opera if they can be used in two contexts. One
context is, of course, the context of these great issues of life that I've read
out to you. If the issues of the environment and the homeless, of AIDS
and gender, cannot be related to questions of love and hatred, vengeance and betrayal, the individual and the family, they won't work as
opera, and you will end up with no more than yet another empty version
of socialist realism.

The other requirement for these issues to count in opera is great music. That's the most important requirement of all. Opera, it seems to me
(if I may approach the subject slightly differently), is about three things:
it's about singing, it's about music, and it's about art. When I look at it
this way, I see a kind of triple failure on the part of opera at this moment.
On the level of singing, I see that the great operas of the past have become increasingly difficult to cast with first-rate singers, and however
they're cast, the results are increasingly poor. In this line, I have often

said that you only need listen to the Metropolitan Opera broadcasts these days, and in particular to the 1989 Bayreuth Festival broadcasts, to know just what a dreadful state singing—at the top—is in today.

Then, if we look at what I see as the failure of opera as music, I think we have to realize that the true test of an opera, and of its survival, is whether it's capable of moving into the concert hall. The great operas of the past exist not only in the opera house (though they surely exist there), they exist as arias that are performed by singers in concert, they exist as overtures, and they exist in full-length concert performance. They exist, in other words, as viable works even when stripped of the distractions of acting and staging. If we look at the operas written in recent years, and each of us will have a different cut-off date over the past several decades, we will find that new opera nowhere exists in the concert hall. In other words, the life of symphony orchestra concerts and vocal recitals goes on without any participation of recent operatic composition.

We must be careful not to blame opera alone for this shortfall in music; the musical problems of opera are no more than an inevitable corollary of the musical problems of music itself. Nor is the lack of marvelous new operatic music, any more than the lack of marvelous new music in general, a matter of lack of support. Everyone talks about the record of Germany in the support of new music, new opera, and so on. What's left of all this? I want to know what's left of the great exemplar of that movement, Stockhausen. What's left of it? What's left of his music? Who wants to hear it? All his records are there. The records are there because the Deutsche Grammophon Gesellschaft and its owners have wanted to expunge the memory of the Nazis in the minds of cultivated people the world over. But the fact is that nothing is left. Where Stockhausen is concerned, you don't want to hear the records or the music, and no one else does either.

Not only is there a shortfall in new opera when it is considered from the standpoint of music. There's the much wider problem of opera as art. I would say that the very existence of our panel today is pretty convincing evidence that opera as art is in a bad way. Because what we are doing here, of course, is talking about everything except the art of opera, about its music, or about its singing. By the way, that applies to me, too. Because I've now been seduced into talking about opera as words, I too have been treating opera as if it were only words.

Everyone now talks about how important it is for politics to be put into opera. Of course we see the proliferation of this idea everywhere. In Europe, we've had the political stagings of Wagner's *Ring*, beginning, I suppose, with Götz Friedrich and continuing with Patrice Chéreau. Lots of less interesting but still trendy directors have gotten in on the act, too. We also have new operas: Anthony Davis—sitting next to me—with *X*, and the Sellars-Adams collaboration *Nixon in China*. Those operas are certainly about politics. They certainly take political subjects, treat them from a political point of view, and attempt to appeal to an audience with a particular political commitment.

Then, too, we have the fad of reworking old pieces. In this country, Peter Sellars is well known for his contribution to this practice. Perhaps I might take a moment to talk about Sellars's Chicago *Tannhäuser*, put on by my friend Ardis Krainik, the general director of the Chicago Lyric Opera, whom I see here in the audience today. I want to share with you my thoughts about how all of you would have felt if the Sellars *Tannhäuser* had not been about the conservative evangelist Jimmy Swaggart but had instead been about the liberal senator Ted Kennedy. Or perhaps if it had been about the equally liberal, but now discredited, former senator Gary Hart. I had actually a rather good time on the plane coming here, thinking of how the characters could be reworked. Gary Hart, of course, would be Tannhäuser, his wife, Lee, would be Elisabeth, and Donna Rice would be Venus; in a cameo appearance, rather like the Italian Singer in *Der Rosenkavalier*, John Denver would be Wolfram von Eschenbach. How would you like that? Would you like to see a classic opera thus represented?

Let me be just a shade more serious. In the late 1930s, the Nazis and their German artistic collaborators attempted to rework the oratorio *Judas Maccabaeus* of Handel. They did it by providing new words that would avoid the stain of the Judaic Old Testament subject; they also commissioned various complaisant composers to provide a new music to replace Mendelssohn's immortal masterpiece in performances of *A Midsummer Night's Dream*. I take it that none of you would be in favor of this kind of updating of musico-dramatic works to reflect present-day politi-

cal realities. You, like decent people everywhere, would reject this blatant and indeed murderous anti-Semitism; I suspect you would be the
first to ask for what can only be called "authenticity."

But beyond the immediate judgment involved here—which it goes
without saying I fully agree with—aren't you then being trapped by the
logic of your position into evaluating art on a purely political basis? If
you reject—as you should—Hitler's political updating of Handel, but
you support Peter Sellars's sociopolitical updating of *Tannhäuser*,
aren't you making a political rather than an artistic judgment? Aren't you
really saying that some politics you like, and some politics you don't, and
if the reworking of opera goes in the direction of the politics you like, fine;
if it doesn't, you don't like it? That means that not opera, not singing, not
music, not art, but politics, is your test.

It is now fashionable to say that opera, like all art, must be "challenging." I don't think that's a fair reading of the history of art: it seems to me
that the preponderance of great art has in fact reinforced and passed on,
rather than challenged and destroyed, the prevailing values of society.
But if we say that art should be a challenge, shouldn't we then go on to
say that art itself should be challenged?

I see people in this room nodding. Well, forces in the Congress of the
United States are now trying to challenge art. You're not in favor of that
kind of challenge, are you? As a matter of fact, not only are you not in
favor of the content of the challenge, you're against the challenge being
made at all; that is, you're against it, in principle, as a human activity. It
seems to me that there is a kind of playing with fire here, in which the
very important, I believe God-given, traditions of our American polity,
the best traditions, are being taken for granted as a backstop by the very
people who are unwilling to admit that these traditions actually exist.
Now, when that happens, you find that the people caught in the middle
begin to lose confidence in the traditions themselves. There is a playing
with fire going on here, and I'm amazed that people whose life is opera,
as is certainly the case for all of you, don't realize quite what the stakes
are in this discussion.

Are we really ready to apply partisan politics as the test for what we
do in opera in this country in the 1990s? Here we are, sitting in Washington, with all the reality of power that suggests. Now if we're going to

apply politics in this way to opera, I think we're redefining opera. We're using opera as a word in quite a new way. Certainly we have never used it in this way in this country before. If we accomplish this redefinition, and make artistic judgments on this basis, I actually would agree that this very subject—opera redefined to mean politics—might be a wonderful subject for an opera. But I have to point out one problem with this fascinating subject. We need a great composer—say, Richard Strauss—to make an opera out of it. But then we're right back to square one with the need for great music. For in opera, music still comes, and will always come, first.

(*The New Criterion*, 1990)

24

BACKWARD AND DOWNWARD

WITH THE ARTS

This spring and summer will witness a bitter fight in Congress, and perhaps even across the country, over the quinquennial statutory reauthorization of the National Endowment for the Arts (NEA) and the National Endowment for the Humanities (NEH). These twin government agencies, first established in 1965 under a common legislative umbrella, together now spend some $300 million on the direct subsidy of the arts and the humanities. Small money, as federal programs go, but the endowments have nevertheless been deeply controversial since their inception, and recent events, all of them concerned with the NEA rather than the NEH, have only served to ensure that the controversy will continue.

The trouble began last spring with the revelation that NEA money had been used to pay for the exhibition of *Piss Christ*, the now notorious photograph by Andres Serrano depicting a crucifix submerged in a vessel containing the artist's urine. Shortly thereafter, it became known that the NEA was funding a traveling exhibition of photographs by Robert Mapplethorpe, containing many homoerotic and sadomasochistic images, including one of a man urinating into another man's mouth and another of a man with a whip handle protruding from his anus; in the expectation of a storm in Congress over this matter, the Corcoran Gallery in Washington, D.C., decided in June to cancel its already announced showing of the exhibition. In November, the NEA first withdrew, and then conditionally reinstated, its funding of *Witnesses: Against Our Vanishing*, an exhibition, more disgusting than obscene, of AIDS-related paintings, photographs, and installations at the downtown Manhattan Artists Space gallery; the part of the exhibition the NEA finally refused to fund was an accompanying catalogue containing virulent anti-Catholic statements proclaiming, among other things, that the Catholic church is a "house of walking swastikas." Just this past winter, the NEA was criticized for its association with a presentation at the Kitchen, the Manhattan avant-garde performance space, of Annie Sprinkle, a one-time prostitute and porn star now turned performance artist; in her "performance" Miss Sprinkle invited the audience onstage to examine her genitals through a gynecological speculum. Though in this last case the NEA denied any direct funding, the fact that it has all along generously supported the Kitchen seemed to bestow an artistic Good Housekeeping Seal of Approval on everything performed there.

The uproar over these various events—and the suspicion that they are only the most obvious examples of an official attitude that in general encourages pornography, obscenity, and indecency—has sparked attempts in Congress by Senator Jesse Helms (R.-N.C.) and others to restrict grants in such areas by both the NEA and the NEH. For the most part, the attempts have failed, although in the process of defeating them, congressional arts advocates were forced to allow some restrictive language in the Endowment's 1990 budget, and to establish a commission to study the NEA's grant-making process, in particular its peer-panel system. The restrictive language is of dubious clarity and applicability; as for the study commission, at this point it seems little more than another hypocritical effort by supporters of public arts funding to legitimize their cause and whitewash the activities of those responsible for its administration.

The truth is that since the inception of the National Endowments there has been little serious discussion, not just of how the agencies should be run from day to day, but of what national policy should underlie their activities. Americans in any case tend to think of "cultural policy" as something slightly illegitimate, the sort of thing that gets promulgated not in a democratic society but by totalitarian regimes like those of Nazi Germany and Bolshevik Russia; and many Americans also still tend to think of culture as essentially a private matter. But now, for better or for worse, the issue of such a cultural policy, and of its place in our national life, is very much on the public agenda.

Where, then, do we stand? I would begin with two contradictory assertions. The first is that in the United States today we have no national cultural policy; though we spend public money, the purposes for which it is spent are random, aimless as to desired outcome, and subject to no accountability either as expenditure or as result. The second assertion is that, on the contrary, we do have a national policy—one that is consciously formed, specific as to desired outcome, and strictly accountable for its results. As I shall try to show, the contradiction is actually more apparent than real: in fact, our present situation is characterized less by contradiction than by a dangerous unity.

We have no national cultural policy: a quick look at the past decade would appear to bear out this contention. There was, to begin with, an effort by the incoming Reagan administration actually to eliminate both Endowments. Then, in 1981, William J. Bennett—by my lights, an excellent choice—was named chairman of the National Endowment for the Humanities in a bruising political fight with no questions asked (by the administration) about the possible fate of the humanities under his stewardship; his replacement, Lynne V. Cheney, also an excellent choice, has been unsupported by White House policy under two presidents and has been left alone to fend off congressional marauders and sniping from the intellectual and academic communities. Under both Bennett and Cheney, the NEH has clung to a strongly held idea of intellectual mission, yet nowhere in the federal government has there been an attempt to apply, say, to educational policy the rigorously reasoned and powerfully written NEH reports on the state of education and of the humanities. The voice of the president in the service of the humanities, or even in the service of a philosophy of humanistic education, has been totally lacking.

The story at the NEA reflects the same absence of policy—but without the redeeming feature of strong agency leadership. In 1981, a chairman, Frank Hodsoll, was chosen for the NEA who lacked a background in art or the arts; the battle for his replacement in 1989 was marked by unseemly competition among various old-boy networks, with the final selection of John Frohnmayer being made on the basis primarily of political patronage. From the beginning, during Hodsoll's regime (1982 to 1989) a series of wise and far-reaching administrative reforms—most, now, under Frohnmayer, a thing of the past—was unfortunately wedded to a refusal to make distinctions between programs and grants, between transience and permanence, between high art and entertainment. Even arts education, for some a quasi-religious cause undertaken on behalf of the nation, ended up after a promising start as a program to hawk the electronic media to our most media-corrupted generation.

Overall, the cry at the NEA has been "presence": the demand that every activity being supported bring the agency to the notice of as many influential people as possible. As was true in the first fifteen years of the NEA, it was felt in the eighties that public support could only be achieved by yoking the agency to the wagons of the glamorous, the famous, and the successful. The White House has abetted this tendency by sponsoring on its premises a mixture of glitz and gloss: Michael Jackson, and now country music. But neither in the Bush administration nor during the two relatively high-minded Reagan administrations that preceded it did anyone ever think that the public "presence" which the agency sought through an orientation to celebrity could be achieved overnight through notoriety. Ironically enough, it has been the function of the now famous Serrano, Mapplethorpe, Artists Space, and Annie Sprinkle cases to bring the NEA a presence in American life it was unable to win in the first twenty-four years of its existence.

Perhaps the clearest sign of the lack of a cultural policy has been the remarkable inability of the NEA and its supporters to undertake an effective defense of these objectionable grants, as well as of the presumed general purposes of the agency. Faced with public outcry, neither agency bureaucrats nor arts advocates at large could do anything more than assert lamely that the NEA, because it relied entirely on peer-panel review, in fact exercised no control over its grant-making. This response was so weak, and ultimately so lacking in philosophical weight, that even seasoned arts administrators—including leading voices at the NEA itself—were soon panicked into claiming that in making provocative grants the NEA was only fulfilling its proper function, since art itself was in its essence provocative. This line of argument, so far from improving matters, merely had the effect of reducing not only the NEA but art itself to being the handmaiden of anger, violence, and social upheaval.

And so for the last several months the struggle over the NEA has been waged entirely in terms of accusation and counteraccusation. Tons of ink and a myriad strident voices have been employed in answering Senator Helms and his supporters, who no more have a coherent policy than do those whom they criticize. Neither side, in fact, has made clear just how and for what purposes NEA money should be spent, if it is to be spent at all. Even more significantly, the president of the United States has been all but silent, close in name only to the activities undertaken on his behalf.

So much for the first assertion. Now for the second: *we do have a national cultural policy.* This policy, some years in the making but now fully discernible, is based on three elements: affirmative action, that is, the preferential hiring of women and minorities to fill both administrative and nonadministrative positions in the humanities and, especially, the arts; a bias toward "multiculturalism"; and, finally, public advocacy and financial support of so-called cutting-edge art. Each of these elements has been, and is, advanced by different forces in American life, and for different purposes, but they partake of a common function and have a common importance.

By affirmative action I do not mean the hiring of highly qualified candidates, who are in fact to be found in all of the groups that make up American life. Nor do I have in mind an actual quota system, though the hand of Congress has been heavy in attempting to enforce just such a system on both endowments. I am concerned with something even more dangerous: the predisposition to require that for each position that becomes vacant, every conceivable candidate of the proper gender or color be sought out. In the area of government arts administration, it is now clear that even minimum qualifications, which often amount to no more than limited acquaintance with a field, are presumptive reasons for hiring. For the most important cultural positions in government, only a record of gross partisan political opposition now serves as a disqualification, and even here the standard is ever more rarely upheld.

Outside government, affirmative action is no longer primarily applied for the limited purpose of bringing minorities and women into traditional activities (as in the case of the hiring of a black bassist by the Detroit Symphony Orchestra last year). Instead it is implemented, from above, as a painless means of winning favor from well-organized and demonstrative groups, while from below it is deployed as a means of altering the traditional activities themselves, in order to transform them into activities for which no social or intellectual consensus now exists. This twin movement, impelled on the one hand by the desire to win immediate popularity, and on the other hand by the principled determination to mount a long-term cultural revolution, is now the most immediate of the factors eroding the life of traditional cultural institutions.

The name of that revolution is multiculturalism, a widespread assault on what is variously called Western, or European, or white-dominated, or male-dominated civilization. To see the multiculturalist bias at work one need go no further than to the pages of *An American Dialogue*, a report on artistic touring and presenting put together by arts bureaucrats and paid for by a powerful public and private consortium made up of the NEA, the Rockefeller Foundation, and the Pew Charitable Trusts. According to this document, the purpose of the arts is overridingly socioideological: to make "a profound impact on American society and the changes that are shaping it."

The exact nature of this "profound impact" becomes clear in the way *An American Dialogue* treats the hitherto exalted status of European-based high art. These imperishable masterpieces, along with the artistic traditions derived from them, are now to be regarded as no more than one kind of ethnic manifestation; in preserving and extending those traditions on the American shore, European immigrants of the past, like peoples everywhere, were merely indulging old instincts and tastes, having brought "with them their hunger and demand for European-style performing arts events." But, the report tells us, we should not grant favored status to this kind of cultural and artistic expression, for we now know that art itself is made up of a "breadth of genres, styles, sources, venues, artists, art forms, and expressions," and that the art of all peoples is equally worthy of preservation and presentation.

It would be tempting to characterize all of this as blather. But I well remember a (failed) attempt several years ago to change the music program of the NEA from one concentrating on classical music and jazz to one open equally to all "world musics," without reference to any serious aesthetic consideration or discrimination; today, the new administration at NEA gives every sign of implementing just such a change as part of its widely proclaimed multicultural agenda. In light of budget limitations, such a policy can only be paid for by taking money away from the large institutions that have been concerned with the transmission of great, albeit "European-style," art.

Nor should we be deceived by the egalitarian rhetoric of the advocates of multiculturalism. Beneath the slogans of equality lurk implicit, and sometimes explicit, hierarchies of favored cultures, often chosen with political ends in mind. According to *An American Dialogue*, art is the product of "cultures and people . . . scarred by centuries of violence against them . . . these histories, and the images and the expressions that have grown from them, must be recognized and supported." Here we come to the true heart of multiculturalism: the frankly instrumental use of culture and art as a device of political consciousness-raising. In the private nonprofit sector, this thrust is already fully internalized. Both the Rockefeller and Ford foundations, to name only the two giants of American cultural funding, have made it clear that they intend to downgrade and even eliminate support for art based on traditional European sources, and instead will encourage activity by certain approved minorities in the United States and abroad. Where they lead, the public sector will surely follow.

The final element in our national cultural policy is the promotion of the so-called cutting edge (once known as the avant-garde). This takes many forms. Sometimes the cutting edge is a fringe movement in such traditional art forms as painting, music, opera, theater, photography, or dance. Sometimes it is a new aesthetic hybrid, such as multimedia art, multidisciplinary art, interdisciplinary art, or performance art. In these latter hybrid activities, the place reserved in multiculturalism for racial or ethnic or national minorities is filled instead by the claims of political radicalism, gender redefinition, and "life-style"—the latter perhaps now little more than a euphemism for florid and variant sexualities.

It hardly needs saying that what gives the cutting edge its current vitality in cultural policy is not the degree of artistic achievement it has displayed but rather its extra-artistic, social content. When I recently asked the woman responsible for arts grants in a great foundation whether she had any idea of just how bad the cutting-edge art she supported was, her answer was swift: "Listen," she said, "I've seen a lot more terrible work than you'll ever see."

The simple fact is that this cutting-edge art, flagrantly exemplified in the Serrano, Mapplethorpe, Artists Space, and Sprinkle cases, more subtly presented in the genre as a whole, is concerned not with art but with advocacy, not with the creation of permanent beauty but with the imposition of hitherto rejected modes of behavior and ways of living. At a conference just this past March on culture and democracy, the art critic Donald Kuspit put it well: the Mapplethorpe photographs, he remarked approvingly, for all their classicizing, half-ironic aspects, serve the purpose of "ultimately sanctifying . . . the perverse subject matter." That being so, it was inevitable that cutting-edge grants would come to be defended by the arts establishment not in terms of artistic achievement but in terms of free speech.

Congress is now beginning to consider the statutory reauthorization of the National Endowments. The real battle, it seems plain, will initially be over the NEA, not the NEH. At this moment, the defenders of the NEA, an uneasy coalition drawn equally from establishment notables and from political and artistic radicals, spend little or no time talking about civilization and permanence, about the past and the future. They certainly spend no time talking about policy, about the large issues that properly underlie any consideration of what should be supported, and why. But neither do those who have the greatest interest in pursuing just such questions. In particular, the great institutions which in the past have been regarded as national treasures, and richly supported by government funds, everywhere stand timorous and silent.

Here is the point of dangerous reconciliation in the contradiction with which I started. For we both do not have, and yet do have, a cultural policy. Until now, our not having a cultural policy has meant no more than the tendency of our national leaders, both public and private, to regard art and culture as trivial, diversionary pastimes, at best mildly amusing or sentimentally uplifting. It has been consistent with this trivializing attitude to use the National Endowment for the Arts as a political cow, ripe for milking. But precisely in this way, our not having a national cultural policy has served to facilitate and consolidate the cultural policy we do have—namely, the effort to exploit the vestigial prestige of art and culture to accomplish radical social and political goals.

What, in the present environment, is the course that should be followed by those concerned with the stability of traditional political institutions and committed to the preservation and transmission of the great traditions of art and learning and the values they embody? It seems to me there are essentially two options.

The first option is to reject in toto the entire apparatus of government support for the arts and, with the arts, the humanities. This would mean an end to the National Endowments, and an abandonment of the idea that one of the tasks of the federal government is to foster a common civilization. Because the rejection of direct government support would now be based not on a theoretical conception of the proper limitations on government, but rather on a gathering perception of the artistic and moral degeneration such support implies, the result would likely be a reexamination of indirect governmental support, in the form of tax deductions, as well. This in turn might lead to a reconsideration of the entire structure of tax deductions for charitable contributions, for the purpose of ascertaining whether such contributions are still today in the widest public interest. What we end up contemplating, in short, is a fundamental change in a whole series of longstanding American arrangements.

The second—and in my judgment the better—option is to refuse to abandon public life to those hostile to the cultural traditions, and the social norms, by which we continue to define—and defend—ourselves. Pursuing this option means continuing to fight, within government and without, in public and in private, for the preservation and extension of our common cultural and artistic inheritance. It means pressing, openly and passionately, for a cultural *policy*—but a policy which, when linked to programs of government support, will help make possible, in Coleridge's great phrase, "the harmonious development of those qualities and faculties that characterize our humanity."

In any case the battle has begun.

(*Commentary,* 1990)

Notes

INTRODUCTION

1. To keep the record straight, I should add that I myself have written one of these upbeat articles, on the 1991 Waterloo Music Festival, of which I am the artistic director.

2. *Public Money and the Muse: Essays on Government Funding for the Arts*, ed. Stephen Benedict (New York: The American Assembly/Norton, 1991).

3. Just how much richer the Metropolitan Opera is than the New York City Opera is shown by a well-founded story that the Met, at a time when the City Opera is concerned with year-to-year operating funds, is now considering a several-hundred-million-dollar endowment-fund campaign.

CHAPTER 1

1. Cornelius Cardew, *Stockhausen Serves Imperialism* (London: Latimer New Directions, 1974).

CHAPTER 2

1. New York: Holt, Rinehart & Winston, 1980. I am indebted to this book for a lucid exposition of the facts of Weil's life.

2. Ann Arbor, Mich.: University Microfilms International Research Press, 1979.

3. These words, not surprisingly, were cut from the 1954 New York revival by the work's adapter, Marc Blitzstein, and replaced by innocuous filler.

4. In this connection it is significant for Brecht's commitment to his position

and for Weill's commitment to Brecht that they both decided to withdraw *Der Jasager* from the Neue Musik Berlin 1930 festival because it had rejected *Die Massnahme.*

CHAPTER 4

1. The entire broadcast is available on a fund-raising album from the New York Philharmonic.

2. Deutsche Grammophon 415 253-1 (LP); 415 253-4 (cassette); 415 253-2 (CD).

3. CBS S32603.

4. NW 277.

5. JJA 197648.

6. *Bernstein: The Art of the Conductor* (New York: Vanguard Press, 1982).

CHAPTER 6

1. I have previously written, in *Commentary*, on Stravinsky (July 1978) and Shostakovich (November 1982); the Stravinsky article was reprinted in my *Music After Modernism* (1979) and the Shostakovich article in *The House of Music* (1984).

2. Horowitz's 1947 recording of the *Toccata* is a fitting monument both to the great pianist and to the entire era of supercharged pianism, now gone, which he exemplified. It is available (or, given the current obsolescence of the LP disc, said to be available) on RCA ARM 1-2717. Of even greater historical interest are Prokofiev's own less aggressive (though equally hard-edged) 1935 performances of the *Suggestion diabolique* and nine of the *Visions fugitives*; they were available in the 1960s, along with other examples of Prokofiev's playing of his own music, on Angel COLH 34.

3. A lovely, dreamy performance of this work by the Russian virtuoso David Oistrakh, recorded (I assume) in the Soviet Union in the mid-1950s, was available many years ago on Westminster XWN 18178. A much more compelling and communicative recording was done as long ago as 1935 by the great Hungarian violinist Joseph Szigeti, accompanied by the redoubtable Sir Thomas Beecham; it was last available in the 1970s on the very choice Szigeti eightieth-birthday album, CBS M6X 31513.

4. Prokofiev's own surprisingly limpid 1932 performance of the Concerto No. 3, made in London with conductor Piero Coppola, is to be found on Angel COLH 34, a disc I have mentioned above. My own favorite recording of

this work was made in the late 1940s by the much-lamented American pianist William Kappell (1922–53); it is now available on LP as RCA AGM1-5266, and on cassette as AGK1-5266.

5. *Sergei Prokofiev: A Biography* (New York: Viking, 1987).

6. In his *The Opera Companion to Twentieth-Century Opera* (1979).

7. Connoisseurs of historical recordings will be interested to know of Prokofiev's own 1938 performance of the Suite No. 2 from *Romeo and Juliet*, now available on a Philips CD (420778-2), and his mentor Koussevitzky's extraordinary 1945 Boston performance of the same excerpts, recently available on an RCA Victrola LP (AVM1-2021).

8. In this era of *glasnost* and *perestroika* it might be salutary to listen occasionally to such a token of the bad old days; the *Cantata* was recently available on a Melodiya/Angel recording (SR40129), coupled with another classic of the genre, Shostakovich's cantata celebrating the thirty-fifth anniversary of the 1917 Revolution, *The Sun Shines Over Our Motherland* (1952).

9. The first American performance of each of these three Prokofiev sonatas was given during World War II by Vladimir Horowitz, who recorded No. 7 in 1950; the performance remains today the standard for the technical brilliance and the cold passion which the pianist, mirroring the composer, brings to the music. This epochal piece of piano-playing was included, along with an equally superlative performance of the Barber sonata, in the RCA LP album LD 7021, now deleted.

10. I am aware of two recordings of *War and Peace*. The first, a 1960 Soviet recording conducted by Alexander Melik-Pashayev and very likely made with the extraordinary cast (including Galina Vishnevskaya) of the 1959 Bolshoi staging, was available (with the usual execrable surfaces) as Melodiya MK 218 D; I have not heard the deleted Angel reissue of this performance. A new CD, recorded in Bulgaria and pressed in West Germany, is now available (with a libretto in English and French) as Fidelio 8801/3.

11. *Prokofiev by Prokofiev*, edited by David H. Appel and translated by Guy Daniels (Doubleday, 1979).

CHAPTER 7

1. *My Young Years* and *My Many Years* (New York: Knopf, 1973, 1980).

2. Material has recently come to light, through a letter by James Methuen-Campbell in the April 1983 *Gramophone*, suggesting that Rubinstein made

at least one disc for a Polish company around 1910. This record, of the Liszt Twelfth Rhapsody and the Strauss *Blue Danube* waltz, is in the possession of the Polish Radio, whence it will doubtless emerge on some appropriate state occasion.

3. DB 1160; currently available on LP as EMI Electrola 1C 151-03 244/5.

4. DB 1161; available during the 1960s as EMI Odeon QALP 10363 (Italy).

5. DB 1257; EMI Electrola 1C 151-03 244/5.

6. DB 1258; available on EMI Electrola 1C 151-03 244/45.

7. D 1746/60; available on Supraphon 1010 2856.

8. DB 1494/7; available on EMI Dacapo 1C 053-10172.

9. DB 1728/30.

10. DB 1762; available on EMI Odeon QALP 10363 (Italy).

11. DB 1915/8; available on EMI Electrola 1C 187-50 357/8.

12. DB 2493/500; available on EMI Electrola 1C 187-50 357/8.

13. DB 1731/4.

14. RCA DM 1016 (78 RPM).

15. Bruno Walter Society BWS 740 (private recording).

CHAPTER 8

1. The LP collection of all the Prokofiev material was available some years ago as Angel (EMI) COLH 34.

2. All the Rachmaninoff recorded performances were available, in five volumes of three LPs each, as RCA ARM 3-0260, 0261, 0294, 0295, and 0296. The works for piano and orchestra (ARM 3-0296) are still available.

3. Seraphim 60183.

4. *Bartók at the Piano 1920–1945*, Hungaroton LPX 12326-33. *Bartók Record Archives: Bartók Plays and Talks 1912–1944*, Hungaroton LPX 12334-38.

5. Though it might be objected that any use of this test recording as a means of evaluating Bartók's playing is unfair because the disc was never released, it seems, from the notes accompanying the current set, that Bartók thought enough of the performance to have given the masters to his son, who cherished them.

6. Sándor was the first pianist to record Bartók's Third Concerto, with the Philadelphia Orchestra and Eugene Ormandy about 1946. Until recently

this performance was available as Columbia Special Products P 14155. Sándor's recording of all the Bartók solo music is available in three volumes as Vox SVBX 5425/6/7.

CHAPTER 10

1. Pearl CLA 1000, distributed by Qualiton Imports (3928 Crescent St., Long Island City, N.Y. 11101).

CHAPTER 11

1. Chapel Hill: University of North Carolina Press, 1989.

2. New York: Summit Books, 1989.

3. Dubal seems to me to have erred in excluding from his recommended lists many classic recordings made by great artists on 78-RPM discs and transferred excellently to LP in Europe. Among the most important of these are performances from the 1930s by the great French pianist Alfred Cortot of works by César Franck and Maurice Ravel—in particular, the Franck Prelude, Chorale, and Fugue and the Ravel Concerto for the Left Hand.

CHAPTER 12

1. Pearl GEMM CD 9474.

2. The Overture to *Der fliegende Holländer* originally appeared on Victor 6547, and I am not aware that it has ever been transferred to LP or CD. *Ein Heldenleben* was available for a time in the 1970s on an English RCA LP, SMA 7001. The Beethoven First Symphony was transferred to LP some years ago on Educational Media Associates RR-501; the Beethoven Third Symphony originally appeared on Victor 7439/45, and does not seem to have ever been transferred to LP or CD. It is to be hoped that Pearl will soon reissue these important performances.

3. Toscanini's performance, from a broadcast, was to be found several years ago in an Arturo Toscanini Recording Association LP album, ATRA-3011.

4. Mengelberg's rephrasing in this passage, as elsewhere, is documented in Bernard Shore's *The Orchestra Speaks* (1938), as quoted in David Wooldridge's *Conductor's World* (1970).

5. Toscanini's Beethoven is mostly now known in the NBC recordings made by RCA in the late 1940s and early 1950s and widely available since then; they may easily be found on CD. An exceptionally stern Toscanini/NBC 1939 performance of the *Eroica* was reissued in the last years of the LP on a Japanese RCA LP, RCL-3348. The First, Fourth, Sixth, and Seventh sym-

phonies, with Toscanini conducting the not-quite-world-class BBC Symphony Orchestra in the years from 1935 to 1939, were available several years ago on LP as EMI EX 29 0930 3. Toscanini's famous 1936 recording of the Seventh Symphony with the Philharmonic is now available, along with a 1933 recording (unissued at the time) of the Fifth Symphony, on a Pearl CD set, GEMM CDS 9373. Furthermore, a 1936 aircheck of the Fourth Symphony was available some years ago on a Swiss LP, Relief 821. Despite many local differences, all these performances, done over a period of almost two decades, are quite consistent in the severity of their approach to the music.

6. Fascinating detail about this practice of Mengelberg's is provided by Bernard Shore in *The Orchestra Speaks* (1938).

CHAPTER 13

1. In this regard, it is a special pleasure here to thank the conductor John Canarina, my friend and fellow student at L'Ecole Monteux in Maine in the 1950s, for his kindness in supplying me with invaluable tapes of all too scarce Monteux recordings.

2. This performance, although interesting in itself, is vastly inferior in finish to Monteux's later remakes of *The Rite of Spring* in San Francisco, Boston, and Paris. It has just been issued in English, accompanied by a 1928 performance of *Petrushka* conducted by the composer, on Pearl GEMM CD 9329.

3. Along with much other choice material performed by some of the greatest French artists of the interwar period, this gem was released in 1987 on a *La voix de son maître* LP set, *Ravel et ses interprètes,* as EMI 2912163.

4. This exemplary performance, so redolent of an era before Bach playing was seen as an archeological enterprise, is just now available on an EMI CD, packaged with two other Bach concertos, played by Menuhin and conducted by Enescu.

5. Many of these recordings were available in the early and mid-1980s in excellent LP transfers on the French RCA *Cycle Monteux.*

6. The Tchaikovsky Fourth Symphony is available on cassette tapes as RCA AGK1-5254 and Victrola ALK1-4772; the Fifth Symphony is similarly available as Victrola ALK1-5385.

7. *Petrushka* and *The Rite of Spring* are now available on a single CD reissue as RCA 6529-2-RG.

8. Monteux's appearances outside San Francisco were so infrequent that during his California years he only conducted the Philharmonic twice, once for two Sunday concerts during the summer season of 1943, and once for two weeks during the 1944–45 regular season.

9. Just how far Monteux was from approving the historical-performance movement may be judged from a story I heard as a young music student in San Francisco. (Though I heard it only second-hand, it has for me the ring of truth.) It seems that when Monteux was rehearsing a Bach keyboard concerto with a distinguished academic musicologist at the harpsichord, disagreements emerged between conductor and soloist—whereupon Monteux exploded in his ineffable Franco-American English: "Now I know why zee peeple 'ate Bach!"

10. This technique includes the use of extreme tempos and dynamic contrasts, and of constant rhythmic displacements and intensifications. The conscious aim, of course, is to compel the listener's attention at every moment; a further aim, which may be conscious or unconscious, is to fasten the listener's attention on the executant as the prime mover in vivifying the music.

11. My copy of this recording, purchased in the mid-1970s, is on Unicorn (England) WFS8.

CHAPTER 14

1. I have adapted this idea from Virgil Thomson's perceptive remarks about Stravinsky: "After giving to the world between 1909 and 1913 three proofs of colossally expanding powers—*Firebird*, *Petrushka*, and the *Rite of Spring*—he found himself unable to expand farther. And since, like Picasso, he was still to go on living, and since he could not imagine living without making music, he too was faced with an unhappy choice. He could either make music out of his own past (which he disdained to do) or out of music's past, which he is still [in 1967] doing."

CHAPTER 15

1. Nimbus CD 5144/48.

2. Angel CD A26 49852.

3. The Hogwood Ninth has just been issued on L'Oiseau-Lyre 425 517-2.

CHAPTER 16

1. Charles Reid, *The Music Monster* (London: Quartet Books, 1984).

CHAPTER 18

1. Edward W. Said, *Musical Elaborations* (New York: Columbia University Press, 1990).

2. I am not aware of the existence of this 1938 Toscanini performance; I wonder whether Said is not referring to the 1939 RCA recording with the NBC Symphony, which has recently been made available on a Japanese RCA LP, RCL-3348.

CHAPTER 19

1. *Lotte Lehmann's Farewell Recital,* with Paul Ulanowsky, piano. Pelican LP 2009.

CHAPTER 20

1. John Carswell, *The Exile: A Life of Ivy Litvinov* (London: Faber & Faber, 1983).

2. The fate of these papers in itself makes up an illuminating chapter in the perils of resistance to Soviet policy: though Ivy, before leaving America in 1943, had entrusted the safe-deposit-box key to "an American friend," some time after Maxim's death she found herself summoned to the Lubyanka prison, where she was faced with, and interrogated about, the supposedly hidden documents. Unfortunately, Carswell gives neither the name of the "American friend" nor even the date of Ivy's potentially fatal encounter with the Soviet authorities.

3. William L. Shirer, *The Nightmare Years: 1930–1940* (Boston: Little, Brown, 1984). In this, the second volume of his memoirs, the famous war correspondent paints Litvinov as directly tied to the Soviet measures he advocated: "Maxim Litvinov, the longtime Soviet commissar for foreign affairs, had staked his reputation and career on building up collective security against Nazi Germany. He thought a united front of the two Western powers and the Soviet Union . . . was the only means of deterring Hitler. . . . Undaunted by Chamberlain's rejection . . . Litvinov called in the British ambassador in Moscow on April 16 [1939] and made a formal proposal for a triple pact. . . . It was Litvinov's last bid to the West to join Russia in stopping Hitler. . . . But Chamberlain stalled, and this was fatal to Litvinov."

4. Both these books are now difficult to obtain, at least in this country. I am indebted to the research collections of the New York Library and Stanford University for making reproductions of them available to me.

5. It should be made clear that, for all Ivy's apolitical stance, she was, for much of the period of her husband's success, aware of the true state of affairs in Stalin's Russia; this is made abundantly plain by Carswell's inclusion of a horrifying extract from a tape made by Ivy in 1960–61 concerning the fate of Rose Cohen, an Englishwoman married to a Ukrainian Communist and murdered by Stalin despite Ivy's attempt to secure the intercession of Harry Pollitt, the head of the English Communist party.

CHAPTER 21

1. By contrast with the reasonably full documentation of Maoist and Soviet policies and their effects, to the best of my knowledge no first-rate account by a major participant in wartime German musical life has yet appeared, at least in English translation.

2. Harvey Sachs, *Music in Fascist Italy* (New York: Norton, 1988).

3. It is a pity that Sachs did not check more closely his attribution of Jewish status to certain important artists. Thus he mistakenly calls the nineteenth-century German and Protestant composer Max Bruch a Jew, as he does the German, half-Catholic, half-Protestant Bertolt Brecht, dramatist and collaborator of the Jewish Kurt Weill. Moreover, it is surely misleading to speak, as Sachs does, of Hugo von Hofmannsthal, Strauss's great collaborator on *Elektra, Der Rosenkavalier, Ariadne auf Naxos, Die Frau ohne Schatten, Die aegyptische Helena,* and *Arabella,* as the composer's "Jewish librettist"; Hofmannsthal was only one-quarter Jewish, and the Strauss-Hofmannsthal works were performed in Germany throughout the Nazi era.

4. In this regard, last season's overpraised *La Bohème* at the Metropolitan Opera was instructive. The most noteworthy aspect of the production was not the conducting of Carlos Kleiber, as refreshing (if unidiomatic) as it was, but the singing: it was amazing to see how little Italianate charm two reigning Italian stars, Luciano Pavarotti and Mirella Freni, had to contribute to this, for them, national classic.

CHAPTER 23

1. It should be mentioned here that the NPR tape of the entire panel proceedings was used as the basis for a feature broadcast by NPR on January 31. In this feature, much emphasis was properly placed on the element of confrontation between Messrs. Hunt and Davis and myself.